Soul of the Grid

Soul of the Grid

✦

A Cultural Biography of the California Independent System Operator

Arthur J. O'Donnell

iUniverse, Inc.
New York Lincoln Shanghai

Soul of the Grid
A Cultural Biography of the California Independent System Operator

iUniverse, Inc.

For information address:
iUniverse, Inc.
2021 Pine Lake Road, Suite 100
Lincoln, NE 68512
www.iuniverse.com

ISBN: 0-595-29348-4 (pbk)
ISBN: 0-595-65990-X (cloth)

Printed in the United States of America

Contents

Introduction: Soul of the Grid

THE CALIFORNIA INDEPENDENT SYSTEM OPERATOR (California ISO) celebrated its fifth anniversary of operations in April 2003. The event marked more than a simple milestone for the organization, however; it represented California ISO's survival through a long and difficult period of turmoil that has come to be known as the "California energy crisis."

Established as a not-for-profit public-benefit corporation to ensure the reliability of electrical transmission systems, California ISO remains the last viable component of the competitive market for electricity envisioned by lawmakers and regulators as part of the state's historic restructuring of utility regulation.

Though not completely deregulated, the century-old system under which electric utilities operated territorial monopolies over generation, transmission and distribution of electricity was supposed give way to a new market-based regime. Restructuring promised lower costs for consumers, a modernized and more efficient power generation system, and a transmission network that would be openly available to all market players.

Instead, half a decade after market inception, much of the competitive universe envisioned by this effort has fallen into disarray and disrepute. And yet, California ISO still stands—not entirely unscathed, but tempered and redefined by the power crisis.

As a long-time independent energy journalist and editor of the award-winning newsletter, California Energy Markets, the author of this book was commissioned by the California ISO to provide a fair, unbiased, and accurate accounting of the corporation's history, from its theoretical beginnings to the eve of its fifth anniversary. The contract specified giving the writer complete editorial control over content and its presentation.

As a result, the reader will find this to be an informed, candid, and uncompromising record of an unparalleled period of California's political and economic history—describing a series of events and decisions that will likely influence national energy policy choices for decades to come.

The occurrence in August 2003 of a widespread, cascading blackout that affected some 50 million people and businesses in New York State, major Midwestern cities, and in Southern Ontario, Canada, serves to underscore the importance of *Soul of the Grid*. This chronicle of California's power crisis and the saga of California ISO will prove to be essential to understanding the intentions and impacts of electric restructuring. In particular, this story highlights the critical interplay of competitive wholesale markets, grid reliability, and the policies meant to foster both.

While this book documents how California ISO came to be and what happened during the first years of its existence, it takes a much different approach than a standard corporate history.

Simply put, this is the story of the people who make up California ISO. The goal is to give a human voice to the history of California ISO that would otherwise be unavailable in the regulatory record or from news accounts and the huge body of analytical work devoted to California's restructuring and the ensuing power emergency.

The writer of this book was on the scene during the entire period and relies on a solid foundation of knowledge for telling the story, based on direct observations, personal relationships, the work of professional colleagues, and boxes upon boxes of data and documentation of these events. Research for the project also involved more than three-dozen extensive interviews with the people directly involved. Many other participants were contacted to help recount specific events.

Readers may be assured that the quotations used, though edited for flow and grammar, and the interpretations offered are accurate reflections of what was said about the events being described. The interview subjects were given free rein to express their opinions and views; indeed, that is one of the most valuable aspects of this work.

There are several overlapping generations in the cast of characters. Among them are those who participated in the policy and market-structure debates that preceded AB 1890; those who were responsible for translating restructuring policies into a practical means of operating the transmission system under the new market regime; the start-up teams that brought California ISO into existence; the engineers and dispatchers who are still struggling to transform a disjointed utility network into a smoothly operating, integrated network. Others include such key constituencies of California ISO as the utilities, customer groups, and members of the organization's boards and committees.

All are part of the California ISO story. Acting together and at times in opposition, they all imbue the organization with its unique and identifiable character and culture—its soul, if you will.

In addition to a fully annotated narrative and the exclusive first-person accounts employed in telling this story, readers of *Soul of the Grid* will find an especially useful set of appendices, including a comprehensive list of bibliographic materials, a glossary of utility terms, an entertaining discourse on industry jargon, and a chronology of important events that occurred during the period under investigation. Finally, there is also a listing of significant individuals who played major roles in the organization, particularly the members of California ISO's governing boards and corporate officers.

When California ISO was being formed, the people hired to work for the corporation recognized its revolutionary role in the restructuring of the traditional utility monopoly industry and wanted to play some part in making that a success.

The earliest hires were recruited with a specific task in mind, to get the new organization up and running by the legislatively mandated date of January 1, 1998. A common joke was that all these individuals came with the phrase "Type A" stamped on their foreheads. They lived up to the highest expectations placed on them by putting in incredible, ungodly hours—even after the start date was necessarily delayed by three months because of computer problems.

The stresses and urgency of the new market never seemed to let up, and even during what some might now consider a two-year period of stable operations prior to the crisis, the demands of a 24-hour-per-day, seven-day-per-week operating schedule did not get easier.

During the extended emergency, the corporation found itself holding together the entire power system, and its employees were asked to perform tasks never expected to be part of California ISO's core mission.

How people dealt with those stresses, sometimes with great humor, makes for a far more fascinating story than would a narrative concerned only with policy or politics. To a large degree, it is a story that has not been revealed publicly, as the successful running of the transmission system on a daily basis was not considered an especially newsworthy item for the mainstream media.

Today, California ISO stands at a crossroads—some might say in the crosshairs—of competing jurisdictional demands and the uncertain future of California's electricity market. The corporation also carries the mixed burden of being a disaster survivor. Its executives and operational staff have been hailed for their heroic efforts to maintain system stability under impossible circumstances *and* vilified by those who claim they did not do enough to avert the crisis. Even as the final chapters were being written, California ISO's most vociferous critics in the state Legislature were targeting it for elimination. Though the organization and its managers survived that particular political attack, there remain several direct threats to California's ISO's very existence and independent status.

Almost two years had passed from the worst of the energy crisis to the time when the bulk of interviews for this project were conducted. The wounds and scars of the power crisis and its aftermath remain visible and somewhat fresh for the people who were interviewed as part of this project. Remarkably, so does the idealism that sparked their decisions to join California ISO. Even if they have left the corporation to go on to other things, most people retain a steadfast loyalty to the organization and a belief in the vision that brought them to the ISO.

Ed Berlin, principal partner with the Washington, D.C., law firm of Swidler Berlin Shereff Friedman, is a keen observer of California ISO and its affairs, having served as its lead outside counsel from 1998 until 2001. In a recent interview, Berlin offered this detailed and telling observation about how the turmoil of California's power crises has affected the organization and its people:

"I think the most remarkable thing is that it has had as little pronounced effect as I would have anticipated it to have. Which is not to say that people there haven't gone through absolute hell and absolute agony, but I would have anticipated that long before today there would have been a wholesale exodus of some very, very bright people out of that organization. And then California would really have a catastrophe on its hands. For reasons that are beyond my ken, that has not happened.

"Sure, individuals have left, but when you look at the core organization that stays intact and the commitment that they continue to have to what they perceive to be their mission, I find it truly remarkable. These are people who, during that whole crisis period, never saw their families and then were subjected to political attack.

"They simply weren't getting paid enough to have to tolerate all of that, and they certainly had opportunities to move elsewhere, where life would have been a lot calmer. And they chose not to. They chose not to because they really believed in what they were doing, and they had developed an amazing camaraderie.

"Had that staff come apart, as I believe it should have, California would be in far worse shape today than it is."

1

The Worst That Can Happen

EVEN in the middle of an emergency, there is a prevailing sense of calm and quiet on the control-room floor at the California Independent System Operator's headquarters. Operators silently and continually shift their focus between the ever-fluctuating load curves shown on their computer screens and the giant graphical representation of California's electrical transmission system that extends some 160 feet across an entire wall of the room.

Envision a map of the state turned on its side, with all natural boundaries or political jurisdictions erased and all topographic features stripped away. The Pacific Ocean might as well be the sea of carpet on the floor of the 15,000-square-foot Control Center as your eyes flow from Crescent City to San Diego, left to right along the imaginary coastline.

Instead of cities and rivers, or even the great bowl of the Central Valley or the extended spine of the Sierra Nevada mountain range, what you see are hundreds of lights and lines connecting them: a huge and dynamic electrical diagram at work 24 hours per day, every day.

The small dots of red or green represent the operational status of every major power-generation facility and transmission hub located in the state. Bright LED digits reveal the amount of power flowing from the plants or across tie lines at that exact moment in time. Points of interconnection, characterized by heavy black lines and identifying codes, indicate the routes and voltage levels for the 25,526 circuit-miles of power lines under California ISO's constant watch.

Some lines extend beyond the imaginary perimeter, the high-voltage interties that connect California with the rest of the Western transmission grid. Bold lines represent 500,000-volt (500 KV) power lines that pull electricity from the expansive Columbia River hydroelectric system in the Pacific Northwest, or draw excess power from coal plants and nuclear facilities in the desert Southwest.

The abstract island of California depicted by this map belies the physical reality of integrated operations among dozens of control areas in 11 states that make up the Western grid, as well as the cross-border ties to Mexico and Canada.

At any time of the day or season, power will be flowing in any and all directions, both into and out of the state. But on average, California is a sink where electric energy drains no matter where it might have been created.

On one particular day, June 14, 2000, the room was especially quiet as operators' concentration focused on the San Francisco region.

A record-breaking day of high temperatures—well above 100 degrees Fahrenheit in the normally cool Bay Area—threatened the stability of the entire system in a way that most California ISO staff members had never before faced.

Conversations among operators and their managers were almost beside the point, except for those telephone calls necessary to secure last-minute resources.

There are no windows to the outside world in the control room, unless you consider the full-length glass lens to the adjacent conference room that gives the area its nickname, "the fishbowl." No way to visually confirm whether it is day or night, sunny or stormy beyond the walls of the ISO building on Blue Ravine Road in Folsom, except for those computer screens and digital readouts.

Still, everyone in the room could see that trouble lay ahead.

Jim Detmers, the managing director of grid operations, had a growing sense of unease about the situation. Pacific Gas & Electric, the Northern California utility where Jim spent his early career before joining the ISO, was projecting an all-time record for electricity deliveries later that afternoon.

Resources were tight because the heat wave extended through much of the region, and imported energy was less available than anticipated. The unplanned outage that morning of a key generation plant in Pittsburg made the situation even tighter.

From long experience in keeping the lights on for PG&E customers, Detmers knew that a widespread and costly system failure was inevitable if loads kept climbing at this pace. And he knew there was only one way to prevent it.

For the first time in the more than two years since it had assumed control over the transmission grid in April of 1998, the California Independent System Operator was about to require that PG&E cut delivery of power to customers in San Francisco, the East Bay and Silicon Valley.

These were not the rare but sometimes necessary voluntary disruptions of service to industrial energy users who had signed discount-rate, "interruptible contracts" with their utilities. Most of PG&E's largest industrial customers already had agreed to shut down or reduce energy use, but the resulting 500-megawatt reduction—about half the output of a nuclear power plant—did not correct the problem.

What was necessary now was to shut off power to specific and identified blocks of utility customers in units of 100 MW. The outages would rotate by hour and affect as many as 100,000 customers per block. By 2:00 p.m., the decision was unavoidable. PG&E would need to drop as much as 200 MW, and neighboring municipal utility districts, even though they were not technically part of the ISO system, would also need to cut some service.

The operators were not even certain they could limit the outages to such small blocks, even though they had previously run simulations to provide assurance that the blackouts would not spiral out of control.

"You know we had never done this back at the utilities," Detmers explained in a pained voice. "You'd pull every trick out of the hat you could possibly think about pulling, and when it came down to giving the order to drop load, firm load, due to just lack of electricity, it was like we failed. I felt like we had failed."

Despite the passage of time and the perspective of having survived nearly a full year of emergency declarations, blackouts and the many, many last-minute saves that characterized the great California Power Crisis of 2000–01, both Detmers and colleague Tracy Bibb still felt the sting of defeat from needing to cut the flow of electricity on that hot June afternoon.

"We failed," Bibb concurred. "We failed," Detmers repeated softly.

In reality, the problem was much more than "just lack of electricity," as measured in unavailable megawatts. Similarly, the decision to shed firm load was not a failure in and of itself but a way of preventing something far worse—a swift and substantial drop in the frequency of power flows that could trip power plants across the entire system, permanently damaging transformers and other sensitive equipment.

To the general public, the job of an electric utility is to keep the lights on at a somewhat reasonable cost, as usually determined by appointed regulators or a publicly elected board. For a transmission controller, however, the operative phrase is "maintaining 60 cycles"; that is, holding a standard level of frequency for the waves of electrical energy that flow from power plants to transmission lines to customers. The cost is secondary.

Through a century of trial and error, of daily success and occasional failure, the American electric industry has chosen 60 cycles as its standard, regardless of whether the voltage level is 500 KV, as on the big interties, or 120 volts running through the circuits and appliances in your home.

The Daily High-Wire Act

Some fluctuation around the 60-cycles-per-second (also known as 60 hertz) fig-ure is tolerable, noted California ISO chief executive officer Terry Winter, but 60 is the magic number to ensure reliable operations for power flowing throughout North America. Anything significantly above or below that level signals trouble. Utility engineers, under the auspices of the Western Electricity Coordinating Council (WECC) or the North American Electric Reliability Council (NERC)—the industry agencies that set reliability standards—select certain fre-quencies as benchmarks for remedial action in order to maintain stability.

Too much demand compared to the amount of generation capacity causes fre-quency levels to fall. An unexpected loss of load, perhaps caused by a lightning strike or a tree falling onto a power line to disconnect customers from the system, will bring a frequency excursion above 60 cycles. Either event can occur, and they do, sometimes daily.

Extreme deviations in either direction cause automatic systems to kick in to try to restore the balance and prevent a cascading outage.

"At 59.56 hertz, the first set of relays drops generation and load," Winter explained. "At 59.3, it's all gone."

Imagine a circus tightrope walker—the utility transmission system opera-tor—hovering without a safety net some hundreds of feet above the ground. The tension of the rope is measured by its frequency response, with power generation acting like a helium balloon to tug the line upward. Electricity consumption, called load, is a weight exerting a downward pull.

As long as the two forces balance each other, and the frequency stays at 60 cycles, the acrobat can successfully cross the chasm that represents each day's sup-ply/demand curve. This equilibrium is measured not just hourly but essentially every four seconds.

But that's too simple of a model, Winter cautioned, because of the complexity of a network system in which thousands of generation sources pump power into the system while millions of load pockets—power users—pull electrons out.

"I use the example in a network," he said. "If you take two chairs and tie a spi-der-web of rubber bands between the two chairs, and you hang all the generators as helium balloons and you hang all the load as weights on this network, you can see as the balloons rise up, the load comes with it. If the balloons start losing pres-sure or generation, the weight pulls it down. And it all flows on this grid, moving up and down. What you don't want to have happen is to suddenly have a balloon break or a load fall off, because then this whole spider web of rubber bands starts popping up and down. If it goes up or down so far that it disconnects balloons or load, then you have what we call the unstable system. It all falls apart."

If unchecked, the frequency fluctuation and resulting voltage instability could spread in a matter of seconds, triggering a massive and cascading outage that might not be contained within the local region. All those dots of light and LED readouts on the big map would go dark. Tens of millions of people from British Columbia to Baja California would flip their light switches or try to turn on their televisions and radios to find out what was wrong, but there would be no juice in the system, no power, no light, and no way of knowing exactly how long it would take to restore service.

It had happened before.

Before the extended California crisis, the date August 10, 1996, was fixed in the memories of utility personnel and control-room operators as the single worst event in the history of the Western interconnection.

On that date, four million people and hundreds of thousands of businesses in 11 states lost power for much of the day. It was the second system outage of that summer but much more widespread than a prior incident in July.

Perhaps it was not as severe as the New York Blackout of 1965, which plunged much of the Eastern seaboard into darkness, or as influential as that event had been in eliciting national policies for the creation of eight separate "reliability regions" like the WECC across North America. Nonetheless, the August 10 outage became the hobgoblin of reliability in the West.

"This should be put in the same category as a nuclear meltdown," said California Public Utilities Commission member Jessie Knight, Jr., at the time.[1] It was an episode that no transmission professional would ever want to see repeated—and certainly not on his or her watch.

Anatomy of a Catastrophe

Occurring during an extremely hot Saturday, when PG&E and smaller public power districts in Northern California were on their way to setting new record peak loads, the triggering event of the August 1996 outage was the instantaneous grounding of power. A heavily loaded transmission line in the Pacific Northwest came into contact with a tree.

This was recognized by the system as if it were a huge, instantaneous increase in demand or a sudden loss of generation.

As you might expect, however, there was a full and complicated set of circumstances underlying the incident. Controllers at the Bonneville Power Administration, the federal power-marketing agency that owned and operated the line, later admitted they had missed some of the warning signs of a potential disaster.

Other utilities affected by the outage blamed BPA for a failure to communicate that three high-voltage transmission lines had relayed out of service earlier in the day, weakening the system in advance of the triggering event. With more warning, they complained, they might have been able to shield their systems from the catastrophe.

At about 3:40 p.m., the 500 KV line connecting the Keeler and Alston substations in Oregon was carrying a full load of power for use in the Northwest and for export to California.

The combination of hot temperatures and being fully loaded caused the line to sag so much that it touched the tree line in a heavily wooded area, immediately shorting the line.

The resulting frequency oscillations set up a cascade of outage events, knocking off line 13 hydroelectric units at McNary Dam, tripping the direct-current (DC) intertie that runs between Oregon and Southern California, and causing a breakdown in the connections between utility control areas—not only between the Northwest and California but also in Nevada, New Mexico and Arizona.

That triggered further outages throughout the West.

The reliability criteria for such a system outage call for "islanding," or separating control areas into autonomous pools so that service can be restored more quickly. The problem was that with so much generation out of service, controllers did not have enough residual voltage support to bring power stations back on line. Huge nuclear power stations at Diablo Canyon and San Onofre in California and at Palo Verde in Arizona fell from full capacity to zero in a matter of minutes. Restoring power after such a "scram" at a nuclear unit can take days. Throughout the system, generation had to be brought back from what operators call a "black start condition."[2]

Ed Riley, now California ISO's director of regional coordination, was an area controller for the Los Angeles Department of Water & Power at the time of the outage. That hot Saturday, he was enjoying an outing with his grandson at Disneyland in nearby Anaheim. "All of a sudden, people start coming out of the rides and there's nothing going on," he recalled. The amusement park was silent and still. "I'm going, 'Hmm, must be a local power outage.' And then my pager went off," signaling that something far more serious had occurred. "So I had to get back to work."

'It's All on the Ground'

To be sure, there had been several other serious system events during the careers of California ISO operators, both before and after the corporation had been created. When Detmers and Bibb reminisced about them, it was like listening to two tall-tale tellers finishing each other's thoughts and trying to top each other's stories.

"The biggest breakup the Western states had ever seen prior to August 10th was December 22, 1982, at 4:29 p.m. I was there. It was burned into my vision. I was there that day," Bibb said. Fierce winds had blown down six 500 KV transmission lines in PG&E's territory east of San Francisco, and the resulting shocks to the grid blacked out up to four million people in three states.[3]

Detmers countered, citing the major windstorm of December 14, 1995. "It blew down lines, and the entire Western United States went unstable," he said.

About 1.75 million PG&E customers lost power for several hours, some for days.[4] "That was the big one you never want to see again, when the wind exceeded 100 miles per hour, exceeded the engineering of the lines and took out the towers. I remember the phone call with the guy in the helicopter. He had just flown from Table to Round Mountain [along the Pacific Intertie in Northern California] and it was still during the storm and they were flying to find out why the lines were out. The towers were gone. They were all laid down for eight miles. Didn't see it when they flew over the first time. They started coming back, and he called me on his cell phone at the window of the helicopter. He was shook up. He said, 'It's all laying on the ground.'"

The two veterans batted about memories of other big outage events, ranging from the 1989 Loma Prieta earthquake centered near Santa Cruz to the 1992 Northridge temblor that wrecked a wide area of Southern California. There was the accidental grounding of energy by a PG&E substation repair crew in December 1998 that left San Francisco without power for a full day and led to unprecedented sanctions against the utility by the new Independent System Operator.

None of it really compared with the August event, which made them "look like a walk in the park," Bibb concluded. "August 10th was catastrophic, because of the magnitude of how many people were off, how many transmission lines tripped out, how many generators tripped off. And having to rebuild the system in many cases from a black start. Yeah, everything ripped apart. Diablo was off, San Onofre units were off, all the nuclear was off."

And yet, the ISO's June 14, 2000, call for firm-load curtailments over a 90-minute period was something these professionals would take far more personally and emotionally than any of the other incidents they had ever experienced. "That was just dealing with our work," Detmers said of the past reliability episodes. "So we were working, doing what we had to do to operate the system, to engineer it, to put the whole thing back together to get the lights back on. We knew what the problems were; it was a storm, it was a quake and whatever. We knew what the problem was and we were dealing with it."

June 14, 2000, was different because of a sense, still lingering, of personal failure.

"In my mind, I pictured people stranded in elevators. I pictured people stranded in stores and checkout lines. All I could think about was the inconvenience, and sitting here thinking…thinking, what rock did we not look under to maybe prevent this," he said.

Detmers, Bibb and nearly everybody else at California ISO knew that June 14th was just the beginning of a long, terrible summer. What they didn't realize was that the situation would turn out to be worse than they feared.

2

The Deal Breaker

ALTHOUGH it is true that the California Independent System Operator was created on September 23, 1996, by an act of California law known as Assembly Bill 1890, the conception of California ISO as a separate and distinct marketplace entity came more than a year before.

For all the late-night lobbying and political compromises that took place during the now-legendary "Steve Peace Death March" to draft AB 1890 and restructure California's energy industry, there was relatively little debate about the form or functions of California ISO or its sibling market entity, the California Power Exchange. In large part, the political compromises necessary to create these two public-benefit corporations, which would oversee transmission dispatch control and utility power purchasing, respectively, had been reached during the summer of 1995.

The vehicle for agreement was a controversial memorandum of understanding (MOU) among utilities, large power users, wholesale energy suppliers and other major stakeholders.

In fact, according to key participants in the MOU process, the decision to separate these two organizations rather than create an all-encompassing power pool or PoolCo, as was being promoted by some, was the last, crucial element in reaching the agreements that would form the basis of AB 1890.

"It was the deal breaker," recalled Karen Lindh, who served as the energy policy manager for the California Manufacturers Association, one of the principal advocates of restructuring in the state. Without that separation of functions, there would have been no MOU, and AB 1890, if it was drafted at all, might have pushed California's restructuring program in a very different direction.

But that's getting ahead of the story.

To fully understand how and why California ISO was created and what its intended role in the new energy environment was to be, it is necessary to step back more than a decade in time. The restructuring debates in California raged through the 1990s and were echoed and amplified in federal policies to encourage the deregulation of industries as diverse as telecommunications, airlines, trucking, and the natural-gas business.

Looking back through the extensive public record, it becomes clear that California ISO has always stood at the uneasy intersection of state and federal interests—or as some have put it, in the no-man's-land between California politics and the jurisdictional authority of the Federal Energy Regulatory Commission (FERC).

The California Coloring Books

The grand compromise of electric restructuring in California was that the incumbent, investor-owned electric utilities, Pacific Gas & Electric, Southern California Edison and San Diego Gas & Electric, should receive full recovery of their multibillion-dollar investment in power generation and delivery assets that might become uneconomic as a result of competition.

The recovery of "stranded costs"—something that would be unheard of in almost any other industry—was the necessary quid pro quo for the utilities to accede to retail competition in the form of what Californians called "direct access," that is, the potential for utility customers to buy their electricity from non-utility marketers or energy service providers.

The reasoning behind stranded-cost recovery was simple from the utilities' point of view. For decades, they had been required by regulators to invest in an extensive network of power plants, transmission lines and substations in order to provide reliable electric service to customers under an "obligation to serve" that was part and parcel of their utility franchise.

In return for committing to this obligation to serve, the utilities were entitled to recover their investments through regulated rates and a "reasonable" rate of return on their assets. Though always contentious, the rate cases that established such findings of reasonableness generally gave the utilities a great percentage of the amounts they requested from regulators. In the industry, this was known as "the regulatory compact."

In a new world of deregulation, where returns would be set by competitive forces and not regulatory proceedings, the compact no longer held together, the utilities argued, and all that installed infrastructure was at risk of becoming uneconomic and unrecoverable in rates. Therefore, they believed they were entitled to full recovery of their embedded costs, with their initial assessments of the price tag reaching more than $30 billion in California alone.

Though skeptical of this entitlement mentality, the largest customers of California's utilities were eager to escape what they considered excessive and uncompetitive utility rates.

Again and again, they had pointed out that utility rates in California were, on average, 50 percent higher than those across the United States, largely as a result of the high costs of nuclear power, required energy purchases from non-utility power generators, and California's embedded policies to encourage diversity of resources (such as wind, solar and geothermal power), energy-efficiency programs, and other social goals.

In comparison to nearby states, the differential was even greater, as the Pacific Northwest utilities benefited from an expansive network of low-cost hydroelectricity, much of it under the control of a federal power-marketing agency, the Bonneville Power Administration.

To remain competitive, California manufacturers argued, they needed to be able to deal directly with the new class of non-utility wholesale power suppliers that were beginning to emerge as a result of federal policies promoting open access to transmission lines. Generators knew that their prospects for selling to utilities were limited, and they, too, were eager to see a new market regime in place.

Consumer advocates, who represented individuals, households, and small commercial segments of the utility customer base, were wary of the entire restructuring scheme. They saw little advantage for their constituents as a result of retail choice and only the certainty that captive customers would foot most of the costs of any transition to competition.

These were the basic positions that had been debated for more than three years in a process initiated by the California Public Utilities Commission starting in February of 1993, with the release of a document prepared by its Division of Strategic Planning titled, *California's Electric Services Industry: Perspectives on the Past, Strategies for the Future.*

Called The Yellow Book for its bright gold cover, the report found that "California's current regulatory framework...is ill-suited to govern today's electric services industry."

The study of historical patterns of regulation led division staff members to conclude that "the commission should exercise its discretion and responsibilities to reform electric regulation, with an emphasis on streamlining and reducing the cost of the administrative procedures governing the industry."[1]

After a year of discussion and a series of public hearings, the CPUC launched a formal rulemaking into possible changes to the regulatory structure on April 20,

1994. This combination rulemaking and investigation, known thereafter as The Blue Book, premiered many of the concepts that would later be adopted in AB 1890, including direct-access relationships between customers and competitive providers, replacement of traditional regulatory review of utility rates with market-based or incentive ratemaking, and the recovery of stranded costs for the utilities over time through a "competitive transition charge" (CTC). [2]

Although the reduction of regulatory costs and utility rates had been an underlying principle of the CPUC's drive for restructuring, the Blue Book did not contain any specific commitment to lowering rates to consumers, relying instead on the premise that more competition would put "downward pressure" on rates—once the stranded-cost liability was erased.

Among market structures proposed to help effect competition was a competitive power pool, such as was being advocated by several academic economists and implemented in the United Kingdom.

In California, the pool concept became known as PoolCo, a quasi-regulated exchange through which wholesale transactions for electricity would flow. Competition to sell into the pool, it was expected, would reduce prices and introduce new generation technologies to replace obsolete utility power plants.

The Blue Book stirred considerable debate in the state and captured the attention of the utility industry throughout the world. As it had so many times in the past, California appeared to be leaping ahead of everyone else by adopting the most innovative and potentially risky policies currently under discussion anywhere.

The Blue Book also put the final nails in the coffin of California's existing program of competition for utility power-procurement contracts, called the Biennial Resource Planning Update, or BRPU. For many people, the BRPU represented the worst aspects of regulatory process, a supposedly two-year auction cycle that became mired in bitter fights over every aspect, including how much power was needed, which generators could participate, what prices ought to be paid, and even allegations of parties unfairly gaming their bids to win the auction.

Limited to participation among "qualifying facilities" (QFs) and other wholesale power providers recognized by a federal law called the Public Utility Regulatory Policies Act of 1979 (PURPA), the BRPU auctions nonetheless resulted in prices well below the benchmark utility costs set by the CPUC. Although dozens of winners of the auctions—including developers of wind farms, geothermal facilities, and natural-gas-fired power facilities—believed they were entitled to 20-year power sales contracts, utilities challenged the awards at every turn, eventually winning a suspension of the BRPU.

As the executive director of the Independent Energy Producers, Jan Smutny-Jones heads the trade association that represented the QF power generators in regulatory and legislative forums. For IEP members, the release of the Blue Book represented the end of their hard-fought campaign to force utility systems open to some form of competition as well as a potential beginning for a new market structure that would embrace non-utility generation. Smutny-Jones saw the Blue Book as "a radical shift" in policy.

"It put us in the mode of having to rethink how we were going forward to do business," he said.

Even though IEP members were talking about building new power plants as "exempt wholesale generators" or "merchant generators" under new rules being promoted by federal regulators, those concepts were still tied to long-term power contracts and "business as usual" with the reluctant and often adversarial utilities.

"The Blue Book changed all that and created a very, very different vision. It was pretty clear to me that the existing way of doing business wasn't going to work, and the analysis wasn't all that complicated. The utilities don't love us and maybe we can find someone else to do business with," Smutny-Jones said. "But by no means was this something that everyone within IEP believed universally was a good idea."

The Blue Book also scared the daylights out of utility investors, who immediately responded by selling their stock in California's IOUs and driving the per-share prices down by as much as 22 percent in the three weeks following its release. Despite an emergency trip to Wall Street firms by CPUC president Daniel Fessler and commissioner Jessie Knight, financial analysts were not optimistic. One key analyst, Barry Abramson of Prudential Securities, warned utility investors, "Returns may be depressed for years to come."[2]

In the Blue Book, the CPUC purposely chose a new term, "direct access," to avoid the preconceptions embodied in a competitive regime, but many in the industry perceived the entire program as a threat to utility earnings and investments—regardless of promises of cost recovery.

Moreover, as time went by, the CPUC process became bogged down in a philosophical dispute between president Fessler and commissioner Knight over what should be the key feature of restructuring: PoolCo or direct access.

Fessler was a former professor of contracts law and a noted scholar on the origins of common-carrier regulation in the public interest. Once described in a *Los Angeles Times* article as "brilliant, if occasionally imperious," Fessler could easily have served as the model for Professor Kingsley in "The Paper Chase."[4] Some weeks after that profile ran, Fessler encountered the reporter, Michael Parrish.

Raising an eyebrow, Fessler said only, "Imperious, eh?" Then he walked away from the startled journalist.

Fessler came to favor PoolCo as the dominant market feature, despite his background in contracts law. This was in part because the "transparency" of pool transactions would provide a way to track electricity prices and established the means for calculating the transition charge and stranded-cost recovery. This opinion had been fostered by nearly constant lobbying from SoCal Edison, which helped sponsor trips for the commission members to see how other countries were conducting privatization of their utility systems.

Knight, a business marketing executive and proponent of less fettered competition, insisted that all customers should be able to deal directly with suppliers, and he believed that a mandatory pool would restrict market options and potential savings.

The dispute between the two regulators impeded progress toward a unified set of policies.

Also, nearly continuous changes to the makeup of the commission had altered the lines of power and alliances during this period. Knight was a relative newcomer to the commission, having been appointed in early 1994 at about the same time as Greg Conlon, a former director for the Arthur Andersen accounting firm.

Two commissioners who had been involved in the early restructuring discussions, Patricia Eckert and Norm Shumway, left between the end of 1994 and early 1995. For much of the following year, the two seats remained vacant, until Governor Pete Wilson appointed former banker Henry Duque and attorney Josiah Neeper to the panel in September 1995.

The Alliances

As a result of 15 years of Republican incumbency in the governor's office in Sacramento, few if any of these regulatory appointees questioned the need or desire to reduce state oversight of utility operations. Their differences were largely a matter of degrees of support for fully competitive markets in electricity services.

In the few restructuring-related votes that were taken during 1995, Fessler and Conlon generally overruled positions promoted by Knight. The two sides came to loggerheads in May 1995 when they issued rival proposed decisions that reflected their conflicting views on a preferred restructuring policy. The split was not resolved with the addition of the two newer members, as Duque tended to side with Fessler, while Neeper joined with Knight.

Among utilities, Edison was the most insistent advocate of PoolCo, and it backed up its cause with a steady stream of appearances by noted economists, especially William Hogan of Harvard, to press for the pool concept.

In arguments and hearings, Edison was joined frequently by SDG&E, although the smaller utility had its own idiosyncratic take on many issues and favored something called "efficient direct access" that was still dependent on a pool-based market.

The state's largest utility, PG&E, committed itself to a market structure that encouraged "bilateral contracts" between buyers and sellers, rather than a pool. The utility's chief executive officer Bob Glynn often said that the company had tried to resist restructuring in natural gas and was still paying the price of customer animosity. This time, PG&E would take the lead in encouraging a more competitive electric market, he said.

Industrial energy users and marketers favored the less restrictive structure embodied by direct access. Consumer advocates were mostly ignored in the debates, as they saw problems with all of the proposals.[5]

At one point during the Blue Book debates, an influential regulatory consultant, Phil O'Connor, offered what he called "the Tehachapi Compromise," named after a range of mountains near Bakersfield that demarked PG&E's service territory from Edison's. Customers in Northern California could pursue bilateral contracts and direct-access arrangements, O'Connor proposed, while Southern California would operate under a power pool.[6] But Fessler at the CPUC insisted on a consistent restructuring regime for the state.

In addition to this debate, the Blue Book contemplated an unbundling of utility services and costs, even suggesting the split of traditional monopoly utility functions into separate businesses for generation, distribution, and transmission of power. Although nearly everyone believed that transmission of energy across high-voltage lines should remain a regulated service, parties differed on the preferred approach to ensure that lines would be open to anyone who needed them.

One of the major industrial groups, the California Large Energy Consumers Association (CLECA), had argued during the very earliest hearings on the Blue Book that utilities "should relinquish transmission facilities to a newly created transmission entity which is integrated and separately owned." At the time, the concept was called TransCorp, with the new entity to be jointly owned by market participants besides the utilities. TransCorp would not only dispatch all interconnected generation facilities, it would serve as negotiator for access to out-of-state transmission facilities on behalf of California market players, and would possibly grow into a regional entity.[7]

Edison's PoolCo included what the utility called an "independent transmission system operator." The terminology reflected the theories popular among academic economists and new directions coming from the Federal Energy Regulatory Commission in Washington, D.C. In Edison's construct, this ISO was part and parcel of the PoolCo structure.

Beginning in July 1995, the utility began promoting what its chief executive, John Bryson, called WEPEX, or the Western Power Exchange, a regional power pool that would also take over control of utility transmission systems. Critics saw the shift as more than a simple change in nomenclature to avoid the baggage that had become attached to PoolCo; industrial customers and generators considered it part of Edison's program to dictate the future of the marketplace.[8]

Barbara Barkovich, a consultant for CLECA whose studies of rate-design issues and regulatory intervention had influenced the original Yellow Book document, saw a very straightforward argument for establishing a separate ISO. "If we had an independent entity managing the grid, then everybody would be treated fairly," she said. That was the position shared by other large power users.

"We were clearly in the camp with the large industrials that were very suspicious of PoolCo and very much oriented toward direct access," concurred IEP's Smutny-Jones. "If the industry was going to get anything out of this, it was access to more customers. At the time, the PoolCo discussion was dominated by Edison, and we were highly suspicious of why they were pushing that model as hard as they were, if it wasn't to maintain market power and control over where the markets would go," he said.

John Fielder, a senior vice president of the Edison utility, explained why the utility favored a single entity. "Our position was that we ought to have an integrated ISO, meaning that the ISO ought to also be responsible for the day-ahead market so that you didn't have arbitrage opportunities among different markets," he said. Enron Corporation, power generators, and large industrial consumers "could not get comfortable" with that market design, Fielder said. "They didn't want the independent system operator to have anything to do with markets, except perhaps real-time markets," he said.

The loose coalition didn't want any kind of mandated power exchange, but if there was going to be one, it had to be separate from the ISO. "It was a deal killer for them," Fielder said.

Despite their differing opinions about the best restructuring policies and the wariness of other stakeholders, the three utilities formed a WEPEX working group to hash out the technical aspects of combining their three separate control areas into one integrated grid operator. The WEPEX working group continued throughout the next 15 months, with the technical meetings conducted on a parallel but distinct track from all resolving policy issues of the regulatory, legislative, and less formal industry forums devoted to forums devoted to resolving policy issues.

The MOU Takes Shape

It took direct intervention by Governor Pete Wilson's office to broker the deal that would become the MOU. Wilson, who had aspirations of running for president of the United States, was getting concerned that the disagreements among his regulatory appointees and the differences in outcomes desired by utilities and large manufacturers were being played out in the pages of major newspapers, including the *Wall Street Journal.* Edison had begun taking out newspaper advertisements promoting WEPEX as a preferred market structure, and the manufacturers responded by directly lobbying Edison's corporate board of directors, pushing for retail competition.

Wilson put two trusted advisers, George Dunn and Phil Romero, to the task of bridging the gap between Edison and everyone else. Many of the parties in the negotiations believed fairness and open access to transmission would occur only if the commercial energy markets were separated from the operation of the transmission grid.

With increasing pressure from the Governor's advisers, a breakthrough came in mid-August 1995, with the MOU parties endorsing full recovery of stranded costs, the creation of a power exchange and a phased-in approach to direct access for all utility customers. The question of consolidation or separation of the power exchange and the proposed grid operator became the last contentious issue to be resolved.

"A truly competitive generation market will evolve only if the transmission systems are operated by an entity with no financial interest in the source of the generation moving across the transmission system," read one of the last draft versions of the MOU.

> "The ISO will be an independent entity, regulated by the FERC, separate from the Power Exchange, and will not be owned or controlled in any manner by a utility owning generation, transmission or distribution facilities. Its principle responsibility will be the scheduling of power transactions, managing transmission congestion and providing non-discriminatory access to the transmission grids of the California IOUs. It will be responsible for establishing the operational controls required to maintain transmission system reliability and

safety. The ISO will provide controls and services which include, but are not limited to, voltage support, spinning reserves, frequency control, load balancing, back-up services and system status information. The ISO shall identify and competitively procure such generation resources as it needs to balance the transmission system and maintain reliability. The ISO should not participate directly in the purchase or sale of power beyond short-term balancing and reliability functions. All users of the transmission system shall communicate their schedules to the ISO pursuant to mandatory protocols which it shall establish. The ISO will provide operating information in a non-discriminatory basis to all market participants."

Responding to this version on August 15, Edison representatives countered with an alternative draft that eliminated almost all the language describing the independent grid controller, replacing it with provisions that called for "creation of a power exchange *with* an Independent System Operator." Though independent of utility control and regulated by FERC, Edison insisted the ISO should be "part of the Power Exchange." In every sentence that had previously described functions of the separate ISO, Edison instead inserted "Power Exchange." [9]

Because of Edison's adamancy about collecting its stranded costs, especially those related to the San Onofre Nuclear Generating Station, and its insistence on establishing the pool as the basis of a wholesale competitive market, the manufacturers and industrials dug in their heels.

"We said there wasn't going to be any deal," Barkovich said. "We simply would not agree to give the utilities stranded-cost recovery unless we got a lot of things we wanted in market structure in exchange."

The disagreement reached all the way to the governor's office, recalled one legislative source in attendance at a meeting held during "the last intense hours" of the MOU negotiations. Republican state senator Bill Campbell, a key supporter of manufacturing interests, reportedly "slammed down his hand and said it's going to be divided or there ain't no deal."

"And in the end," Barkovich said, "we finally arrived at the MOU in which there would be an ISO and a PX, and all the rest of it." The "rest of it" included a commitment to full recovery of utility stranded costs, although the prospective dollar amount was left to be decided by regulators. There would be a period of time during which utilities would collect a surcharge on distribution rates that was inescapable by customers.

Direct access would be allowed for all customers, but on a graduated schedule that allowed large power users to enter the market first. There was also recognition that, while the CPUC would need to approve the MOU provisions for CTC collection, there must also be a new law passed to establish a legal grounding for the entire program in order to derail a possible citizens' initiative being threatened by consumer groups that might undermine the entire restructuring program.[10]

Though an agreement by the parties was publicly announced in mid-August, it was not until September 14 that a final version of the MOU was signed and presented to the CPUC. The proposal provided for an ISO that would be operated separately from the power exchange.

The MOU helped bring a near consensus on some of the toughest issues in restructuring. Given an opportunity to comment on its terms as part of CPUC review, even the ratepayer group Toward Utility Rate Normalization (TURN) grudgingly saw a positive aspect. "If the MOU makes it any less likely that PoolCo will be the adopted market structure for California's electricity market, TURN believes we are all better off." Still, TURN felt that consumers would on the whole be worse off, even under the future dictated by the MOU's terms.

Among the most critical voices weighing in on the MOU was that of the California Energy Commission. CEC attorney John Chandley, who was the agency's liaison on restructuring matters, questioned the proposed split in market functions between a PX and ISO. "The MOU signers have failed to demonstrate that this forced separation makes any sense, that it solves some real problem, or that it makes the system operate better, more efficiently or more fairly." He also foresaw that the ISO might be unable to deal effectively with transmission congestion and that the separate markets might allow "arbitragers to exploit the resulting inefficiencies."[11]

The split between Fessler and Knight came to a head in late December, as the commission considered two rival proposals, each as thick as the San Francisco–area Yellow Pages. Despite their extended speeches in support of a direct-access future, commissioners Knight and Neeper lost out on a 3-2 vote that approved a revised decision melding Fessler's restructuring proposals with the terms of the MOU.

Among other key policies adopted in this comprehensive decision was a mechanism to "encourage" utilities to divest their non-nuclear and nonhydroelectric power generation, setting up an auction process to sell these old facilities to new market players and devote the sale proceeds to buying down the stranded-cost account.[12]

The Legislature Steps In

However, that ruling, called the "Preferred Policy Decision," did not stand as the last word on restructuring policies in the state, because certain influential members of the state Legislature did not trust the CPUC's actions or the motives of market stakeholders.

Robin Larson was at the time a legislative adviser for then-senator Steve Peace. Peace, a San Diego–area Democrat, served on the energy and utilities committees in both houses of the Legislature and was one of the few lawmakers actively paying attention to restructuring. He didn't much like what he was seeing.

"Senator Peace was adamant that the product would move to the Legislature because he didn't trust Fessler," Larson said. Several times, she used the term "hijacking" to describe how Peace was taking over the restructuring debates from the regulatory agency. "There was that friction between Steve Peace and Fessler. He didn't want to leave it to the CPUC. He wanted to make sure consumers were protected and various other things."

Peace, along with Jim Brulte, a Republican Assemblymember from Rancho Cucamonga, formed a special committee of six lawmakers from both political parties and legislative houses. They took over the task of crafting a new statutory platform for redesigning the state's utility industry.

Peace, known for possessing both a brilliant analytical mind and a mercurial temper, had previously worked with Brulte to forge a political compromise on workers' compensation issues. Together, they thought a similar deal could be reached on restructuring policies. But more than simply restructuring the rules of the power game, Peace was also considering legislation that would do away with the CPUC entirely, and he headed a related joint committee on regulatory reform.

A series of severe winter windstorms during late December 1995 and the resulting extended power outages for up to 1.7 million PG&E customers in Northern California gave the lawmakers grist for their initial hearings, which were held in the CPUC auditorium in San Francisco.

Despite Fessler's stance that "Safety and reliability concerns are not being changed at all" under the restructuring plan, Peace and colleagues were not convinced.

"As I watch deregulation unfold, there's an apparent lack of focus and attention to issues other than sweeping statements from the commission," Peace stated. "There's nothing in place that gives us any sense that questions of reliability and services have been answered. I don't think you want us to be responsible for having allowed the erosion and deterioration of services."[13]

Although Fessler would soon turn the presidential gavel over to Conlon and rarely set foot in the Capitol for committee hearings, Peace was unstinting in his criticism of the commission's effort and the involvement of special interests in drafting restructuring policies.

"As noble as these representatives of economic interests may be, the public process is frankly served better by them not engaging in what is often self-delusion of higher purpose," Peace declared at a committee meeting. "Anytime someone tells me, 'I'm just trying to do God's work here,' that is when lawmakers should step in. Our job is to do God's work."[14]

Part of the Peace strategy was to reduce adversaries to ashes with his withering wit and to browbeat parties into a submissive state where they would agree to almost anything just to end the torture. And so, the legislative process to craft a restructuring law became known as the "Peace Death March."

To help process the complex issues into legislation, the committee hired John Rozsa from the California Energy Commission to support Peace's advisers Larson and Dave Takeshima, who was a former lobbyist for Edison. The resulting bill, AB 1890, carried Brulte's name as main author but was cosponsored by the entire committee.

While industry participants had been all-consumed with issues of structure and cost recovery, the critical issue for lawmakers was to provide some clear benefit for average consumers. This was done with a mandatory 10 percent rate reduction over four years for households and small commercial customers that would be financed through issuance of nearly $7 billion in public bonds, repaid through rates over a decade. Even though ratepayer advocates bristled that the resulting debt service would wash away any apparent short-term savings, the deal provided sufficient political cover for lawmakers to claim that restructuring would be beneficial for all customers.

Since no one could agree on exactly how much utility investment was truly stranded, the law called for basing CTC collections on the difference between utility costs (including the expected lower price for power bought in the PX) and existing retail rates minus the 10 percent reduction. A rate freeze would remain in effect for utility customers over a four-year transition period, or until the utilities fully recaptured what they considered stranded costs.

Most importantly, full direct access for all customer segments and an entirely new market structure were to take effect no later than January 1, 1998.

When complete, AB 1890 was presented as a fully formed, predigested package to the Senate and Assembly, where it was passed with little further debate and unanimous approval.

Hailed as a landmark change in the history of electric utility regulation, AB 1890 carried grand expectations. "Every time a resident of this state flicks on the electric switch, they pay 40 percent more than residents across the United States," proclaimed Governor Wilson during the signing ceremony held at a San Diego–area manufacturing plant.

"The legislation I am signing will end that by ushering in a new era of competition, making California the first state to dismantle its electric monopoly."[15]

A Separate Piece

Despite the intensity of debate or heavy criticisms of the policies that had resulted from the CPUC's 30-month process, the end results of the "Peace Death March" did not appreciably alter the components of the MOU that established California ISO and the PX.

Even though AB 1890 radically amended the existing Public Utilities Code to effect a new, potentially more competitive electric services industry in California, the law provided remarkably little guidance as to the nature and responsibilities of the new transmission controller.

Part of the reason for this was that, all along, the WEPEX working group had continued meeting on a parallel track, although it became clear that its technical deliberations frequently spilled over into policy determinations.

WEPEX had also become the vehicle for an increasing interaction with FERC, as the utilities drafted a set of operational policies for filing in Washington to address sticky issues of power scheduling, bidding rules, congestion management, and creation of ancillary service markets. These policies were drafted with special consideration for how FERC was proceeding in its deliberation on open-access transmission policies. And certainly, during 1996 the federal regulators were paying more attention to the details of the WEPEX proposals than they were to the state Legislature's deliberations.

This sense that WEPEX had become the de facto forum for ISO and power exchange matters occasionally troubled CPUC president Fessler, who feared the group was too tightly controlled by the utilities. "It would appear that the three jurisdictional utilities alone have voting rights and that other vital members are there in an advisory capacity," Fessler wrote in a letter to the utilities.[16]

His concerns were echoed by many non-utility parties who increasingly felt shut out of the decision process, especially consumer advocates who foresaw market players dominating the proposed board structure and a lack of concern for achieving a "least-cost" outcome in balancing system needs.[17]

Although the utilities' April 29, 1996, package of filings to FERC did not resolve all differences, it established many of the key decisions that would later become embedded policies, including creation of a stakeholder governance structure and proposals for congestion pricing for transmission services. But there was still controversy over the filing. SDG&E had gone so far as to make an alternate filing to promote points that it had lost during the deliberations, such as a more powerful ISO that would impose least-cost criteria on generation dispatch decisions. SDG&E, however, later withdrew its competing filing.[18]

Even as the legislative committee was drafting AB 1890, the WEPEX proposal for funding the new market entities with up to $250 million in loan guarantees (later raised to $300 million) was being approved by the CPUC—although on that recurring 3-2 split vote. Additionally, the CPUC's August adoption of WEPEX plans for setting up governing boards for the two entities—a 15-member ISO board and a 17-member PX board—set the stage for later governance provisions in AB 1890 that ratified the concept of having utilities, market players, and other "stakeholders" be key participants in governance.[19]

As a result of this implied deference to the WEPEX group on "technical matters" and the structural compromises of the MOU, many issues that later became all-important for the ISO during California's energy crisis were barely discussed in the AB 1890 sessions.

"There wasn't a lot of debate about the separation of functions," Larson remembered. "They were givens, they were understood: This was what the ISO's going to be responsible for, but we're not going to tell you how to do it reliably because the utilities have been doing this for years. We're going to make it known that you're going to be independent, that your mission is open access."

There was little or no discussion in the legislative hearings about the ISO's operation of a spot market for balancing energy needs, she added. "It was apparently a given that it would be such a small last-minute, real-time function that would mimic what the utilities used to do that it wouldn't really be that important. I guess there was a presumption that we would run this thing the way the utilities did."

Also, she said, the feeling among drafters was: "They'll probably hire a bunch of utility people anyway."

The key provisions of AB 1890 affecting market structure were chaptered as Sections 330 through 379 of the Public Utilities Code. "In order to achieve meaningful wholesale and retail competition in the electric generation market," the law reads, "it is essential to do all of the following: Separate monopoly utility transmission functions from competitive generation functions, through development of independent, third-party control of transmission access and pricing...this competition will best be introduced by the creation of an Independent System Operator and an independent Power Exchange."

Other provisions directed the ISO to ensure efficient use of the system and to maintain operational standards "no less stringent" than those set by the Western Systems Coordinating Council or the North American Electric Reliability Council. The ISO was directed to develop maintenance and repair standards for transmission systems and conduct reviews of serious outages, and the law authorized "appropriate sanctions" against transmission owners if their practices caused or extended outages.

The new law recognized federal jurisdiction by directing the utilities to "jointly advocate to the Federal Energy Regulatory Commission a pricing methodology for the Independent System Operator that results in an equitable return on capital investment in transmission facilities for all [ISO] participants." In other words, the new ISO would need to file a tariff with the federal government in order to recover its costs of operations.

Probably the most direct and extensive requirement imposed by the state was that within six months of FERC tariff approval, the new California ISO in consultation with other state agencies was to present a report to the Legislature detailing: a) operating and reliability criteria, b) economic costs of outages on high-voltage lines, c) options to prevent or mitigate such outages, d) communication protocols needed to give advance warnings of outages, e) need for additional generation and voltage support equipment, f) transmission capacity additions that might be needed, g) the adequacy of existing or prospective provisions for reliability, h) mechanisms for enforcing transmission rights-of-way for maintenance, and i) recommendations for improving electric system reliability.

The heavy emphasis on reliability was a direct outgrowth of earlier concerns from the winter storm outages of December 1995. These concerns were amplified by the massive system collapse that hit the West on August 10, 1996—just as negotiators were putting words to the hard-fought concessions in the AB 1890 package.

The realization that a diverse generation resource base and energy conservation had been critical in restoring service and minimizing the impacts of the outage also helped give environmentalists one of their few victories in the AB 1890 debates.

Just a month before AB 1890 was completed, bill author Brulte had boasted at an annual conference of the California Manufacturers Association, "We're going to roll over the enviros" in the restructuring process. Now, pressure from liberal Senator Tom Hayden helped put into the bill as much as $540 million over four years to preserve and encourage new "public-goods" programs.

Reliability concerns stemming from the windstorms of the previous winter had also prompted the lawmakers to add hundreds of millions of dollars to PG&E's base rates for tree trimming and system maintenance.

Recognizing that responsibility for ensuring electric system reliability would soon be transferred from utilities to the ISO and the market, AB 1890 added something that had not been envisioned in the MOU—a five-member Electricity Oversight Board (EOB) that would create the rules and appoint the members of governing boards for the ISO and PX, and serve as an appeal board for decisions of the ISO board.

Membership in the EOB was split between three appointees of the governor and two nonvoting legislative members. Importantly, membership for the EOB and for the California ISO board was limited to California residents, and a simple majority of the ISO board was required to consist of persons unaffiliated with the electric utilities. That established what later became the stakeholder board of governors.

According to Larson, there was no misunderstanding at all that California was ceding transmission and market operations to federal authority, but it wanted a way to maintain the state's interest.

"I remember we said that decisions could be appealed to the EOB, and the EOB confirms the appointments. So that was the state's way of protecting itself given that, yes, we understand this is a FERC jurisdictional entity," she said.

In the early policy formulations on restructuring, CPUC president Fessler had recognized the fundamental shift in jurisdiction that was soon to occur as a result of market reformation: "I deem the market for electricity to be governed by a transmission grid which embraces more than a dozen Western states, two Canadian provinces, and the Mexican states of Baja California Norte and Sud. To describe this market is to depict a political problem. We have no institution or combination of institutions which can easily and effectively monitor industry performance within this market nor police against discrimination, anti-competitive, or unfair dealings."[20]

Rather than simply shifting responsibility to FERC, however, Fessler declared a policy he called "cooperative federalism" that he hoped would allow California to exert a continuing role in establishing the rules for the new marketplace, even while deferring to the interstate nature of electricity generation and delivery.

Cooperative federalism was a concept few really understood, but it basically told federal regulators, "We know this is in your ballpark now, but please let us determine how to play the game." As it turned out, the provisions of AB 1890 seeking to maintain a firm hand over California ISO would set up the first important conflict between federal regulators and California over the new market structure.

Deregulation at the Federal Level

Entire libraries of books have been written about the evolution of regulation in various commercial industries and the growing trend of "deregulation"—seemingly coinciding with the administration of President Ronald Reagan in the 1980s—that soon swept through telecommunications, transportation, banking, and natural gas. Successes seen in one industry in reducing inefficiencies of government intervention in markets were routinely offered as proof that similar savings could be achieved in another.

When disasters occasionally struck, such as the multibillion-dollar savings and loan debacle, they were explained away by free-marketeers as failures of individual market players, rather than a failure of the marketplace created by deregulation.

In time, prominent economists, including Alfred Kahn and Paul Joskow, became popular cheerleaders for open markets, even in what some observers called "The Last Monopoly"—the electric utility business.[21]

In many respects, electricity deregulation at the federal level was a direct outgrowth of the restructuring of natural gas markets in the 1980s, although that trend began with decontrol of wellhead pricing limits a decade earlier. In between, the turmoil caused by the oil embargo of 1973 and the Iranian revolution of 1979 had led the federal government to actually place restrictions on the use of natural gas by utilities to produce electricity—although non-utility developers of cogeneration projects were given incentives to sell to the utilities under a law initially introduced during the Jimmy Carter administration.

Richard Hirsh, a utility industry historian at the Virginia Polytechnic Institute, credits this law, the Public Utility Regulatory Policies Act (PURPA), with breaking down the barriers to utility systems that had been built up through many decades of regulation. While much of the utility industry's concerns with PURPA focused on provisions related to ratemaking standards, natural-gas use, and conversion of power plants to burn coal, Hirsh recounted that few lobbyists paid much attention to Section 210 of the act, titled "Cogeneration and Small Power Production."

Evidently "added as a way to benefit one senator's constituent"—a waste-to-energy plant in Saugus, Massachusetts—this provision ultimately became one of the most significant and contentious aspects of PURPA. Hirsh wrote, "PURPA immediately created new classes of participants in the electric utility community."[22]

The law's directive that utilities must buy power from "qualifying facilities" at or below their otherwise "avoided cost" of production or purchase was to be enforced by FERC and administered by state agencies.

Rules favoring PURPA transactions became a hallmark of state regulatory policies in California and a few other states. By the mid-1990s, QF power was responsible for more than 10,000 MW of California's resource portfolio—and for a large portion of what utilities claimed to be their "over-market costs."

Even a federal mandate to sell to utilities was not enough to make real competition happen, however, and QFs became vanguards in the drive to force utilities to provide "open access" to their transmission systems. In that regard, QFs found support among "transmission dependent" municipal utilities and other public power entities that had long been at the mercy of investor-owned utilities when attempting to access distant power supplies.

Conflicts over interpreting rules for moving power across utility transmission systems became commonplace at FERC.

Open Access to the Future

Open access for wholesale power transactions was instituted as a public-policy imperative with the passage of the National Energy Policy Act of 1992 (EPAct), a law that was actually far more concerned with the country's growing dependence on oil imports than with electricity matters. Still, noted Hirsh, EPAct "offered much to those advocating the use of free market principles in the utility system."[23]

It created yet another new class of competitive power suppliers, the "exempt wholesale generators" (EWGs), which were excused from restrictive rules on corporate structure and finance that applied to interstate utility operations under the New Deal–era Public Utility Holding Company Act (PUHCA).

The newer law allowed utilities to freely enter competitive markets by approving international development subsidiaries and allowing them to build, own, and operate EWGs located in service territories other than their own. Although the law stopped short of letting FERC approve "retail wheeling" to accommodate direct power sales from non-utilities to end-use customers, EPAct gave states the right to authorize such transactions, thereby providing the legal platform upon which California would construct its Blue Book policies for direct access.

Martha Hesse, who served as chair of FERC during the Reagan years, was a driver of the agency's gas pipeline restructuring policies.

After returning to private industry following her tenure in government service, Hesse in October 1995 provided an audience at a San Francisco conference about electricity transmission issues with her vision of the eventual impacts that transmission open access would provide, predicated on results in other deregulated industries: "First of all, there will be little defined service territory, if at all. Generation will be fully competitive, with market-based rates, not cost-based rates, and not really connected to any service territory. Distribution utilities will probably be independent companies, common carriers, like natural gas [pipelines]. Transmission will be a common carrier, like in gas, where you don't need to own the pipe or the wires to transport, and customers will pay a transport fee only. Companies, like MicroSoft or Visa, will offer group electricity rates, something like what we know in telephones now as MCI and Sprint, and some of these groups will offer 'green power' or non-nuclear power."[24]

Although a staunch Republican and a free-market advocate, Hesse was expounding a vision of competition that has been shared by just about every commissioner appointed to FERC from 1980 to the present day, regardless of his or her political affiliation.

"I'd say there was uniformity regardless of party affiliation, uniformity and agreement on the need to move forward," said Steve Greenleaf, a former FERC policy staff member who had served as adviser to commissioner Don Santa. "A lot of it comes down to individual leadership, and I thought Betsy Moler was a phenomenal leader of the agency. But you had Don Santa, a Republican, and while they disagreed on particular points, they were well aligned on the overall policy objectives. It really never came down to a party issue, a political issue. Everybody thought that's what made sense."

Needless to say, the entrenched utility industry was up in arms against open access, declaring—in much the same manner that AT&T had argued against access to its telephone lines—that the end result would be higher costs and less reliable service for all. Proponents of competition countered that such warnings had proved false after the breakup of Ma Bell into regional companies and that, in fact, requiring long-distance telephone lines to become common carriers had provided great benefits for service and innovation.

Building upon the EPAct requirements, FERC in 1995 issued a notice of proposed rulemaking (NOPR) to consider broad policies for open-access transmission, but it tacked on a related investigation into how utilities might recover "stranded costs" as a result of such competition.

In a nod to the increasing urgency of issues raised in California's restructuring effort, FERC also scheduled hearings and technical workshops on everything from power pools to principles that should govern independent system operators. The NOPR became known as a Mega-NOPR for its broad sweep.

The key decisions that eventually resulted from FERC's rulemakings, Orders No. 888/889 issued on April 24, 1996, became the cornerstones of electricity wholesale market restructuring policies across the nation. Order 888 required transmission-owning utilities to accommodate other parties' wholesale power transactions with services that were "comparable" to what they reserved for their own needs. New rules for non-discriminatory access to market information, under the Open-Access Same-time Information System (OASIS) requirements, carried the principles of competition further.

FERC chair Moler, an appointee of Democratic president Bill Clinton, put the impact of the new orders in straightforward terms: "The future is here—and the future is competition. There is no turning back."[25]

It seemed that deregulation had become a fast-moving train, no matter what reluctant utility monopolists or worried consumer advocates said. As Martha Hesse had told that San Francisco audience a few months earlier: "Get past denial and get on with it. Accept the new world as it's going to be. Don't say, 'FERC can't make us do that.' You know they can and they will!"[26]

At the Intersection of State and Fed

In some respects, FERC was playing a game of leapfrog with California in devising and revising its regulations affecting utility competition. Where the early QF industry in California had grown reliant on the provisions of PURPA to guarantee market opportunities in the BRPU auction process, by 1994, FERC chair Moler was already eying a more extensive competitive marketplace to replace the limited competition QFs could provide. Her adverse ruling on a petition from California's utilities challenging the auction had all but killed the BRPU.

Although Congress had specifically prevented FERC from allowing "retail wheeling" for power users, California used the EPAct authority to pioneer policies promoting customer choice and direct access. As the federal government was just beginning to grapple with stranded-cost concepts, California parties had already reached a compromise for full recovery of such costs.

When SoCal Edison offered a proposal for an "independent transmission system operator" in the Blue Book proceedings that would be followed with more detailed standards in the WEPEX filings, it was FERC's Order No. 888 that fleshed out exactly what an ISO ought to be by enunciating eleven ISO principles:

- Governance should be fair and nondiscriminatory, with rules that prevent control or even the appearance of control by any class of participants. Boards should be independent of any individual market player or group.

- There should be no financial interest in the economic performance of any market participant and strict conflict-of-interest standards are required.

- ISOs need to offer open access and all services under a single, unbundled, systemwide tariff.

- ISOs have a primary responsibility to ensure short-term reliability of grid operations.

- ISOs should have control over operations of the interconnected transmission facilities in their regions.

- ISOs should identify constraints and be able to take actions to relieve constraints, employing established trading rules.

- There should be appropriate incentives for management and administration.

- Ancillary service pricing policies should promote efficient use of and investment in generation, transmission and consumption.

- ISOs must comply with OASIS requirements.

- There need to be mechanisms for coordination with neighboring control areas.

- ISOs should adopt an alternative dispute-resolution process to resolve disputes in the first instance.

These principles both reflected what California stakeholders had proposed as part of the MOU agreement and established deeper requirements that the newly formed California ISO would need to live up to.

Although it is uncertain in retrospect whether FERC ever fully bought into Dan Fessler's "cooperative federalism," it is true that the federal agency initially gave a great deal of deference to California's fledgling market reorganization.

IEP's Smutny-Jones recalled being part of a group of stakeholders, led by industry lobbyist D.J. Smith, which traveled to Washington to meet with the California congressional delegation. "It was probably one of the few times that the entire California delegation got together," he said. "Dogs and cats, Republicans and Democrats, they were all in the room. And the message was 'Hands off of California. Leave our market design structure alone. We don't want PoolCo. We want what we've got; leave us alone.' And so FERC did."

3

In Dave Freeman We Trust

THE TELEPHONE CALL came at an unusual point in S. David Freeman's career. The nationally known "utility repairman" was actually between jobs.

The government-asset privatization policies announced by Republican governor of New York George Pataki meant that a New Deal/New Frontier/Carter-era Democrat was no longer welcomed as head of the New York Power Authority (NYPA). That's where Dave Freeman had gone to work as general manager in 1995 after leading the Sacramento Municipal Utility District through a remarkable transition to fiscal stability following the closure of SMUD's troubled Rancho Seco nuclear project.

It wasn't Freeman who made the decision to shutter the unreliable nuke; Sacramento voters accomplished that in June 1988.[1] But after being hired by the SMUD board about a year later, Freeman successfully directed the district into an era of stable rates and a diversified portfolio of energy resources that gave full measure to energy-efficiency programs and solar power, along with modern and more reliable natural-gas generators. Once Sacramento's program was in place and its budget on track, Freeman also was wise enough to turn the reins over to a homegrown crew of managers as he went on to find his next challenge in the Big Apple.

The Power Authority, brought into existence in 1931 by New York governor Franklin D. Roosevelt, seemed like it might be a natural fit for Freeman. NYPA was the prototype for the federal power agencies that Roosevelt created after he took over the White House during the Depression, and its hydroelectricity from Niagara Falls and turbines along the St. Lawrence River made it a national leader in clean energy production.

Among other jobs on an impressive résumé, Freeman had been in charge of the Tennessee Valley Authority from 1978 to 1981, and he had advised President Jimmy Carter on ways to break free of fossil fuels following the Arab oil embargoes that caused repeated price spikes in jittery energy markets. As principal author of the Ford Foundation's seminal energy policy study, *A Time to Choose,* Freeman had literally written the book on the promotion of renewable resources and conservation programs to stem the anticipated boom in costly nuclear power or dependence on environmentally (and politically) unsound oil-fueled electric generation.[2]

Those ideas formed the basis for Carter's National Energy Policy, including the National Fuels Act and PURPA.

In hiring Freeman, NYPA's board proclaimed a need for policy changes along the lines of his alternative-energy visions.

But the new executive made waves at the near-dormant public-power agency beginning with his first week on the job, when he appeared on television observing that NYPA didn't have nearly enough women or minorities on its payroll and promising that he would "get to it" as soon as he settled in. He also instituted an immediate 10 percent budget cut and put the agency on notice that its entire way of doing business was subject to review.[3]

That Freeman also preferred to run things from a Manhattan office rather than at the Power Authority's White Plains headquarters did not sit especially well with the entrenched bureaucrats. In all ways, he was an outsider and a maverick. They never could get used to the Tennessee drawl, the cowboy boots, the Western way of looking at the world, or the folksy sayings that Freeman employed as attention-getting devices with the media. So perhaps it was fated that Freeman would not last very long at NYPA.

Not that this near-legend of the electric utility business was idling after he'd hung his trademark Stetson on the New York skyline. As he sat out the rest of a three-year contract with NYPA, Freeman got involved with a nonprofit group trying to promote solar-power technologies in developing regions of the world, and he was still on the media's A-list for calls from reporters whenever an energy issue reached the front pages or daily news broadcasts.

This particular call from California, however, was something different.

"It was one of the more unusual phone calls I've ever gotten in my life," Freeman recently reminisced. "I was in New York City, having left the Power Authority when Pataki took over, and just kind of recharging my batteries when I get this phone call. On the line is Dan Fessler, the head of the PUC, and Chuck Imbrecht, chair of the Energy Commission, and someone from the governor's office, probably [Phil] Romero. At any rate, I made some smart-ass remark about did I fail to pay my taxes or something? I left the state in good shape, I thought."

The regulators told Freeman of their dilemma. Although the electric restructuring bill AB 1890 created two new public-benefit corporations to take over utility functions, the state constitution prohibited the new entities from starting until the next year. "They were stuck until January to create the boards, and I was the person that had enough respect from the munis, the industrials, and the utilities that they thought I could come back here and break the logjam," Freeman said.

It was supposed to be a very short-term assignment, Freeman was told, just a couple of months in order to issue requests for proposals for systems, infrastructure, and equipment. "You need to get into RFPs and purchasing equipment for both the PX and the ISO. They said there's all these stakeholders, and it's planning, planning, planning." He chuckled at the memory. "I said, 'Sure.' So I came back. And it ended up being about a year rather than a couple of months. The governor did not have boards to appoint in January or February or March or April or anytime."

The electric utilities had been ordered to hire two "trustees" to oversee the $250 million in utility-backed loan guarantees that had been set aside for the Power Exchange and the California ISO during the interim period while the Electricity Oversight Board could come up with a group of two dozen stakeholder representatives for each of the new governing boards. Because financial firms that the IOUs approached for the job were wary of potential liabilities, the utilities were unable to find any takers.

The clock was ticking on the mandated market start date of January 1, 1998.

"I was hired under one of the most unusual orders that the PUC had ever issued," Freeman continued. "They put out an order directing the utilities to hire me—by name. And I remember that I said, 'Well, I'm not going to sit down and negotiate the contract with these people. I'm going to be the trustee.'"

The CPUC ruling repeatedly pressed the sense of urgency: "There is insufficient time between today and the date the ISO and PX must be operational to delay developing the hardware and software necessary for these new entities to reliably provide new services."[4]

To get the trust agreements in place, Fessler directed his adviser Camden Collins to negotiate with the utilities to finalize Freeman's contract within ten days.

"It was a rare job in that I really had no boss," Freeman said. "On the other hand, the deal was that if I went along with the recommendations of the stakeholders group, I was automatically being prudent. I had the authority to reject their recommendations, but then if there was a later audit or questions, I was on my own to prove that I was prudent. So I had every incentive to go along, but I had the authority not to go along, which made it workable. It was a perfect balance, and there weren't that many disagreements."

The task itself was hard to conceptualize because of the complexity of entirely restructuring an established industry—and even harder to explain. Freeman once said that when he was flying to the West Coast and tried to describe to a fellow passenger what he was about to jump into, he was met with a blank stare. "But if I said, 'I'm helping to break up the utility monopolies,' they immediately got what it was about and were all for it."

Freeman took up residence in San Francisco in October 1996, borrowing offices from the Skadden Arps law firm at the Embarcadero Center. A trustee without portfolio, he also had to borrow staff and just about everything else. One thing he could not borrow, though, was extra time to get the job done.

Staring at Half Dome

The WEPEX working groups were at the time the closest thing to the kind of governing boards that AB 1890 envisioned, and most of the same people who had been meeting endlessly on WEPEX technical matters migrated over to what became known as the Trustee Advisory Committee (TAC).

A few individuals were enlisted to support the trust, including John Flory, who focused on market-design issues, and Dianne Hawk, an employee of Barkovich & Yap, who had been representing industrial concerns at the WEPEX meetings. Other staff members for the trust were Bob Logan and Angelina Galiteva, though Logan soon left after a few unhappy run-ins with Freeman.

"It was a pretty intense time," Hawk recalled. "At the beginning of November '96 I was hired by the trust. For the next year and four months, I worked 14-hour days. I didn't do anything besides sleep after I worked."

Today, many of the people who were involved in the WEPEX and TAC groups have a hard time distinguishing when one entity dropped off and another began. What they remember is one long, non-stop meeting in some hotel or another as the various committees hashed over issue after issue.

"I've probably seen the ballroom of every airport hotel in California," quipped Jan Smutny-Jones of the Independent Energy Producers. "There were certain faces and names that I kind of recall, but I don't remember how things officially changed. They sort of unofficially migrated over from the sort of energy salon we had going on, you know, talking about market structures, into something that was more formal in terms of trying to advise Dave."

The first job for the trustee staff was to figure out exactly what needed to be done, what kinds of contracts were necessary, and to finalize the RFP documents that the WEPEX group had begun to put together. The lease for California ISO's

Folsom facility had been signed by PG&E in late December; the PX's location was still open to debate.

The WEPEX board in January awarded Duke Engineering and Services the contract to be project manager for the ISO, with the job being to oversee design and implementation of the energy management system and scheduling infrastructure. Duke also was hired to take on responsibility for human resources.

That was just the start. In February, the trust announced a slew of contracts with companies large and small for components of California ISO's new market and grid-control operations:

- Asea Brown Boveri (ABB) was contracted with for dispatch and data-management infrastructure.

- ABB Systems Control and Perot Systems would devise the scheduling, transmission assessment, congestion management, bidding, settlements, billing and administrative systems.

- IBM would handle hardware and other computer systems.

- Utility Translation Systems (UTS) took on data acquisition.

- Buildings and property management were assigned to Shoji Hara and Wasano Hara Trust; Turner Construction; and Lincoln Properties.

On the Power Exchange side, Coopers-Lybrand was named project manager and OM/Hand-El of Norway won the contract for developing the bidding, settlement, billing and administrative systems. MCI was tapped for communications hardware and software for both the PX and California ISO.[5]

Many people have since compared the start of California's new energy market to gearing up for the D-Day invasion during World War II, or to preparing for the Apollo 13 mission to put an American on the moon.

Hawk saw her task in terms equally daunting, if less militaristic: "Looking up at Half Dome. I've got to get from here to there and I don't have any crampons. I have no ropes. I have nothing."

The metaphor had practical implications. "There was not an organizational plan either. There was no project plan for how to do that, how to get all those things in place, for how to switch authority. We went from the WEPEX board, and those people switched to the TAC pretty much to the person. There was a whole lot of discussion about how to get people on staff to finalize these RFPs and get the whole process going. And it was really important to me that it wasn't just loaned staff from the utilities. That we had to find a way of paying people from other stakeholder groups to be involved," she said.

Meanwhile, the trust staff formalized the TAC group structure and meeting process. Just keeping track of the dozens of advisory committee members, their alternates, and correspondents was a massive undertaking. Although they were supposed to be two separate entities, there was a good deal of overlap between the ISO and PX committees, and discussions frequently crossed lines.[6]

Elena Schmid, who was acting director of the CPUC's Office of Ratepayer Advocates, sat on the ISO committee, trying hard to keep a focus on transmission issues.

"When we talked about the Power Exchange, I left the room or stood up and didn't participate because I didn't want the two mixed up," she recalled. "I was very clear from the beginning that the energy and transmission should be separate, so it always bothered me that the boards were together."

Until the new market entities completed the incorporation process in May 1997, which finally severed the Siamese twins, there was only the fuzziest sense of authority. "So really, who had the authority to tell whom to do what?" Hawk puzzled. "Where were the lines of authority? Nobody defined them. That was one of the hardest things for me, to make decisions and to get something started and then have somebody somewhere stop and say, 'We don't like that.'"

Some of the difficulty stemmed from the basic incompatibility of policy determinations set by the CPUC and AB 1890. "You know, the PUC pretty much said, 'Here we have these conceptual things, why don't you figure out what to do and bring back a blueprint for us.' They really weren't involved at all."

Another problem: "Many decisions were made on the basis of political policy as opposed to technical information," she said. "There were a good number of decisions made at TAC that I passed messages to Dave and said we can't do that on implementation."

For some people on the TAC, and even some of the vendors, the trustee support staff had little or no standing. To this day, it's a sore point for Hawk. "I will never allow myself to be put in a position again where I have intense responsibility and no authority."

While Freeman was an expert horse trader from way back, he himself was unsure about how much he should impose on the group decision process. After all, the trustee had a specific purpose, and it did not necessarily include deciding all of the market or technical issues that were needed to create entirely new markets.

"We didn't have a lot of broad policy issues. It was nitty-gritty implementation questions, and the right answer would appear," sometimes after a lot of back and forth, Freeman said. "You know, these were intelligent people. I mean, I was able to help facilitate the discussions with humor and kidding people and all that, but they didn't trust each other."

As had been true of the WEPEX group, the strongest base of technical expertise came from utility personnel, particularly Vikram Budhraja of SoCal Edison and Jim Macias of PG&E, both senior vice presidents of transmission. The nontechnical stakeholders might argue, and they constantly did, about issues of market power or what the best bidding procedure might be, but for those "nittygritty" issues of how the transmission system worked and what that meant for market operations, decisions often were swayed by those with the most utility experience.

Dianne Hawk found Budhraja to be especially influential. "Vikram was always fascinating for me to watch. The way he worked people, the way he worked a room is he sits and listens and listens and listens and doesn't say anything. Then when he does talk, people tend to listen because he hasn't said anything. Vikram became very influential and I think even more so once the trust started because he had a very good grasp of the technical information and he is politically very facile. He would make some correction in the technical argument; sometimes it was a critical one and sometimes it was subtle. He could then launch from there into an alternative approach. And it was very hard for most of the people on that committee to argue with him."

While admitting it was logical to defer to those with utility experience, Smutny-Jones sometimes felt that the new market demanded a new way of looking at the system. "It occurred to me at the time that we had Silicon Valley down there with all kinds of very smart people that were inventing all kinds of new stuff. Rather than assume that the existing group of people who'd done utility service over the last one hundred years should continue to do that, maybe just asking the question, 'Is there a better, cheaper, easier new way of doing this?' would have made some sense. That didn't happen."

Time was a critical constraint on every decision, Smutny-Jones admitted, but he believes the lack of an independent view of how transmission might be reconceived led to certain consequences later on. "Was it fatal? No, but did it cost money? Yes. Did it cost time? Yes. Did it have an outcome in terms of where we ended up? Yes."

Schmid concurred that the urgency of the deadline frequently precluded the ability to look at bigger issues. "The mindset that was going on at the time was 'How do we make this work?' There was hour after hour, day after day, and week after week of solving this problem, solving that problem, but never, 'Gee, should we not do this?'"

"Once there was a compromise, there wasn't enough time to put in to developing and relating what was desired in terms of the design of a market and relating that to how one could do it," Hawk said. "People were just moving so, so fast. Didn't have time to do that. I can't tell you how many times I said, 'I don't have time to do that.'"

Legacy Decisions

"Decisions that were made or not made way back then continue to have huge reverberations today," observed Mike Florio, senior attorney of the ratepayer group The Utility Reform Network and a TAC member.

It may be easy in retrospect to identify "legacy decisions" made by WEPEX or the TAC that would later prove costly and problematic when the California market turned sour.

At the time, though, Freeman was most concerned about getting contracts in place and meeting the statutory deadline. "We were dedicated to making 1/1/98," he affirmed. "You know, 'Ours was not to question why, ours was to do or die.' And it was made very clear to us that we were losing money every day that this new system that was going to save money didn't go into place."

Still, there were some issues he believes were sources of later problems. One was the decision to employ a "single-price" auction for bids on the Power Exchange, under which the price bid from the last generation resource necessary to meet expected load would establish the price for all other generation during that hour.

While consumer advocates on the committees, particularly Eric Woychik, complained that this would drive the price of energy higher, detailed analysis from Stanford economist Robert Wilson argued otherwise. The single-price auction was promoted as more efficient and less likely to engender gaming of bids by generators under the market conditions expected in California.

A related issue was whether the bid price should reflect only the energy commodity, or whether it should also reimburse the generators for their capacity, or fixed, costs. This was known as the "single-part versus multipart bidding." The bidding issues remained among the most contentious elements of the market system even after the trustee set up shop, Hawk said. "I can't tell you how many conversations there were where people talked past each other on that one."

In the end, a single-price auction was chosen, but it didn't sit well with Freeman. "I remember being very frustrated about the bidding system," he said.

One of his fears was that entities with access to very inexpensive hydroelectricity, such as the Bonneville Power Administration, would collect windfall profits under a single-clearing-price auction.

"I said we've got a system now where we're paying for hydro power at a much lower level and if everybody's going to get the same price, it's going to result in higher, not lower rates. And I remember Wilson telling me that maybe we can change it in the future."

To this day, Freeman regrets the choice. "That wasn't the only flaw, but it was a major one."

For many people, one of the biggest "mistakes" made during this time was the selection of MCI to design, install, and maintain a communications network for California ISO at a cost of about $5.8 million per year for five years. The system was set up to accommodate as many as 2,000 users and would allow a variety of access speeds for dial-up, ISDN, frame relay, or leased lines that might be employed by various classes of generators and scheduling coordinators. Costs per scheduling coordinator had been estimated from $1,000 per year for individual SCs to $22,000 annually for the largest and most sophisticated clients.[7]

The problem was that the California ISO system never had anywhere near that number of users and the costs per user skyrocketed. Although some people pointed to new developments in Internet networks, the mind-set of the time was that only a proprietary system would provide adequate security and functionality for the new grid-control operation.

Another issue was the forced separation of the PX and the ISO, which Freeman felt affected everything from their locations to the way they could and could not communicate with each other and the systems that were built to accommodate them. It was, as many people have observed, a "religious issue," sacred and inviolate, that stemmed from the MOU agreement but meant that as the largest market participant, the Power Exchange could not have any special access to California ISO systems or data.

"We had the dilemma that the PX and the ISO had to talk to each other and not talk to each other," Freeman said. "This was mainly Jesse Knight's big deal that there had to be religious separation. And frankly, it was that line of thinking that damn near killed us. We could not locate the PX in the ISO building; we had to find a different location for it. It was expensive and time-consuming and didn't make any sense to me."

Among those arguing most vociferously for separation in every way were CPUC member Knight, who saw it as the only way to prevent utilities from controlling both markets, and large customer representatives, including Barbara

Barkovich on behalf of CLECA and Dian Grueneich for the state of California's Department of General Services and other clients who expected to participate in the commercial direct-access markets.

Additionally, noted Florio, power marketers promoted the idea that the biggest threat to the market was residual utility market power. "The loudest voice arguing that those separations had to be made was Enron," he said. It was an argument that went all the way back to the MOU and the earliest WEPEX filings. "There was a very strong antiutility sentiment that existed around that time…that seemed to be led by Enron but had a lot of large user representatives on the same side that said, 'In the end the utilities just did whatever the hell they wanted and didn't pay attention to us.' Now, I never saw much evidence of that, but that was the perception."

Given everything that happened in the power crisis—with new revelations still coming out today—Florio found the determination that the markets be separate a "sinister" aspect of the market-design debates. "You know, I think it's conceivable that this whole thing was designed to allow somebody to rip everybody else off. It would at this point take a lot of convincing for me to believe that this wasn't the agenda because I saw things happening that made no sense," he reasoned.

Whether deliberate or simply an artifact of the political compromises, one very real consequence of the forced separation was that the market-transaction systems for two different vendors designed the two corporations and bundled their data differently. The Power Exchange treated all energy schedules for its day-ahead market as individual transactions, while the ISO aggregated all the deals into a single bundle. When it came time to run simulations of the market, the two systems refused to communicate with each other.

"There was a big glitch there," Freeman recalled. "If we hadn't discovered that and gone on and completed them without integrating them, God, it could have taken another year."

"I was subsequently appalled at the inability of the PX and the ISO systems to communicate," agreed Smutny-Jones. "It brought back visions of the fiasco in the desert when they were trying to rescue the hostages in Iran and they found out that the Air Force and the Army radios didn't communicate with each other." He traced the problem to the bidding among software developers for the PX system, which drew five bids but none that really seemed perfect. "There was a decision to redo things and bring back the people from Scandinavia. I think we very naively believed that all you had to do was translate this from Norwegian or

Swedish into English and load it up in the computers and it would work, and that isn't what happened."

Smutny-Jones winced at the recollection. "When I look back on this, the fact that this thing got built and actually working by March 1998 was nothing short of a miracle."

Within the big 1/1/98 deadline was an entire series of milestone dates, dictated by regulatory decisions, contract terms, and other factors. Freeman knew he and his small support team could not do it all by themselves. "I had the issue of making a filing with FERC by April. There were no boards, and so I just figured that we need to keep this show on the road, so we hired this law firm out of London. It's a firm that had done similar work in Great Britain, and they came in, and with the staff we put together the necessary filing and just asserted the authority to file on behalf of these agencies."

The British firm hired by Freeman was McKenna & Company, which had recently established a Washington, D.C., practice under the direction of attorney Fiona Woolf. In anticipation that restructuring policies would soon be taking the U.S. by storm, McKenna also hired some American attorneys who had familiarity with FERC procedures.

The so-called Phase II filing, amounting to 1,600 pages, would need to be completed by Woolf's team of a dozen attorneys in ten weeks. At the time, Freeman acknowledged the strong influence that the British model would exert on the new California market, calling Woolf "the most experienced attorney we could find. She *is* the UK experience."[8]

A Completely Baked Cake

Adding to the complexity of process to bring about the new market structures was Governor Pete Wilson's appointment in February 1997 of the members of the Electricity Oversight Board. Wilson named as chair Roy Anderson, the former chief executive officer of Lockheed Corporation, along with ex-banker Lewis Coleman and attorney Archer Pugh. A month later, two nonvoting legislative appointees, Senator Steve Peace and Assemblymember Diane Martinez, were added to the panel.

Like the trustee, the Oversight Board had few resources, and it borrowed office space at the California Energy Commission's building. "The board has no appropriations," lamented chair Anderson at the group's first meeting on March 20. "We must rely on the kindness of a sister agency." Staff members, provided "on loan" from the CEC, were Gary Heath as executive director, Erik Saltmarsh as chief counsel, and Sharon Howell as executive assistant.[9]

From the very start, tensions arose between Martinez and Freeman. The lawmaker from Los Angeles immediately questioned whether the trustee should be overseeing both market entities and whether Freeman even had the authority to make the massive FERC filing that was due March 31. She worried that lines of jurisdiction would be muddied and openly fretted that the trustee groups were not concerned with consumers' welfare.

Freeman was adamant. "This matter has been thought through very, very, very thoroughly, and the filing we're going to put through is completely within our jurisdiction," he said, although he later apologized for not seeking input from the Legislature.[10]

Still, Martinez demanded that she be provided an advance copy of the filing, telling the trustee and the Oversight Board that she planned to read it, in its entirety, during her upcoming honeymoon vacation.

At more than 1,600 pages and weighing over 25 pounds, it would be impossible to summarize all of the elements of the Phase II filing with any justice—let alone describe the subsequent responses from interested parties that parsed and criticized nearly every component.[11]

In its prior order on the Phase I filing, issued in November 1996, FERC had directed the California parties to provide detailed bylaws and conflict-of-interest standards, and to explain how the proposed structure for California ISO met its previously articulated principles governing ISOs. The federal agency had also deferred final determinations on such issues as treatment of market power, bidding procedures for the PX, and the crucial matter of governance by the state-appointed Oversight Board.

All of those matters and more became part of Phase II:

- The ISO tariff, defining responsibility for grid reliability, scheduling, and pricing, as well as congestion management, ancillary service markets, billing settlements, and system expansion.

- The PX tariff that described bidding rules.

- Bylaws for the two organizations.

- Transmission-control agreements that turned over control of the utilities' high-voltage systems to the ISO.

- A market-monitoring plan from the ISO to assist in detecting "anomalous" behaviors, potential gaming by participants, such as taking advantage of system constraints, and other design flaws.

- A set of "must-run" contracts with power generators, especially those recently sold by the utilities, located in key areas or necessary for reliable operation of the grid.

- Open-access "transmission owner" (TO) and distribution service tariffs for use of the wholesale power-delivery system by third parties.

- Market-power mitigation plans for the three investor-owned utilities.

- Explanations of how existing contracts would be honored under the new system.

The massive filing also contained some elements not previously considered in the Phase I filing, such as an explicit obligation of the utilities to construct new transmission facilities that the ISO finds to be needed for economic or reliable operations, and a proposal to limit the amount of money BPA could collect from its bids into the Power Exchange.

On this last point, Dave Freeman was stubborn, contending that BPA could make between $50 million and $100 million each year by selling its cheap hydropower at natural-gas generation prices. Instead, the Phase II filing proposed forcing BPA to sell at a negotiated energy price unless the Power Exchange clearing price was lower. He called it a "fair and simple way" to reduce BPA's market power.[12]

The proposal, which FERC eventually rejected, was just one of many contentious matters contained in the filing.

Despite it all, Freeman looks back on the filing as an overall success—criticisms from lawmakers, consumer advocates, and municipal utilities notwithstanding. "I think everybody accepted the fact that it was good that we made the filing, and nobody was questioning the open-access rule. I thought it was a good rule; it was at the heart of what we were trying to do, and there was no state versus federal government fuss in our hands at the time. We didn't see any conflict," he said. "Everybody was moving toward deregulation arm in arm, you know."

Freeman claims he presented the tariff filings as "works in progress" that could be refined as time went by and circumstances warranted. This is certainly true given that some 50 amendments have been proposed to the California ISO tariff since the start of market operations.

However, there was something unique about the 1997 California ISO tariff filing that would come back to haunt the organization in subsequent years. Beth Emery, who became the ISO's first general counsel, explained that, unlike electric utilities, which file for tariff authority under Section 205 of the Federal Power Act, the ISO design was based on Section 206 authority.

To the lay public, the difference might be inconsequential, but there were very real consequences of the decision.

Under Section 205, utilities are able to make changes to their rates and operational rules without waiting for approval from FERC. If someone else objects or problems arise, the changes can be suspended pending a hearing or regulatory order. Under Section 206, however, every change, major or minor, needs to be filed as a tariff amendment, subject to scrutiny, challenge, and an order, before it can take effect. More than anything else, Emery maintained, this constraint has made it very difficult for California ISO to have the flexibility it needed to adapt to changing market circumstances.

The attorney, now with the law firm of Ballard Spahr Andrews and Ingersoll, said that when she became general counsel, she was presented with "a completely baked cake" in the form of the seminal California ISO tariff structure.

"We had a set of rules developed that were a compromise made by a bunch of people on the committee, each arguing their point and any time anyone was concerned that somebody was going to get away with anything, they wrote down to the umpteenth detail what they wanted to do to constrain the ability. As a result, they created a set of procedures that were almost impossible for us to operate under. And so we spent a huge amount of time basically trying to get people to understand we couldn't run it that way," Emery said.

Proposals built into the tariffs, such as a power-dispatch program that updated system status and accepted bids every five minutes, proved too costly, infeasible both technically and politically because no other control operator in the West could handle that capability.

For Emery, it signaled a severe disconnect between reality and the politics of system design. "Someone always told me that the original thought was this was all going to be done on a turnkey basis and the consultants were going to hand the keys to a CEO on the day of start-up."

As if.

4

The People Movers

WHAT gives an organization life?

You can make the case that the California Independent System Operator was conceived as a political compromise, blessed and funded by the CPUC's policy determinations, birthed by passage of AB 1890, endowed with a legal identity upon incorporation, and launched on its market mission via federal tariff filings. You might even argue that the skeleton of infrastructure, the shell of its leased building and the arterial network of communications and energy-management systems all gave form to what was up to mid-1997 little more than an idea on paper.

The ingredients necessary to breathe life into an organization, though, are not contracts or leases, regulatory decisions, or even acts of law, but people. California ISO was something that had to be created from scratch, and it would require some pretty smart and dedicated people to do the job.

From the start, three different levels of people were needed: a board of governors to be selected by the Oversight Board as specified in state law; an executive management team that, by all rights, ought to be chosen by the new board; and staff-level personnel with the proper experience in operating critical utility transmission systems. The Power Exchange had its own staffing needs, which differed somewhat from those of California ISO, but it seemed that vendors and consultants could accomplish much of the initial work on the new electricity bidding system. For California ISO, though, trustee Dave Freeman knew he had to start somewhere and soon.

"I didn't have any clear authority to hire people," Freeman recalled. "This system was being built and had to start working, we thought, by January 1. There was no way it was going to run all by itself. So I just started hiring people, and nobody stopped me."

As had been expected, the most obvious choice of prospective staff would come from the utilities that were relinquishing control of their systems to the new grid operator. There was, nonetheless, a strong sentiment from some members of the trust advisory committees that key personnel, and in particular the chief executive officer, should be recruited from outside the state.

The lingering distrust of California's incumbent utilities also left residual concerns that a wholesale transfer of control operators from the big three IOUs would somehow diminish the independence of the new organization and put other market players at a disadvantage.

Still, utility transmission experience in some form seemed to be an entry-level credential. The core of initial recruits turned out to be the "loaned" utility staff members who volunteered or had been assigned to work on the technical details of system design for the WEPEX group during the previous two years.

"We were looking for confident and experienced people, and the only place they existed were in the utilities," Freeman explained. "Since we were taking over the control function, there were obviously people up for grabs. And we grabbed some of them, I think the best ones, the central players who could run the grid, which was a life-or-death function."

Although a Duke Energy subsidiary had been contracted to handle human resources for California ISO, the arrangement was terminated early—largely because of irreconcilable differences over how the task ought to be done. Duke Engineering had also been relieved of its role as California ISO project manager after it failed to take responsibility for costly problems with the roof of the new headquarters building in Folsom.

Freeman turned to the PX project manager, Coopers-Lybrand, to fill the gap. In late February 1997, Randy Abernathy, who had begun an HR practice for the firm in the San Francisco Bay Area, found himself called in for a special audience with the sometimes-crusty trustee.

"I had no clue who Dave Freeman was, so my first introduction to him was my interview for doing the HR stuff," Abernathy recounted. "Freeman just started firing a bunch of questions at me. It was obvious he was just testing me. I told him no when I thought no, and he said, 'OK, you've got a presentation tomorrow in front of the TAC.' And that was boom! Off and running."

Abernathy had been mostly working with start-up technology firms in the Silicon Valley—a far different world than the highly structured electric utility business. "The first recommendation I made to the trust advisory committee was, 'You need to hire seven people with these kind of skills. Don't put job descriptions on them yet, because you don't really know what structure you need. Nobody has done this before, right? Let's bring these guys in and figure out what you need them to do.'"

The idea might as well have come from Mars—or Cupertino. "I remember Vikram Budhraja said, 'You've got to have work charts. We've got to be able to tell these people what they're going to do. We've got to give them a clear structure.'" Abernathy retold the story with amusement. "So I went home that night and drew little boxes around each of those seven areas and I put titles on them, and said, 'OK, here are the seven people.'"

One thing that immediately struck Abernathy about the organization was that it seemed to expect it would be staffed completely by operational people. The original organizational chart for California ISO had 195 positions, he said. "There was a general manager, there was one attorney, there was an assistant GM for administration who was going to do HR and finance. There were two finance people. There were no client relations [staff]. There were no lawyers other than a general counsel. There was no training. It was just operators and engineers."

He was dumbstruck by the oversight, and let the trustee committee know about it. "This is great, this is your talent to get things started, but who is going to take care of them? You need to pay these people. You need somebody to find them for you and actually make sure they get in and that you comply with all the laws that are necessary to run a business in California. It's going to have to be an organization, not just an engineering function. They had built this like it was a subsidiary of a utility. All of the infrastructure was kind of assumed." That was something that needed to be changed.

The first few people to be hired would represent the basic functions of the new organization, but they were merely on the tip of the pyramid of staffing needs. "We knew that there were a couple of core types of jobs that we were going to need. We put titles on some of them; some of them we just described as areas," Abernathy said. "We did big, broad pay scales and said these are the kinds of skills that we need to fill these positions. We ran ads in the *LA Times*, the *San Francisco Chronicle*, the *Sacramento Bee*, a San Diego paper, and we had 10,000 résumés in about a month."

California ISO also tried a new approach to recruitment by posting its job notices on the Internet, advertising for "grid operator" and "dispatch control" positions. The unexpected result was an outpouring of response from Russian taxicab operators, as well as police and fire department dispatchers from all over the world—people who thought this job in Folsom, California, might be a wonderful new career opportunity.

Whatever it was.

The First Hires

The first operations person officially hired for California ISO was Kellan Fluckiger. At the time he was working for Idaho Power, but Fluckiger was something of a utility "rounder" with prior stints at Pacific Gas & Electric and Arizona Public Service. Long involved in reliability and wholesale-market issues, Fluckiger was a member of the boards of the Northwest Power Pool and the Western Systems Coordinating Council. He had helped write many of the rules that governed system reliability and security coordination among utilities in the Western interconnect.

"I was heavily involved in the Northwest attempts to form an ISO; it was called Indego at the time," Fluckiger said. "We were aware of WEPEX and all the stakeholder meetings and things that were going on, the legislation that got passed ordering the creation of the whole thing."

Some of the "loaned" utility staffers and consultants hired by the trust had been making an outreach to their counterparts in the region, which is where Fluckiger first had contact with the formative group in March 1997. "That started some discussions that happened very fast over a period of months," he recalled. "The folks I met with identified me as someone they wanted. So I got a job offer very quickly from the trustee, literally within three or four weeks of meeting them, and came to work in May of '97." For the first several months, Fluckiger's checks were drawn from the trustee's account.

Other early hires included Jack Allen, a Southern California Edison information systems specialist; Ziad Alaywan, a PG&E engineer; and Ed Riley, who represented the Los Angeles Department of Water & Power on several of the WEPEX developmental teams.

Alaywan had been conscripted by his boss Jim Macias to provide technical support during the WEPEX period and went on to help develop real-time energy-control systems for the new ISO. He had been considered a real up-and-comer at PG&E, rising to a supervisory position in less than ten years—something that in a previous era might have taken 20 years to achieve. However, the normal career path for utility control operators was being drastically altered by deregulation.

"At first people thought, oh well, this will never happen," he said. "I would say 99 percent of the people on the floor at PG&E didn't believe this was going to happen. They thought this is going to be an experiment, and this is all PUC/government BS. I just had a different perspective on things. You know, this might be interesting. I believed you could open up the system and still retain reliability, and I wanted to be part of it. I said, I'm young; if it failed, fine, I can do something else."

"Something else" became everything else for the first California ISO hires. Not only were the recruits responsible for buying, building, and overseeing development of the needed systems and hardware, they were told to find others like themselves who could run the transmission system.

Riley ticked off the priorities: "The first job was to get all this infrastructure in place, get some computers so we could start writing operating procedures and protocols and part of the tariff, and spending a lot of time flying back and forth between here and Southern California, doing interviews and recruiting staff. There was many a plane ride with Kellan, Jack, and Ziad sitting in these little back-to-back seats, leaning over, writing stuff and making notes, talking about things." It was a lot of fun, Riley remembers, but all-consuming. "We put in 16-to-18-hour days, seven days a week."

Though much deeper into his utility career than Alaywan, Riley carried a "start-up mentality" and a depth of experience that made him stand out from the typical utility lifer. "I've always been one of the start-up guys," he explained. "When I first started with L.A. as a steam plant operator, after a year and a half, I went to substation operations and was one of the original crew members at Sylmar DC [intertie terminus] when that was being built. And when I went down to the dispatcher's office, I did a lot of shift work first, then I got real interested in the computer systems." When LADWP decided to build a new computer system for power dispatch, he was also on that team.

"I had 29 years on and off with the city of Los Angeles and they were good years," Riley continued. "But I really wanted to, I guess, end my career with some notoriety. I wanted to be the first, to be there first. So that's why I'm here."

In many ways, Alaywan and Riley epitomized the people who would sign up for California ISO, and not by coincidence. Their attitudes toward change and challenge were exactly what were being sought.

"We hired people who really wanted to do this. We wanted the best," Fluckiger said. "Jack, Ziad, and I probably interviewed 400 people in two months. The first criteria for me, before technical expertise, was 'Why do you want to do this?' Without the right answers to that question, the right feeling, that isn't what we need. We need somebody who really wants to do this because it's cool, 'cause I can make this work, this is the new stuff, this is where I want to be. And so that by itself weeded out all the people that were sort of married to the old utility, stodgy, trudgy kind of activity. And so we had a whole houseful of people. The only company I had ever worked for where every single person really wanted to be there."

Abernathy, who eventually became California ISO's vice president of human resources, concurred with the sense that the new organization required something beyond mere technical proficiency. "We were very thoughtful about the type of culture that we wanted to build here. There was an early bias, especially with the utility folks that we were hiring, to find those who were not satisfied with the utility environment. We specifically looked for people that were kind of driven crazy by the bureaucracy."

People with the "right stuff" needed to be smart, flexible and able to put every-thing they had to the task of starting the new organization. "We had lots of tech-nical talent," Abernathy recounted. "Then the question was, OK: Do you understand what it's going to mean to work in a start-up environment? Do you know what you need to do? Are you the type of person who can collaborate with a group of other people? Are you the type of person who's not going to get defen-sive when somebody asks you throw your idea on a table in a room full of 10 or 12 very smart people, all of whom are going to have different ideas about it? Are you able to stand up and discuss that stuff? Are you able to put it together in a way so that it's a solid idea? That people can understand it, that you can express it well, that, theoretically, it will hold operationally, it can be implemented? And so we searched out those specific kinds of folks and said, 'If you're like this, great. We'd love to have you. If you're not, sorry. We appreciate your interest, but this is probably not the best match for you.'"

Not everyone fit the bill, he said. "I can remember having a lot of really frank discussions with a number of utility and regulatory people, many of whom still come back to haunt us, that applied for jobs here that we had rejected early on because all of the feedback on them, everything about the way they worked was, you know, they were very siloed in their thought process. They were not terribly flexible, they certainly didn't deal well with anybody being critical over what they thought, or they were information hoarders."

Economics also dictated the selection process. While the trustee and the board of governors allowed recruiters to offer pay and benefits that were more favorable than the normal utility packages, the offers appeared most attractive to veterans, like Allen and Riley, who were close to retirement anyway, and to a younger gen-eration, like Alaywan, who might never have the chance to climb to the top of the utility scale.

"We could hire guys who were close to retirement from the utilities because the utilities were pushing them out" with early-retirement packages, Abernathy said. "Or we could hire really young guys. But guys between the ages of 38 and 48, we couldn't touch because where they were in the curve of the utility retirement plan, they were in too deep to leave and not far enough along that they could take early retirement."

"We knew we were making midcareer changes for lots of people," added Fluckiger. "I didn't want to hire 3-year, 5-year people. I wanted 15-year veterans that knew exactly how to do the different pieces; that's exactly what I wanted. We expected to pay for it, we did. Our salaries were higher. We pissed the utilities off a little because we raised the bar. We had to raise our own salaries to keep some people, and, in that sense, ISOs around the country got mad at us a bit because they didn't have that same kind of premium."

California ISO was not the only new type of company actively recruiting from the ranks of utilities. The utility corporations themselves were establishing wholesale marketing and power generation affiliates, and such firms as Enron, AES, Southern Company, Houston Industries, and Williams were all expanding aggressively in California and other regions. Even financial houses, such as Morgan-Stanley and Koch, established power and fuels trading arms.

California ISO also needed to draw on skills that were not traditionally associated with electric utilities in such areas as customer relations and information services.

That put the grid operator in direct competition for talent with the high-flying technology companies in Silicon Valley and San Francisco.

Jerry Fry, now California ISO's director of human resources, was at the time working for Cooperative Employment Services, a firm that helped find workers for state government jobs that had been subcontracted to fill California ISO positions.

"We knew we had to have a comparable benefits package to what the utilities had," Fry explained. "The one thing that we had then and still have difficulty matching is the old retirement system. Almost no company formed since the 1990s has been able to offer a pension system like the old utilities are locked into. We knew we had to pay more than the going rate at the utilities to get anybody to leave because the retirement system was so good. We found by experience to get people to leave the security of the old utilities, we could get their attention at 10 percent. We could get them to leave at 20 percent."

But money wasn't the prime motivator for most of the people who eventually gravitated to Folsom, Abernathy said. "They were there not because they couldn't find another job and make a lot more money, but because they were going to do something that, when they were done, having their name associated with it would be a great thing."

There were plenty of interested candidates. "We started in May," Fry remembered. "The first time I met with Randy Abernathy, he handed me 900 résumés and said, 'Here, start hiring.' Over the next seven months, I think we provided about 120 or 130 employees we found out of 10,000 résumés we received."

Search for the Top Guns

By May, the formalization of California ISO and the Power Exchange as public-benefit corporations was falling into place. Freeman and the trust were still nominally in charge of system development, but it was time to turn policy decisions over to the formal boards.

Once again, it seemed, the same stakeholder representatives that peopled WEPEX and the trust advisory committees were tapped for the new boards, although the dictates of state law and federal policies meant some new faces were taking their places in the crowd of governors for each corporation.[1]

One newcomer was Ken Wiseman, a Fresno-based business executive, who had worked for oil firms and agricultural interests in the Central Valley. A self-described "maverick Republican not to be trusted by conservatives," Wiseman had some prior exposure to electric competition as a consultant for the Agricultural Energy Consumers Association.

Michael Boccadoro, a lobbyist for the AECA, had been serving on the TAC for California ISO, but active lobbyists were frowned upon as members of the new stakeholder boards. Boccadoro suggested that Wiseman apply to the Oversight Board for one of the consumer representative spots. "I show up in San Francisco and all these people know each other," Wiseman said. "This is totally boring to me. I don't know any of these people, and they're all jockeying for position, they all want the ISO."

He hadn't prepared a speech but described his brief pitch to the board in this way: "I'm a customer. This is my background. I've managed companies. I've been a state employee. I don't have any axe to really grind other than I'm a believer in markets that are watched. I've been in the produce industry. It's a market. I think I can contribute."

On his way out of the meeting, Wiseman said that Jan Smutny-Jones approached him, saying, "Well, greased-lightning. It's clear that we have one member of the ISO."

In short order, Wiseman found himself on the search committee for an executive management team, along with Elena Schmid from the Public Utilities Commission, Vikram Budhraja of Southern California Edison, and Terry Winter from San Diego Gas & Electric, who served as chair of the group. "I said, well, this HR committee. I do that. I've hired a lot of executives. I don't know any of you people, but I know how to put management teams together, so I think I can help."

Because of the consensus opinion that the new CEO should come from out of state, the group quickly identified their top candidate in Jeff Tranen, a utility executive from the New England Electric Supply System (NEES). But Tranen did not want to start in California until he had completed the job of selling NEES' portfolio of power plants—as it turned out—to a PG&E affiliate.

That put more pressure on filling the second spot, that of chief operations officer, and according to Wiseman, there was plenty of competition. Fluckiger put in his name for consideration. Jim Macias, the head of PG&E's transmission arm was back and forth on whether he wanted the job. Kent Palmerton, who had been the manager of planning and contracts for the Northern California Power Association, also applied for the gig.

Wiseman said that he had his own favorite candidate—Terry Winter. There were several things about the utility veteran that especially attracted Wiseman. One was that, like Wiseman, he seemed to have a low tolerance for what appeared to be near-constant bickering over the minutiae of system operations by board members who were supposed to be concentrating on policy matters.

"These people, they ought to go and run the grid and get off the board," Wiseman frequently thought to himself. "This is not anything to do with policy. Or it got into old wars and people posturing. Either way, I would get up and just leave; I need to get a drink of water. The guy I kept running into who was doing the same thing was Terry Winter."

Wiseman also perceived a kind of old-fashioned integrity in Winter that resonated with his own upbringing. "We both came up in agrarian small towns heavily influenced by church politics, and both of us for that reason are not particularly partisan, are very independent," he said. "Terry says, 'I don't do politics, I do church.' Yeah, right. That's where I learned politics, at church."

Even though Winter was supposed to be in charge of the executive search committee, Wiseman began pressing him to take the COO job. "After Tranen said he can't come for awhile, I said, 'Hey, how about you?' And he said, 'No, no, no, no, no, I'm not the right guy.' So we'd look at some more résumés and we'd talk with some more people. And I'd go, 'Hey, what about you? Come on, you can do this. This is perfect for you. You don't want to be in charge. You hate politics; you love operations. Run the operation. You love Tranen, you know you can work with him. You know who your boss is gonna be. Take this.' So he agreed to put his name in."

The decision, when it became known, did not sit well with many of the other candidates, Wiseman admitted. "That dynamic was awesome, as you can imagine with all that posturing going on," he recalled. "I realized we had some real talented people. I could also see we had some people who were brilliant technicians but really missing parts."

He offered this analogy: "When you have an interview and somebody just wants to talk about what's under the hood, instead of how are we going to get the car down the freeway. That was really when we made the decision. And that was Terry because you saw that his thing was, 'I know what's under the hood, but I know how to get the car down the freeway. This is where I think we can get black tires, and this is where we can stop for gas and water.'"

Though their personalities could not have been more different, Wiseman said, Tranen and Winter proved to be perfectly complementary in their roles. "Jeff was the right guy for start-up because he was very political and he was very ambitious and he was very focused. Sometimes he wasn't really interested in hearing all sides because he knew what he had to get done. Terry, on the other hand, was much more deliberate, willing not to take action before he checks out the whole landscape. They're both brilliant men."

While officially chief operating officer, Winter took on the role of interim CEO beginning in July. All of the pieces were falling into place. The core group of California ISO employees was going to start moving into the new Folsom headquarters in August.

Entrances and Exits

Meanwhile, the stakeholder board of governors was settling in. There were still lots of disputes over technical matters and some friction with the trustee staff, but by and large, what Dave Freeman referred to as "the Tower of Babel" was giving way to a more unified sense of purpose.

With separate boards chosen for California ISO and the PX, each organization began developing unique characteristics. Mike Florio, the TURN attorney, was one of a half-dozen members who sat on both boards of governors. "The culture of the two boards was extremely different," he said. "The PX was more like a corporate board. The board was there as a set of advisers to help management be successful. People exchanged ideas and sometimes had little squabbles, but in the end, nearly every vote was unanimous."

In contrast, the ISO board was prone to continuing debates and competing visions of how things ought to be, Florio said. "Even though there was an ethic particularly at the beginning of, you know, you leave your vested interest at the door, you couldn't leave your views of what was good and what was bad at the door."

From the beginning, the size of the board was unwieldy, said Barbara Barkovich, who represented industrial interests. "I don't believe in big boards," she said. "I think the expectation was that once the institution was established and people could see that it was designed to run the grid and didn't have an agenda, people wouldn't have the sense that they had to have a seat at the table." At some point, the board would shrink to a more manageable size, she expected.

In July, the PX board announced the appointment of Don Ritchey, a former executive with Lucky Stores, the supermarket chain, as its chair. Ritchey, who had experience as an outside director on corporate boards for SBC Communications, the McClatchy Newspaper group, and the Rosenberg Foundation, brought that kind of traditional corporate vision.

At the same time, the PX board hired Dennis Loughridge, the president of BHP Power, as president and chief executive officer. In October, George Sladoje was recruited to become executive vice president. Sladoje, a former executive for the Chicago Stock Exchange and the Chicago Board of Trade, filled the Power Exchange's need for someone from outside the utility industry who could apply his experience in exchange, trading and scheduling operations to the new power market. Sladoje would eventually replace Loughridge as CEO for the exchange.

The California ISO, for better or worse, tended to stick with leaders drawn from the same pool of experienced stakeholders and utility managers. Although the EOB's first choice for chair of the board was Dick Ferreira, assistant general manager of the Sacramento Municipal Utility District, the decision did not go over well with SMUD administrators, so Ferreira resigned after chairing a single meeting, though he remained a governor.

Almost immediately, the job was handed over to Jan Smutny-Jones, head of the Independent Energy Producers. "I happened to be sitting in the Oversight Board hearing when that occurred," Smutny-Jones recalled. "Gary Heath, who was executive director of the Oversight Board, came down from the dais and said, 'Hey, would you mind being sort of the interim chair?' At the time they were looking for a former CEO of a corporation to take over as chair of the ISO. I said, 'Sure I can do that for awhile.' Well, they never did successfully find anybody."

With the new boards in place, and at least some of the top executives identified, Freeman made the surprise announcement that he was resigning from the trust to become general manager of the Los Angeles Department of Water & Power. "The boards were being formed; they just didn't need me any more," he said. "There was a feeling by the board members that they wanted to take charge and as long as I was there as trustee, there was a duplication of responsibility. It was just time for the job of trustee to be over, and it coincided with the time when this opening came up that I was interested in."

The announcement generated mixed feelings among California's regulatory community. CPUC president Greg Conlon called Los Angeles mayor Dick Riordan to see if Freeman's new job offer could wait until the start of market operations. "I think Riordan told him they needed me worse," Freeman said.

In his last formal appearance as trustee, Freeman on September 3 updated the CPUC on the status of progress toward the January 1 start date. Although he assured regulators that everything was being done to hit the deadline, his report was less optimistic than some were prepared for.

"There's a good chance [the ISO] will be operational by 1/1/98," Freeman said. "There's also a good chance it might not make it."[2]

The main problem proved to be the design differences in communications systems built for the PX to transfer its hourly schedules to the ISO. The problem had been discovered early enough to avert disaster, he said, but it "still poses serious risks to the project" because contractors were projecting that a complete fix might not be ready until late December.

5

Folsom and the Birth of the Electric Grid

EVEN NOW, 135 years later, it is not hard to imagine what Horatio Gates Livermore saw and heard as he stood on the banks of the American River where it curves past the town of Folsom.

For all the changes that have occurred in the intervening decades, including the damming of upstream river flows to create the Folsom Lake Recreation Area and the construction of a modern American River Bridge to carry a steady flow of cars between Folsom and nearby communities, the scene from this point remains much the same as it was back then. Tall bay trees shelter a quiet cove at Grinding Rock. The swish of their branches overlays the gentle sound of water lapping at the Lake Natoma shore and the honking calls of snow geese or other migratory birds.

Just up the hill from this serene park stands the historic Folsom Powerhouse.

Perhaps Livermore would be disappointed that his dream of creating an extensive industrial complex in Folsom had never reached fruition as he had envisioned it, but he could be justifiably proud of what had been accomplished. From that site emanated the nation's first high-voltage alternating-current system to transmit electricity over long distances for municipal and industrial use.

A native of Maine, Livermore was one of thousands of individuals lured to California in the early 1850s by the promise of finding gold, although his real fortune was made through lumber, mining franchises, and the political connections he'd formed as a state senator. He also carried to the West a vision of a new manufacturing community modeled after that of Lowell, Massachusetts. This modern hub would employ the latest technologies of hydropower generation to replace traditional mechanical waterwheels with steel-forged turbines and electrical wires.

Folsom seemed ideal for the venture, and not solely because of its fortuitous location along the river. The terrain featured just enough of an elevation change to easily accommodate construction of diversion canals and penstock to boost the pressure of Sierra Nevada water that would run through hydroelectric turbines.

The town was already a center for gold mining and commerce, boasting of the first flour mill built along the American and the terminal for the Sacramento Valley Railroad, the first railroad company in the West. Folsom residents were also proud of the town's role as a key stop for the short-lived but highly regarded Pony Express mail service in 1860.[1]

Livermore and his two sons, Charles and Horatio P., had taken control of the Natoma Water and Mining Company and purchased several thousand acres of land along the river with plans to send lumber downriver to a mill in Folsom. By 1868, they had approached the state of California with a novel plan under which they would donate land and provide electricity for the construction of a new prison facility in Folsom. In return, they would use convict laborers to build a dam upstream, divert the water through pipes and a power station before allowing the water to flow back into the river.[2]

Easy to imagine, the plan took decades to accomplish, and Livermore did not live to see the completion of the red-brick powerhouse or witness the thrilling moment in 1895 when the rush of water through three turbines sparked a landmark in electrical generation.

Faced with financial boom-and-bust cycles and extended delays in construction of the granite-walled Folsom Prison, the Livermore brothers were forced to scale back their father's grand vision of a hydro-based industrial center for the town. Instead, the elder son, Horatio P. Livermore, conceived of the idea of transmitting the electricity generated at their powerhouse some 22 miles to downtown Sacramento, where it would be used to power streetcar lines and provide street lighting.

The first power flows occurred in July of 1895, but the venture received widespread acclaim on September 9 during a "Grand Electrical Carnival" held to celebrate the 45th anniversary of California statehood. Strings of thousands of electric bulbs emanated from the substation at Sixth and H streets to drape a tent pavilion on the street and outline the E.G. Atkinson Building with a brilliant electrical light. Folsom's new power station was hailed as "the greatest operative electrical plant on the American continent" by the newspapers that sponsored the festivities. The coming "age of electricity" was saluted by a volley of shots from militia riflemen and hailed with a parade of brightly lit floats that were pulled by the street trolleys.[3]

Although a similar experiment in long-distance transmission of electricity that originated at Niagara Falls, New York, was far better publicized—largely because of the involvement of such notable persons as Thomas Edison, George Westinghouse, and J.P. Morgan, respectively, in conceiving, building, and financing the venture—the Folsom Powerhouse was completed and operating commercially more than a year before the Niagara plant delivered its power the full 11 miles to Buffalo, N.Y.[4]

The Folsom plant used the very latest in equipment from the recently incorporated General Electric Company, especially a new three-phase alternating-current (AC) system that had been successfully pioneered just two years before at the high-head Mill Creek hydro facility in Southern California. The plant's four generators, which had been shipped by boat around Cape Horn, produced a little over 3,000 kilowatts, or 3 MW, of electricity that would be conducted at 11,000 volts via 60-cycle, three-phase current—the system that would eventually become the basis for standardized power-transmission networks in the United States. Technology historian Thomas Hughes summed up the relevance of this development in this way: "Industry did not need to move to the water-power site; the power had traveled over small wires to industry."[5]

In June 1895, a *San Francisco Call* article discussing the soon-to-be completed power station also described a hydro mania apparent in the West: "A new kind of hustler has arisen, and within the past three or four months he has been rapidly multiplying and filling the earth. He is the promoter of new electrical enterprises, and especially the promoter of schemes for the long-distance transmission of electric power. The air of the whole Pacific Coast has all at once become filled with talk about setting up water wheels in lonely mountain places and making them give light and cheaply turn wheels in towns miles away."[6]

Despite its pioneering status, the Folsom plant was not to be the centerpiece of electrical production and transmission for long.

Unfortunately for the Livermores, their main asset, access to Sierra-based water, was threatened by a severe drought just a few years after they began operations. In order to meet their contracts for supplying power to Sacramento, the Folsom facility needed to buy the output from an even newer plant built in 1899 by San Francisco entrepreneurs Eugene deSalba and John Martin. Named after financial backer Riggs Colgate, an heir to the Colgate soap and perfume dynasty, the Colgate plant on the middle fork of the Yuba River transmitted its energy more than 60 miles to Sacramento, over a 40,000-volt circuit.

The pace of innovation was quickening, and by 1900, more than two-dozen hydroelectric stations were in operation in California, stretching from Eureka to

Pomona. Advances in transmission, such as the construction of a then-record 142-mile-long power line from the Sierra projects to the San Francisco Bay Area, helped bring electricity to California's booming cities in April 1901. The wooden poles and hastily strung copper wires were soon replaced with engineered towers of steel capable of spanning the half-mile gap of the Carquinez Strait and withstanding harsh winds from the bay.

Another breakthrough, documented by the *Journal of Electricity, Power and Gas*, was the tying together of several hydropower stations at distant sites, "to be operated in unison as a single station as easily as if they were combined under a single roof."[7]

Martin and deSalba soon became electric empire builders, and through purchase and consolidation they created a network of electric generation and distribution companies that stretched from Chico to Stockton and beyond. Merging their holdings in the California Gas and Electric Corporation with their acquisition of the San Francisco Gas and Electric Company, deSalba and Martin in October 1905 formed the Pacific Gas and Electric Company. Capitalized with more than $45 million in stock and debt securities, the company was able to survive the Great Earthquake of 1906, while many of its competitors collapsed. PG&E would continue its expansion by swallowing less capitalized firms and would soon become one of the largest public utilities in the nation.

Among the many early acquisitions made by Martin and deSalba was the original Folsom Powerhouse, which continued operating as part of PG&E's system until it was replaced in 1952 by a more modern 160 MW hydro plant built at the new Folsom Dam.

As breathtaking as the Northern California achievements in electrical transmission were, they were eventually eclipsed by the even longer lines built to move southern Sierra hydroelectricity to the Los Angeles area. The leading developer of the Southern California system was Henry Huntington and his Pacific Light & Power utility, formed to power Huntington's extensive streetcar lines in the booming and sprawling metropolis.

In 1913, Huntington completed the first development of the Big Creek hydroelectric complex and its 241-mile transmission line to Los Angeles. After Huntington sold his interests to competitor Southern California Edison in 1917, the Edison Company also pursued an acquisition program of smaller utilities until it rivaled PG&E both in the size of its territory and in operating an interconnected system of generation and transmission that covered tens of thousands of square miles.

Taken together, these investor-owned electric companies and a growing community of public-power utilities and water districts put California in the forefront of electricity generation and consumption. Writing in December 1899 about the integration of hydropower and electric lines, George Low, the founding editor of the *Electrical Journal* trade publication, offered his readers this vision of the new electric utility industry: "For not many decades will pass before the Sierras will be studded with power houses from the mountain streams of the Southern California Water Company in San Diego to the McCloud River in Siskyou, whence transmissions will be run to all cities, towns and industrial centers, and these transmissions will be interlinked as intimately as are those of Southern California today."[8]

Low was correct. From its beginnings as a 3 MW power plant on the side of a river with a short 11-mile-long wire connection to a population center, the California network was by the 1930s equal to, and in some ways more impressive than, any in the large industrial states of New York, Pennsylvania, or Illinois.[9]

California ISO Moves to Folsom

Interestingly, when members of the WEPEX advisory groups were selecting the site for the new California Independent System Operator's headquarters, the role that Folsom played in the birthing of the electric utility industry was not much of a consideration.

The policy determination that California ISO should be operated separately from the Power Exchange was given a physical dimension. A compromise was reached that the PX would be located in Alhambra, not far from Edison's headquarters building in Rosemead, while California ISO would reside somewhere in PG&E territory or possibly in San Diego. A compromise within the compromise decided that each entity would have a backup facility located at the other's site.

Ziad Alaywan, who in 1996 and early 1997 was PG&E's liaison to the WEPEX technical group on logistical matters, was one of four people assigned to find a site for California ISO. "We had a site in Folsom, here, we had a site in West Sacramento, we had a site in Santa Rosa, we had sites in San Diego, L.A., and Fresno," he recalled. "You know, nobody wants to live in Fresno, San Diego was too far in the south, and Santa Rosa didn't have any airport nearby."

Increasingly, Folsom moved to the top of the list because of the availability of a building in a business park at Blue Ravine Road that had formerly housed Intel Corporation offices and a Bank of America check-processing center. The building was fully wired for the kind of extensive communication network that California ISO would need. The price seemed right, Alaywan recalled, "something like 68 cents a square foot for this building."

Also important was the fact that Folsom sat on solid ground and to the best knowledge of anyone had not experienced an earthquake in tens of thousands of years. On behalf of PG&E, Alaywan and his boss Jim Macias signed the lease on the building at 151 Blue Ravine Road. "They gave me the key," he laughed in recollection. "I came here and I've got the key, but I don't know what to do with it."

The reality of the big decision hit soon after, he said. "They used to send me the bill, and I said, 'Oh my God! This is how much this thing costs!'" He knew *he* couldn't pay for it.

To put costs into perspective, the new Folsom control center would be the central monitoring station and command post for the fifth-largest integrated electricity network in the world.

Three into One

By the time California embarked on its historic electric restructuring, the combined system to be put under California ISO control comprised 25,526 circuit-miles of high-voltage lines, with major interties connecting the 11 states in the Western interconnection and stretching from British Columbia to Mexico. It was anticipated that at any given moment, California ISO would be responsible for dispatching power from a thousand individual generators to meet consumers' demand for electricity, with an hourly load ranging from 20,000 MW to as much as 50,000 MW.

Besides the systems being turned over by the IOUs, California ISO also had to integrate—or at least accommodate—power flows from and between California's dozens of public power utilities and irrigation districts, and the state's water project, and maintain control over the import and export of electricity from the Pacific Northwest and the desert Southwest.

The largest generation facilities were owned by the utilities—ranging in size from the huge nuclear complexes at Diablo Canyon and San Onofre to large "central station" power plants and smaller "peaking" units scattered throughout the system. But nearly all of the IOUs' gas-fired power stations were being sold to other companies. In addition, California's commitment to non-utility power supplies meant there were hundreds of smaller QFs that were hooked into the system.

The change in the state's market structure meant that, soon, most of these facilities would no longer be centrally controlled and dispatched. Decisions about operational availability and use would rely on market forces and competitive price signals, not least-cost planning regimes subject to regulatory review. Although its federal tariffs and contractual arrangements with certain "must-run" plants gave California ISO nominal control over dispatch, the new market would be nothing like the old system.

The giant map board being installed in the control room of the Folsom building illustrated a single, interconnected grid of power plants, substations, and transmission paths. That concept was a fiction; or at best, it was a goal for the new market to achieve.

In theory, power could flow from any point in the system to any other point on the map, and an energy sale or financial transaction might well involve electricity generated in Canada being delivered to Mexico via California lines.

The reality was that because each utility had constructed its network to meet its own needs and not those of an integrated wholesale market, the Western transmission system was anything but seamless.

Armando Perez, director of transmission planning for California ISO, was at SoCal Edison for nearly 30 years. "When I was in control of the generation and the transmission, I could substitute generation for transmission at any time," he explained. "A lot of the system was planned for the ability to control generation. Once you move into the kind of market that we have, we don't really have any control over the generation or know which of them are going to be running at any particular point in time."

By all accounts, there was a vast difference in the systems operated by PG&E, Edison and San Diego Gas & Electric.

In some cases, it was a matter of geography or investment decisions made at the corporate level. PG&E territory, for instance, covered vast mountainous regions prone to severe winter storms and served a greater number of "load centers" in the cities and towns of Northern California. Its transmission system was considered problematic and required a great deal of maintenance.

Edison, in contrast, had what some operators considered a gold-plated network, tightly configured to deliver energy to the major population centers surrounding Los Angeles. Though frequently subjected to Pacific windstorms, Edison's system hardly ever experienced the same amount of outages as PG&E, in part because the utility traditionally installed a lot of reinforcement equipment at major substations.

The old joke among control operators, according to Alaywan, was that "when PG&E has a storm, half the system goes down. A storm comes to Southern California, everything's fine—or at least in better shape than PG&E."

Jim McIntosh, a veteran PG&E control operator who later became director of grid operations at California ISO, concurred that "maintenance practices have always been somewhat of a struggle" at PG&E. "If Edison needed another transmission line, or they added a generator that needed transmission, they needed three lines but put four lines in. PG&E would never do that. They'd put three lines in and if one went out of service, you'd do what we call contingencies."

Contingencies often involved rerouting flows to restore service, he explained. "That was just kind of their design philosophy." Too often, it meant interruptions to power flows for some customer or another. "You know, there are places down in Edison's territory where they can have four or five lines and lose two of them and not have a problem. PG&E, if you lose two lines anywhere, you're probably blacking somebody out by the time the second one goes out."

The condition of SDG&E's network fell somewhere in between. San Diego and southern Orange County were fairly discrete markets, and SDG&E had only a few major generation facilities. Instead, it relied on the 500 KV Southwest Power Link to import energy from Arizona for much of its needs while interfacing with the Mexican utility system for limited import and export opportunities.

Ed Riley, California ISO's director of regional coordination, who put in nearly three decades at the Los Angeles Department of Water & Power, summed up the differences among the IOUs in blunt terms. "The San Diego system is a mess. The PG&E system is a bigger mess. The Edison system is pretty well designed, they're pretty solid," he said. "You can't really blame anybody, it's just the way it was."

It would be an important part of California ISO's job to plan upgrades and fill in holes in the systems so that system reliability would be as good or better under the new market.

Islands in the Gulf

The big control areas hung together on the backbone of the Pacific AC Intertie, twin 500 KV lines that could carry thousands of megawatts between the Northwest and California. However, the energy transfer capability between the territories was severely constrained.

Historically, the most constrained areas were in PG&E territory, particularly the Path 15 bottleneck in the Central Valley and the limited transmission lines flowing into the San Francisco Peninsula. Edison's most problematic area, Path 26 east of Bakersfield, faced the additional challenge of being the conduit for scattered wind and geothermal facilities not owned by the utility.

The municipal systems were like dozens of little islands in the Gulf of IOUs, but they too had joined in constructing some major interties to access out-of-state energy supplies, with sometimes troublesome links into their local distribution systems. LADWP, along with smaller southern munis, operated a DC Intertie that brought excess Northwest energy to the Sylmar terminus in northern L.A. county.

Similarly, a group of Northern California munis joined to construct a 500 KV California/Oregon Transmission Project, called the "third AC" line, but they still relied on parts of the IOUs' network for final delivery of the power at the south end. Various joint agencies formed by munis added to the web of high-voltage lines within the region.

At its core, the mission of the new independent system operator was to take this hodgepodge of infrastructure and run it as one seamless marketplace, while providing nondiscriminatory access to the system to all market players—even if, as in the case of the munis, they were not California ISO scheduling coordinators.

This task was made even more challenging by the decades of animosity that had been built up between the public and private utilities over access to the grid. The munis had fought long and hard for their interconnection agreements to use transmission at predictable costs, and they were wary of any element in the California ISO tariff structure that might seem to impose higher costs or diminish their flexibility.

The introduction of new market players—power sellers, generators, and other scheduling coordinators—who also demanded fair and economic access to the transmission system was another complicating factor in the transition to the new market structure. It meant that the physical system would have to be reconfigured and operated with consideration for existing entitlements as well as for the demands of a competitive marketplace. Those battles were being fought both at governing board meetings for the new market entities and in the hearing rooms at the Federal Energy Regulatory Commission. The disputes figured directly into the ways that California ISO staff would need to design and operate the transmission system.

California ISO's official mission statement—"Reliability Through Markets"—reflected this tension. The job would require the development and installation of an entirely new computer network to track all the flows, schedules, and status of facilities. The Folsom map board offered a picture of the network, but the real work was silently conducted by the computer systems being devised by contractors and ISO staff.

"Buying the system was the easy part," Alaywan reflected. "The hard part was integrating it all together to make it work. That's what we did for about a year, trying to hook up all these pieces together to make it work."

He admitted that it could not all be done at once, and for the first year of operations, California ISO would continue to rely on the network configurations employed by the utility control areas to acquire and monitor the flow of information about the flow of power throughout the statewide system.

Out of the Bunkers and into the Daylight

There was another somewhat revolutionary aspect to the siting of grid operations in Folsom. For the first time, the business of transmission would be done in a visible way. Federal rules required transmission operators to provide an Open-Access Same-time Information System (OASIS) computer network for capacity availability and pricing data. At California ISO, the public (mainly through its intermediaries in the media and government) also would be allowed access to the control room, albeit in a manner that acknowledged the legitimate security concerns of the network hub.

To be sure, California ISO's headquarters does not advertise itself or stand out in any obvious way from any of the other nondescript buildings in the landscaped office park on Blue Ravine Road.

Any hapless visitor who might attempt unauthorized access or even try to take photographs of the building without permission will almost immediately be confronted. "I'm going to have to ask you for that roll of film," the ever-polite but armed security guard will say as he calls for backup on his walkie-talkie.

Still, the entire atmosphere of the California ISO complex masks this devotion to silent, effective guardianship, and it's a far cry from the way that utilities traditionally maintained an almost paranoid secrecy about the location and operations of their control rooms.

"When I was in L.A., everything—*everything*—about the control center was secret," Ed Riley reminisced. "It was a secret location up in the hills, and nobody was supposed to know where it was. And the only way you got there was by going downtown and coming out with somebody" from the public information office. "When they first put up the building, they had a DWP logo on the front," Riley continued. But the head of operations had it filled in. "He wanted no recognition at all it was a department facility."

Other former utility operators told similar tales about the isolation of their energy control centers. "Ours was a bomb shelter," recalled Tracy Bibb, an ex-chief operator at Edison, who is now the director of scheduling for California ISO. "We could have thunder and lightning right overhead and somebody would say, 'Does anybody hear anything?'" He laughed. "No windows."

PG&E used to house its control room in what California ISO vice president of grid operations Jim Detmers called "the dungeon" until it was moved to a secluded, somewhat idyllic location on the 15th floor of the utility's Beale Street headquarters. "I looked out over the bay," said Detmers somewhat wistfully. "Whatever trouble you had with the PG&E system that we're still dealing with now, after you get done with the problem, you turn around and look out over the bay and go, 'Wow, I'm OK. Everything's nice. I can relax.' It was the place to be."

It's possible that some of the serenity at PG&E may have come from knowing that even if the president of the utility wanted to visit the control room, he'd have to wait for someone to let him in. "Even if you've got a card, they've got to buzz you in. If they don't see you, they're not going to let you in," said Alaywan. "You know, dispatchers don't like people on the floor," he explained.

"Here it's different. We went from that environment to what we call the fishbowl."

From the beginning, California ISO's communications department wanted to make the engineers and operators accessible, and for public information officer Stephanie McCorkle, that meant bringing reporters and their cameras right into the control room.

"With television, unless you can give them a visual, they're not going to do the story," she said. "So to get TV to tell the story, I had to get them into the control room. To get anyone, even print, to do the story, you had to get them into the control room. And there's something magical about that control room. When you walk in, you see the importance of the place, and it just puts a visual to what's going on in there. Otherwise it's so hard to describe."

A System of Values

In recounting the formation of utility networks in California and elsewhere from the vantage point of the early 1980s, historian Thomas Hughes did not specifically consider how the possibilities of industry restructuring or deregulation might alter these systems. Nonetheless, his summary comments seem especially prescient.

It is difficult to change the character of large electric power systems, he suggested. "Those who seek to control and direct them must acknowledge the fact that systems are evolving cultural artifacts rather than isolated technologies. As cultural artifacts, they reflect the past as well as the present. Attempting to reform technology without systematically taking into account the shaping context and intricacies of internal dynamics may well be futile. If only the technical components of a system are changed, they may snap back into their earlier shape like charged particles in a strong electromagnetic field. The field must also be attended to: values may need to be changed, institutions reformed, or legislation recast."[10]

For all the emphasis on new technology, systems, infrastructure, laws, and policies that were basic necessities for the new California Independent System Operator to accomplish its mission of ensuring "Reliability Through Markets" and open access, the hardest part of the job would be to reshape the attitudes about the transmission system that had been built like steel towers across the span of decades.

6

Countdown to a New Market

ON HIS FIRST DAY of work at the new California ISO building, communications director Patrick Dorinson was being given a tour by Terry Winter.

They stood in the area that was going to become the conference room. "The fishbowl" that was the control area would eventually be separated by a huge glass window, but at that moment, the space was open and seemed vast in its emptiness. Construction workers were everywhere. "This is going to be our control room," Winter explained.

"We're looking at it, and there's nothing," Dorinson recalled. "My first reaction was, 'You've got to be nuts. By December 31st? We're supposed to be up and running and tested and taking over?' I didn't know how this thing was going to work. I knew eventually it would work, but I thought, 'Why did they ever compress this thing in this time frame?'"

Unlike most of the new California ISO hires, Dorinson did not have a utility background, and he readily admitted that all he knew about electricity was that it came from an outlet in the wall. His most recent job, however, had been as an associate deputy assistant secretary for communications at the Department of Energy in Washington, D.C. That's where he had heard about California's restructuring program and the fact that Dave Freeman was the trustee for the new market organizations. As a political fund-raiser for the Democratic Party in California, Dorinson knew Freeman as an early contributor to President Clinton's 1992 election campaign.

"I was looking to get home to California. I was done with Washington. Done with Clinton and politics," he said. "I figured out where Dave was, and I called him up. It didn't take him long to get back to me. He said, 'Hey, you know we got this thing going out here and we're really going to put it together.' I said, 'You got any room for some PR people?'"

"In fact, we do," Freeman responded.

With a note of support from the trustee, Dorinson was flown out to San Francisco for an interview and, in short order, he was offered the job of heading communications for the ISO. "I thought this was very interesting, and it was new. So why not jump into something that nobody's doing and use it as a learning experience? Who knows where it will take you."

While his 15 months at DOE probably helped seal Dorinson's shot at the position, it was a prior job at the National Aeronautics and Space Administration (NASA), working on the international space station project, that gave him a better understanding of the monumental task at hand. "It was Apollo 13. We've got to do this. We don't have any options," he said. "The atmosphere was 'Just get it done.' Money wasn't really an object, although we didn't go overboard. But it was like we've got to do it, and we've only got so much time."

Dorinson was able to hire Stephanie McCorkle, a public information officer at the Sacramento Municipal Utility District. A former television news reporter in coastal California and in Austin, Texas, McCorkle had met Freeman when he headed up the Lower Colorado River Authority. When it came time for her to look for a life after TV, Freeman helped steer her to a job with SMUD, where he had become general manager. In the fall of 1997, she migrated over to the California ISO with a couple dozen other ex-SMUD employees.

McCorkle brought to the ISO's communications department an understanding of the electricity business, familiarity with the state's few active energy reporters, and a sense of mission derived from the public-power agency. "I brought a muni thinking to what we were doing," she said. "There's a sensitivity issue in terms of your meetings being open as possible, and I tried to promote openness in terms of public information. SMUD was a not-for-profit, too. It was a community-owned asset."

One example of this sense of openness to the public was the first media briefing and facility tour held by California ISO on October 2, 1997. It would be reporters' first opportunity to see the new facility—even in its unfinished state—and to meet with CEO Jeff Tranen, who had finally settled in. Also on hand were Winter and Kellan Fluckiger, who now sported the title of director of operations and engineering.

One reporter likened the communications staff to "nervous realtors at a Sunday open house." Even though only a handful of journalists showed up that day, the question on everyone's mind was whether the new market would start on time.

Tranen responded with characteristic confidence. "People know what needs to be done. What makes it complex is that so many things are being done at the same time," he told the journalists. "If you don't tell people something is impossible, they'll get it done."

Tranen's certainty was counterbalanced by Winter's caution about the challenges that still lay ahead. By this time, the communication problems between California ISO and Power Exchange systems were common knowledge, and even though consultants and staff were working on a fix, Winter was forthright upon questioning. "You bet it makes me nervous," he said. The good news was that California ISO anticipated that it could start testing the revised power-scheduling software by early December, leaving just enough time to get it right before the market start.[1]

If possible, the already strident pace of market implementation gained even more urgency upon Tranen's arrival. In a recent interview, he remembered being impressed both by how much had been accomplished by the trust, board, and initial staff when he arrived at Folsom, and by how much was still to be done.

"I was employee number 70-something," he recollected. "We were going from 70 to 200 or 300 employees, staffing up the organization from both in and outside California and working with consultants to bring systems on line in an incredibly short time."

Tranen had helped develop the New England ISO, and he recognized how different California's situation was. In the East, the grid controllers evolved from existing power pools and were really spin-offs from joint utility agencies. Grid controllers at NEPOOL, at PJM, and in New York had essentially just exchanged their employee badges for ones that said ISO and kept doing the same jobs they been doing all along.

"We literally created an organization from scratch," he said, adding that "the most enjoyable and exciting" part of his job as CEO was to see how people from different companies, cultures and even ideologies could all throw in together to reach a common goal. "People signed on knowing they would work enormously long hours. You don't sign on to work 60 to 80 hours each week without that commitment."

The Breakfast Club

But the goal was not just to make a deadline, he said. It was fundamental to the task that system reliability could not be put in jeopardy. "There was an absolute assumption of reliability, first and foremost, to keep the lights on."

And, it seemed, Tranen expected no less of himself than of his crew. He presided over meetings every weekday at 7:30 am. As time drew closer to the January

1 start date, the meetings were extended to Saturdays and Sundays. Using a small table as a desk, Tranen was either scribbling furiously on a notepad with a mechanical pencil or scrawling on a white grease board as all the directors and managers offered their status reports. "I used to be a teacher," he told the assembled group. "So pardon me if I teach you."

Dorinson did not attend every meeting for the technical staff, but one stands out in his memory. "He drew a little timeline, and then he asked all of us to predict if we were going to make 1/1/98. Everybody's going 80 percent, we're taking percentages. I said 95 percent and gave a nice little PR speech, and they all started cracking up. And then it was just back to work," he said.

They were what Dorinson called "iron pants" meetings, during which there was a lot of coffee but no bathroom breaks. Tranen never seemed to need a break, and since he barely even ate, the sessions turned into marathons of endurance.

The meetings were lively and contentious, Dorinson recalled. "There was a lot of back and forth. There was arguing. And I'll admit to you that I didn't understand a lot of what they were arguing about—I'm learning as I'm going—but it was always constructive arguing."

Randy Abernathy, vice president of human relations, was especially keen on monitoring the interaction of all these Type A individuals who had been recruited into the organization. "We had lots of people with very strong beliefs about certain stuff, but they pretty much set it aside because the mission was so singular. Everybody understood it. Everybody was crystal clear about what needed to be done, and it just coalesced," he said.

No single individuals dominated the meetings or the discussion, and leadership on an issue or task could come from anyone in the group.

"It was an interesting dynamic because they would step up where they really had something to offer and take leadership responsibility, but an hour later on a slightly different subject, they would step in the background and be a good soldier and do what needed to be done. What we just started doing was tapping into where those people had the greatest strengths and using them for those roles." The dynamic extended throughout the organization, Abernathy said.

To illustrate, he told this story: At one early "all-hands" meeting, someone raised the idea that there would need to be an emergency notification system. "We've got to be able to communicate. Can somebody get some pagers?" One of the administrative assistants immediately volunteered to make calls to pager companies. "The next day, we had a rep out here with twenty pagers so that we could communicate with each other."

Even with such a group of problem solvers, though, there were times when simple things slipped through the cracks. While the technocrats focused on the big task of market start-up, it was sometimes unclear who was responsible for making sure that the trash was emptied at night.

The Gang's Almost All Here

Coincident with Tranen's arrival, the California ISO executive team was being filled out with the hiring of Charles Smart as chief financial officer, Dennis Fishback as chief information officer, Susan Schneider as vice president of client relations, and, finally, Beth Emery as general counsel.

Emery began her law career at the Rural Electrification Administration and then became an assistant to Mathew Holden, one of the original five members of the Federal Energy Regulatory Commission after it was reformed from the Federal Power Commission.

Later in private law practice, Emery still tracked FERC issues for a large generation and transmission cooperative and was well aware of California's pioneering efforts to build an independent system operator.

One October evening, she got a call from an attorney friend from the New England Electric System who had considered following Tranen to California but who decided she did not want to leave Boston. She asked whether Emery might be interested in interviewing for the general counsel job. "Are you kidding?" she said. "That's like asking a rocket scientist if they want to work on the Mars project."

There were other possible candidates, she was told, including Ann Cohn, the Southern California Edison senior attorney who had helped carry restructuring through the California regulatory process. But it turned out that Cohn, too, felt the timing was not right for a location change.

Emery, however, was ready. "They brought me out and interviewed me, and 30 days later I was in California with my family and the car and all of the house and everything." She and her husband flew out to Folsom for a weekend and within a day had found the only available house for rent in Granite Bay. "Everything just kind of fell into place."

Well, almost everything. Her husband, a headhunter for legal firms, closed his D.C.–area business and took on the role of corporate husband. "He spent a month trying to figure out how to fit everything from a huge house in Virginia into this tiny little rental house," she said.

Meanwhile, Emery was still in Washington, but putting in 18-hour days trying to balance the needs of her existing clients while getting started on her new
job. "I had to wind down a practice and turn things over to other partners," she
explained. "I was in the middle of a debt structuring for a co-op and a refinance
and some FERC proceedings and a merger case. I basically had to get all that
transitioned. Tranen had me on conference calls from the moment I accepted, so
for that 30 days, I was on two- and three-hour conference calls from airport
lounges and other places, trying to come up to speed at the same time I was trying to wind down all the stuff in Washington."

When she finally landed in California, the days did not get any shorter. She
took her place at the 7:30 a.m. meetings, where she was quickly impressed by
Tranen's energy and intellect. "Everybody has their pluses and minuses," she
explained. "He had this just superhuman ability to take all of these incredibly
complex, mind-numbing issues and just drill down and drill down and stick at it
until he could get it into some sort of recognizable order that he could then
explain."

As general counsel, she saw the other side of the CEO's job, which was not
just to make sure the new market was going to become operational, but also to
keep key constituencies—the board of governors, lawmakers, state and federal
regulators—up to date and confident.

As a result of FERC's rulings on the ISO tariffs, Tranen also had to win certification from the three CEOs of the transmission-owning utilities that the market
could begin without affecting system reliability. "The consultants were all saying,
'You can't start, no one ever starts this kind of software project unless you go
through testing. All these things could go wrong.'"

She recounted this story: At one meeting where the options were being considered, CIO Fishback joked that no matter how much you test software, as soon
as it's up and running there are problems. "And Jeff's like a laser," Emery said.
"'Well, what do you do about that?' he asked. Fishback responded, 'You have a
contingency plan for everything that will go wrong.'"

Tranen lit up at the suggestion, she recalled. 'What if we have a contingency
plan? We'll do this and this and this for anything that goes wrong and then the
utilities can certify that we're not going to affect reliability because we know that
no matter what goes wrong, we'll have a fallback position.'

"That was really the key to getting started on time," Emery said. "So we
started this huge book of contingency analysis." To a large degree, contingency
analysis meant system redundancy. The ISO didn't just have a communications

system connecting all the generators to the grid-control network; it had backup landlines and cell phones.

Tranen also began crossing milestones off his checklist. At every meeting, the directors needed to not only explain where they were on their piece of the start-up puzzle but also hit target dates in order to keep to the plan. The group remained confident that 1/1/98 was still a possibility and that no matter what happened, California ISO could keep the lights on.

Perhaps too confident, reflected Kellan Fluckiger. "Through November, everybody still thought we could make it," he said. "You know, we would have these meetings where Jeff would say, 'What's your sense? 50 percent? 80 percent?' And because we had a room full of 'we can do this no matter what' people, we all estimated too high."

Maybe it was that some individuals didn't understand how all the pieces fit together, Fluckiger suggested, and how problems in one area might hinder another. "But it became clear to me toward the end of November that it wasn't going to make it and the only question was what is the adjustment we need."

Independently, Terry Winter was reaching the same conclusion. "We got into later October and we put in the energy-management system, we put in all the electric markets and we were moving pretty confidently that we would be able to make it by January first." Still, what troubled Winter was the settlements process—basically, getting the accounting invoices and payments done in a reasonable time. The English pool and grid operator had stumbled on settlements, but the government continued bankrolling transactions.

"I said the worst thing we can do as ISO is to start this market and then find out we can't settle. The financial risks were huge. Well, when we got to about the first of December, the emotional thing was huge in my mind because we'd been literally working day and night for the last nine months."

He shared his concerns with Tranen. "I said, 'Jeff, I am really nervous, our settlement system has not been tested. Everybody tells me it will work fine, but you know what? Until I see it done, I don't think we can start."

Tranen took the concerns under advisement. In retrospect, he described the "delicate balance" he was trying to maintain, even though he too was becoming convinced that January 1 was no longer feasible. "You don't want to take the pressure off. When do you formally delay? If you do it too soon, the pressure comes off."

The balance point came in early December, but he and Winter kept pushing the schedule. "So we had a week of back and forth, bring everybody together, and of course they were all optimistic because they'd been running so hard for so long and they had a lot of success," Winter said.

Whenever there seemed to be a breakdown in one system or another, everyone would jump on the problem, rewrite the software code, and get things running again. "We got this almost false expectation of how great we were," Winter said.

Finally, though, the message was coming through at the morning meetings: The settlements process was too uncertain. Both Tranen and Winter agreed they could not tell the world that they were sure all the systems would work properly. They informed board chair Jan Smutny-Jones as well as Senator Steve Peace and Assemblymember Jim Brulte of the decision. All concurred that it would be a mistake to start out without full confidence.

Next, the executives told ISO staff. "You know, I just had some people literally sit down and cry, because they had such emotion about making that day," Winter recalled. "One lady came up to me and said, 'I just went home and cried all night long. Now I'm ready to get back to work.' So they dove right back into it."

The formal announcement that the new electricity market would be delayed came on December 22. Although the Power Exchange publicly said it was ready to start, insiders knew that there were just as many uncertainties down in Alhambra as in Folsom.

But the lack of confidence in settling transactions was not the only problem lurking in the California ISO system. A week before Christmas, the engineers discovered a problem with the data-acquisition programs. Everything seemed to be multiplying.

Ziad Alaywan described it as "multiple schedules" for every generator on the grid. "You know, like you give me a schedule. You're going to generate here and deliver here. And I accepted that. Then I look at it and there were two schedules for the same transaction. And later on we're seeing three schedules for the same transactions. Exactly the same. We couldn't figure out why every time we receive a schedule, sort of double, triple, and quadruple. It was weird. It didn't show up in testing. Obviously, we couldn't go live with something like this."

With only three systems in the world configured like California ISO's, there were not too many people who could even begin to diagnose the problem. One was in Canada, one in New York, and another somewhere on the East Coast. Because it was Christmas, they were unable to fly out to California.

There was nothing that could be done, so for the first time in months, Winter told his operations staff to take three days off to be with their families. A few engineers would work out the corrections over Christmas week, teleconferencing with the software experts to solve the mystery.

"Thank God we had made that decision," Winter reflected. "That took a lot of the sting out of the decision not to go forward when we suddenly realized we would have been dead in the water."

So, 1/1/98 as a mission statement was finally put to rest. To soften the blow, California ISO organized a family day in early January, to thank everyone for their hard work and sacrifice before they resumed the nonstop job of getting the new market in place.

The day had a Western theme. The communications department had a special poster created with a picture of a covered wagon crossing the Western plains and the slogan "Blazing New Trails in 1998."

One by one, California ISO employees lined up to sign their names to the poster, as if it were a manifesto or pledge. To this day, the picture hangs on the wall at California ISO headquarters as a reminder that, as with California pioneers' journey across the continent, the impossible *is* possible, but sometimes it takes longer than expected.

7

The Hour Ending 01

THE DELAY in opening California's new electricity marketplace was met with indignation from state regulators, an overall sigh of relief from industry quarters, and a shrug of indifference from the general public. Despite a wave of consumer-oriented newspaper articles beginning in December heralding the market changeover, Californians still had little clue as to what to expect when the new regime finally took hold.

During the first public meeting of the California Public Utilities Commission following the announcement, commissioner Jessie Knight openly wondered whether it was possible to recoup from California ISO software vendors some of the expected $40 million in extra costs attributed to the delay. "Who of us would build a house without timelines and penalties [for contractors]?" Knight asked.[1]

Among those most critical of the decision to defer were energy traders and big power marketers that had already entered contracts for electricity deliveries beginning January 1. Enron Corporation complained bitterly to the CPUC that the delay "represents the failure of the government institutions" that had been mandated by legislation and regulatory policy. "It is extremely disturbing for a delay of this nature to be disclosed literally at the last moment before direct access was scheduled to occur," the company stated in a filing. Enron president Jeff Skilling pinned the blame on the Power Exchange, an entity that Enron never supported, and on the incumbent utilities.

Power schedulers from surrounding states said they wished they had gotten advance notice of the deferment but generally went on with business as usual. "I'm kind of glad they delayed," said one. "It would have been a hell of a thing if it didn't work."

Others admitted that the California Independent System Operator's computer systems were not the only aspects of the market that needed fine-tuning.

Julie Blunden, Western regional director for Green Mountain Power, pointed to continuing problems with the utilities' processing of direct-access service requests (DASRs) from the new energy service providers. Besides, she suggested, the delay brought with it a burst of media attention that served as another reminder that consumers would soon be able to exercise a choice of energy providers. "There may be an unintentional effect of increasing overall awareness to the benefit of marketers," Blunden said. [2]

The electric utilities had begun accepting DASRs in November, but there were big delays in processing some requests because many of the larger customers would need new electric meters that measured energy usage on an hourly basis.

Although the utilities claimed there was no backlog of servicing new meter requests, some of the larger customers complained about being put on hold for installing new equipment pending site visits from utility personnel.

Residential customers did not face technical delays, but to prevent unauthorized switching—called "slamming" or "cramming"—regulators required a verification system whenever a new service request was entered. The utilities were reporting thousands of "error status" DASRs that they said needed to be investigated.

By the end of December 1997, the CPUC reported, some 31,800 customers had entered new switching requests, with slightly more than 11,000 households, over 15,000 commercial or industrial accounts, and about 5,000 agricultural customers asking to buy non-utility power. Given the size of the overall California utility market, with 11 million electric meters, the numbers were miniscule.

The previously feared "land rush" to direct access was more like a trickle, and San Diego consumer advocate Michael Shames claimed that the lack of any kind of market savings being offered to households and small commercial customers meant that restructuring was really just a "rush to nowhere."[3]

More than 300 new ESPs had initially signed up with the CPUC, evidently thinking that their only barrier to entry was the $100 filing fee and believing that they would be able to simply buy discounted energy from the Power Exchange for resale to consumers.

Few were prepared to post required bonds or meet other regulatory hurdles. By the end of January, CPUC staff had revoked certification for 113 of the ill-prepared new marketers and launched investigations of several who seemed to be offering "pyramid schemes" instead of true energy services. Only about three-dozen ESPs ever actively participated in the residential retail market, according to CPUC records.

Many of the lofty expectations expressed for California's energy market were colliding with reality.

CEO Jeff Tranen in late December had told regulators and the governing board of the crucial problems with settlements accounting that led to the delay decision. Just before the New Year, he publicly revealed the mysterious dilemma of multiplying energy schedules—albeit in vague terms. Even before the delay was called, however, there were grumblings among market participants that the scheduling glitches were just the tip of an iceberg big enough to sink the new market.

In a letter to executives of California ISO, the PX, and the utilities, a group of would-be scheduling coordinators had warned that a half-dozen "essential features have neither been delivered in a usable form or tested properly."

The letter questioned the readiness of all the major data and communications systems and added that a lack of understanding about all of the market costs and a dearth of training by ISO staff about emergency operating practices threatened both the viability and reliability of the new market.[4]

Most of the problems stemmed from the rush to meet the legislated deadline and all of the subordinate deadlines that went along with making 1/1/98. Because the federal tariffs said that only certified scheduling coordinators could move power over the ISO system, there had been a last-minute rush to sign generators, sellers, and end users to contracts.

California ISO client relations vice president Susan Schneider proudly proclaimed "50 contracts in 30 days," but the achievement had come at a cost. An "us against them" mentality was developing between market players and California ISO, which was being seen as the new monopoly trying to force its decisions on everyone else.

Although there was a "scheduling coordinator users group" (SCUG) stakeholder process to get California ISO customers on board and up to speed on the rules and protocols, many participants felt that they were being pushed into uncharted territory and that there was insufficient interaction with California ISO operators, who would be deciding whether power schedules would make the hourly dispatch cut.

Special arrangements had to be worked out for federal power agencies that could not commit to the California ISO, while munis still held to their demands for recognition of existing contract rights.

By early January, though, the executives of both market organizations felt confident that the countdown to the new market could resume with a new target date of March 31. PX CEO Dennis Loughridge reassured skeptical reporters that the new date was "doable."

Privately, Tranen expressed his conviction that even though the postpone-ment had been necessary, there could be only one delay or the entire project would lose credibility. That meant the pressures on California ISO staff never let up because next time there could be no excuses.

Ziad Alaywan recounted the feeling among the staff. "You have worked for a year to get [to 1/1/98] and then find out you need more time. We had to over-come that, and it wasn't too easy because people had worked really hard. It wasn't because of politics; it wasn't because of a utility; it was because the systems were not ready. That put more pressure on people. You know, a lot of people had done their part, but the problem was somewhere else."

Still a little perplexed by the computer glitches, Alaywan said he went to work each day with one question: "What else is going to happen?" He redoubled his efforts at testing the system and was in Tranen's and Terry Winter's offices every day to give the executive officers a status report on any new problems. The meet-ings with Winter tended to be much shorter.

"We can talk to Terry for half an hour and then figure out what it is. With Jeff, he needed to know everything about everything. Everything about every-thing about everything!"

He laughed at the memory. "Jeff," he protested at the time, "I've been here for six hours. If you really need me to fix this, I need to leave. With all due respect, I need to go do it."

It became something of a routine. "He kept asking me more and more every day, so I was like, 'Can I go? Can I go now?' Every day. 'Can I leave?'"

Tranen's stock response was, "Well, I need to know so I can assess the risk," Alaywan said.

"And so we tested, and we tested, and we tested it. I was the optimistic guy around here, and they knew that about me. They take what I tell them and they kind of notch it down a little bit."

Another Day, Another Employee

The frantic pace of hiring California ISO staff continued well into the rainy win-ter of 1998. "During the first 250 days after incorporation, we hired a person a day," recalled Randy Abernathy, the ISO's vice president of human relations. "Bringing somebody new in, telling them what they needed to be able to do, get-ting them up to speed, getting their families here. I was probably here 18-19 hours a day. I'd be here, I'd go home, take a shower, say hello to my wife, maybe eat something, come back."

By January, the "full staff" of 300 employees was crowding the offices on Blue Ravine Road, which had expanded into an adjacent building. Even more consultants were brought back for another shot at getting the new systems ready to go live before April.

Relocation assistance for the new hires had become something of a sideline for the HR staff. "Everybody came to Folsom brand-new," Abernathy said. "We had information on schools. We had information on what was happening in Folsom and what kind of support activities there were. We had lots of information on the neighborhoods."

"For the early start-up crowd, Folsom was a detriment," Abernathy said. "You said Folsom and everybody thought—the prison."

One advantage was that housing prices were moderate, especially compared with the Bay Area and Los Angeles.

The constant flow of newcomers translated into a rapidly appreciating real-estate market. "We developed a good relationship with four or five really good realtors. I could get their undivided attention because I was bringing in a boat-load of people."

Different neighborhoods and communities attracted different demographic groups of employees. "If you had a couple come in and they had young kids, you sent them to El Dorado Hills," he said. "If they were at a little higher level so they were going to make a little more money and they had kids, they went to Granite Hills because that was the killer school system. A lot of the retiree guys who didn't want to deal with a commute came to Folsom."

The assistance was especially welcomed by the "trailing spouses" who were saddled with all the responsibilities of settling in while their partners worked day and night on start-up. Informal social networks were encouraged, and Abernathy's team would try to match families that had children in the same age groups. "Early on there was a lot of impromptu socializing that would happen. Birthday parties, 'we finally got this done' parties. People would find a reason to go spend time together, away from work, if only for a few hours. Just to blow off steam, to reconnect."

The California ISO staff was booming right along with the town, which was experiencing a population explosion because of expansion at Intel Corporation and the other high-tech companies that were locating in the area. Rapid changes were apparent not only in the burst of housing development but also in the constant construction of commercial and retail space along Folsom Boulevard, Iron Point, and other key arterials.

At the beginning, there was hardly anywhere within walking distance of the headquarters to go for lunch, except for an old diner that staff jokingly referred to as "the ISO cafe." Otherwise, the choice of available food was limited to Pop Tarts and power bars from a vending machine or whatever people could scavenge from conference rooms where the seemingly never-ending start-up meetings were held.

"You could go across the street for a sandwich," recalled Beth Emery, the newly arrived general counsel. "But there was never enough time to go out. We were in that conference room hour after hour after hour, day after day after day."

Agenda Items

Suddenly, it seemed, it was March and everything was still touch-and-go. Tranen reported on the status of systems and some new glitches during an all-day meeting of the board of governors on March 11. Things were not perfect, he said.

The software that had caused the big delay had run just one day without any problems and four days without any significant problem. "We're on a curve towards start-up March 31," he said. "There's a low likelihood of bad things happening [but] I'm happy that today is not start-up."

If Tranen's tone seemed less confident than usual, he was decidedly more upbeat the next day in a presentation to the Electricity Oversight Board. "Our belief is we will be able to start on March 31," he told the board.[5]

The oversight board's agenda also included regulatory updates—on March 4, FERC had rejected an appeal of its October decision overruling EOB's state-granted authority in several matters of ISO governance. Federal regulators again dismissed any attempt to limit California ISO board membership to state residents, and it denied any role for EOB as an appeals court for California ISO board decisions. FERC suggested a less formal role for EOB as a mediator of disputes internal to the ISO and PX.

Another matter under EOB consideration that day would eventually further the rift between state and federal governance. The state board voted to reject adding Eric Woychik as a consumer representative to the California ISO board to replace Bill Ahern, who was taking a job with the California Coastal Commission. EOB member Lewis Coleman told colleagues that the League of Women Voters had sent a letter of protest to the board, citing work Woychik had done as a consultant for some energy service companies.

While several of the California ISO governors objected to Woychik's appointment for other reasons, the allegations of conflict of interest were somewhat ironic. Throughout the WEPEX and TAC era, Woychik had represented consumer groups, and he carried the endorsement of The Utility Reform Network (TURN) and the Utility Consumers' Action Network (UCAN) for the spot on the California ISO board.

FERC later ruled that the consumer gadfly be given a seat on the California ISO board.

Many people on the board had a hard time dealing with Woychik's strident personality and near-obsession with pointing out market-power opportunities and other flaws in the new system. Even his consumer-watchdog ally Mike Florio, senior attorney for TURN, recognized that parts of the Woychik "package" were "his sense of outrage" about many of the decisions that led to the prevailing market structure and his unwillingness to give up an argument.

California ISO had a "collegial board," Florio noted. "You have to work with these people. Eric advocated in that forum the way you would advocate at the PUC and became ostracized as a result. If you're going to work with people over a period of time, you can't just denounce them as evil or stupid or both and expect them to talk to you the next week as if nothing had happened. But unless you were willing to throw a tantrum like Eric, you couldn't get a hearing."

Also on the March 11 agenda was the introduction of a new stakeholder group, the Western Power Trading Forum.

Executive director Gary Ackerman explained that his group was meant to make sure that the needs of scheduling coordinators would be brought to the attention of California ISO operational staff as they were devising market rules and systems. He supported the establishment of a client-relations department within California ISO because it represented a change from the old utility mentality.

"My focus was definitely on client relations because I saw that as something completely different," he said. "Now you had a group that was earnest about working with customers, customers being the scheduling coordinators."

Because everything was so new and systems were constantly being altered, there was frustration on both sides of the equation, he said. "I think the tension was that people who were interested in becoming a merchant generator or scheduling coordinator couldn't get answers to any of their questions. Probably because answers did not exist."

A Really Hard Day's Night

"Frankly, I don't even remember my first day at work," said Deane Lyon, California ISO director of operations support and training. Even today, Lyon sounds a little unsure about his original job when he arrived in autumn 1997, except that he was hired as a "security coordinator," to make sure that the rules for regional system reliability were being followed.

"What I was trying to do at the time was try to read some of the tariffs and the protocols that we were going to be required to follow, and they weren't even completely developed yet. And get to know my way around the building and see what needed to be done," he recollected.

Within weeks, however, he was moved to grid operations. "No matter what your title was back then, nobody really had a specific job. You found your niche and you found a way that you could best contribute. Certainly, there was a line of authority. I reported to Ed Riley. You took direction from them and you looked at where your talents were best utilized and you focused your efforts in that area."

Mostly, each day involved testing and retesting the system. "We called it 'going on control,' where the IOUs would turn the system over to us for test runs for periods of time, making sure that things would work the way we thought they should," Lyon said. "There was actually a point before 1/1/98 when we started working rotating shifts, covering the place 24/7 to get people in the mode of monitoring such a big system and interacting with the participating transmission owners and making sure we had the communications down."

When the big day finally came, Lyon logged on as shift manager, starting at 6 pm for a 12-hour overnight turn. "The night we went live, the night we took over control and combined these three control areas into one, we did it at midnight, what we call Hour Ending One, on the first of April," he said.

Despite all the testing and dry runs, things did not go completely as planned. "I've described that day as the most exhilarating, most exciting, and most terrifying day of my life," Lyon half-joked.

Jim Detmers, head of grid operations, recalls that he felt much the same way. "Night one was one of those days that took the life out of me," he said. "All I can remember is sitting across from this table right here and Deane Lyon is sitting in the other chair and we had to take over control. We're looking at each other; we're taking over control. All three of the IOUs are on the phone, and we had them muted. We're looking at each other going, 'Oh, my God. We'd better not do this. We'll never be able to figure it out, because we don't have a control number.'"

He explained that the control number is an algebraic sum of all the energy transactions entering and leaving the network over the 26 intertie points that mark the boundaries between California's grid and the adjacent control areas in the Western interconnect. An unexpected computer glitch was preventing the ISO's energy-management system from making the calculation.

Within the state's system, there was a lot of wiggle room because loads on various transmission paths did not appreciably change during the middle of the night. Without configuring the entire control area to that net figure, however, the frequency might suddenly shift from 60 cycles. All the other regional controllers' computers would sense something was wrong, and a host of automated systems would kick into place to try to rebalance the system—with potentially dire consequences.

In short, it was a nightmare. "It's five minutes to midnight on March 31st and we didn't have the number," he repeated. Remembering the moment seemed to strike Detmers with a sense of panic. "Now what do we do?"

Somebody grabbed Jeff Tranen's white planning board from the conference room, and brought it into the control room. Operators frantically began calling all of the other control areas to find out what numbers they had coming into California for HE 01, and they started jotting down all the numbers with the corresponding intertie points. Somebody else grabbed a calculator to tally the net figure. "While we're deciding that, we had to tell the investor-owned utilities, 'You're going to have to retain control here for at least another 10-15 minutes,'" Detmers continued. "We took it on the half hour…and we operated the system. We did that for about a month."

Listening to the story, probably for the hundredth time, outage coordinator Tracy Bibb couldn't resist jumping in. "Well, it wasn't *quite* that long," he jibed Detmers.

"It *felt* like a month, Tracy."

"I think it was a solid week," Bibb retorted.

"It was a couple of weeks. It was a couple of weeks we operated without having the right control," Detmers conceded.

The story of HE 01 carries a mixed message of humility, determination, and pride that seems to characterize how California ISO operators conduct their work. It tells of the fierce dedication to maintaining system reliability—"keeping 60 cycles"—that drives the operators every minute of every day, and of their on-the-fly resourcefulness based on an intimate understanding of the physical system.

Those things had become standard practice as the new independent system operator asserted a new way of doing business, and it would come to the fore again and again during the crisis.

But the tale also illustrates their stubborn conviction that no matter how difficult things are or might get, the new market organization was going to survive. And it doesn't matter what the old utility guard might say or think. "We had a big confidence barrier we had to overcome," Detmers said. "We had money bet against this place. We had lunches bet against this place. We had all sorts of things bet against this that made us do what we did."

Bibb added, "There are people today that will make little snide remarks on the phone like, 'Oh, you guys still there?' And we've been here five years. Get used to it, pal. Because we're not going away."

8

Money Changes Hands

PEOPLE CELEBRATED the start of California's new energy market in varied ways.

Dianne Hawk had remained as the restructuring trust's liaison to the California ISO and PX boards and managers for another six months after Dave Freeman's departure. There was still a fiduciary responsibility to ensure that the trust funding was being spent properly, but Hawk felt more friction whenever she tried to assert any kind of direction to the new management. Finally, her job was done. "I woke up that first morning, flipped the light switch on and said, 'It works!' Two hours later, Hawk was aboard a plane bound for St. John in the Virgin Islands. There, she said, she "sat on the beach for two weeks" staring out to sea.

In Folsom, the grid operator's staff, family members and invited guests were served cake and praise for the successful transfer of operational control. CEO Jeff Tranen hailed the event as "the culmination of everything I've worked on for 27 years." In a burst of market sentiment, Tranen posed a rhetorical question to the crowd: "Do you believe that our system of democracy and capitalism has driven enormous gains in technology and quality of life, at a lower cost, because of competitive effort?"

On that day, there were few doubters in the room. "Energy policy will no longer be made by utility executives or policy wonks, but by consumers," declared California ISO board chair Jan Smutny-Jones.[1]

Some observers simply reveled in the moment. "For me the biggest thing during start-up was watching not just the guys that had been here, working so hard, but watching the community of spouses and kids and everyone else enjoy that day as well," recalled Randy Abernathy.

The communications department had planned a major media event, with short speeches by the executives and an assistant mayor on hand to formally inaugurate Folsom as the new center of California's electric system. With a deft sense of high-tech showmanship, a produced video wiped images of the three big utilities' logos into the new California ISO emblem—a square of blue and gold with white cascading waves, signifying the current of electricity flowing through the grid.

Communications director Patrick Dorinson was satisfied but not over-whelmed by the turnout from the media. Except for the week when the start of the market had been delayed, getting mainstream reporters to pay attention to the new organization was proving tough.

There was always a degree of interest from the specialists who wrote for trade publications and the national financial press, but the daily newspapers and broad-casters were more concerned with the retail aspects of restructuring and what it would mean for consumers' monthly bills.

"Pitching the story was difficult," he said. The general feeling was "So you're new. So what?" Even on that first day, a local TV reporter had told him, "This is probably the last time I'm going to be out here, unless something screws up. If you guys are running things and everything's fine, there ain't no news," Dorinson recounted. "You should be happy about that," added the TV guy.

If anything, the Power Exchange was more likely to be in the headlines, as that was where the commodity price of energy was being set on an hourly basis. "We weren't a money center; we were supposed to be the silent operator," Dorinson said.

The reliability markets being run by California ISO were intended to be a very small portion of the state's $26 billion annual electricity industry. Most of the ancillary services that were now being opened to competition—with obscure technical names like spin, non-spin, regulation, and replacement—had never before been visible to the public or had a price tag attached to them.

The Market Monitor

One of the theoretical constructs of electric restructuring was that the day-ahead price of power would become a public reference point, available for publication in daily newspapers in the same way that the weather forecast might help people decide how to dress.

A high price for electricity was thought to offer a price signal for consumers to use less power or to defer consumption to less expensive off-peak periods. But the rules of restructuring in California maintained a retail rate freeze for up to four years. That effectively mitigated any "price-responsive behavior" by consumers during the transition period and meant there was little or no general media inter-est on a routine basis.

The PX day-ahead price averages were compiled in the commodities table in the *Wall Street Journal*, along with the contract prices for New York Mercantile Exchange (NYMEX) electricity contracts, and several industry newsletters incorporated the pool price in their indexes and market reports. Few people paid any attention to the California ISO market prices.

Few, of course, except for the scheduling coordinators and generators that would end up arguing over the cost of the new power-delivery services and Anjali Sheffrin, California ISO's director of market analysis. The former head of resource planning for the Sacramento Municipal Utility District, Sheffrin had joined California ISO in 1997 to be the in-house monitor of transactions in the new ancillary services markets. Like many of the new employees who came from the highly compartmentalized utility industry, she was both energized and slightly perplexed by her lack of a job description.

"It was my job to define it," she explained. "What do I do? So the first thing I said to myself was, 'I can't be the first market monitor, right?' There are markets that must have monitors.' I discovered there are monitors in commodity markets; there are monitors in stock markets. Those are the first places I visited to learn how to do my job because no one had told me how."

During the whole period of restructuring policy debates in California and nationally, the proponents of change relied almost exclusively on a frame of reference derived from the deregulation of airlines or trucking or telecommunications. Few seemed to explicitly recognize that electricity markets were more akin to the real-time financial markets. Even natural gas differed from electrons because it could be stored, and other fuels could be used as substitutes when prices spiked. Sheffrin found a much better parallel in the stock market run by the National Association of Securities Dealers, popularly know as NASDAQ.

"NASDAQ was a really good model because their market had just been subjected to a Department of Justice investigation of manipulation. I wanted to see what they were doing as a result of that," she explained. "They were wonderful. They let me sit on the [exchange] floor. Because NASDAQ is all electronic, it was a lot closer to what our market was going to be."

Her biggest surprise came when the market monitors actually made telephone calls to traders and companies if they noticed unusual price changes in a stock. Their powers seemed quite broad, she realized. Monitors could demand information about why prices were moving and even inspect a company's books. If something seemed suspicious or prices too volatile, the monitors could halt trading in a stock while they investigated.

Up to that point, her perception was that these markets pretty much ran by themselves or under guidance of Adam Smith's "invisible hand" to keep people honest. "But the reality was they worked very hard to make sure things run effectively because they know the consequences of a loss of confidence, and nobody can withstand a loss of confidence when it comes to trading stocks."

Sheffrin carried that new understanding with her back to Folsom, along with a copy of the NASDAQ market rules. It became a reference as she wrote up the market protocols that needed to be filed with federal regulators before California ISO could begin operations.

Her other job was to identify members of a market surveillance committee, which had been mandated by FERC. The committee was a panel of three independent economists who would watch the new marketplace, report on problems and make recommendations if it seemed that there needed to be additional protections. The big concern was that a board of governors composed of market participants or transmission owners might try to influence policies to the disadvantage of others.

For the time being, though, Sheffrin was the main person responsible for watching how well market prices matched expectations.

"I knew I was in trouble the day before the market was going to operate because we had some price spikes and we couldn't explain them," she said. "We were here literally until three or four in the morning trying to figure out if things are ready or not. It was pure panic because, I thought, I shouldn't have anything to do for the first couple of weeks until the data started rolling in." She couldn't in good conscience sign off on the market, or recommend that the utility CEOs certify things were ready for operations, until she understood the problem.

Was it a software glitch, or was somebody making aberrant bids? "After an excruciating evening, it was determined it was the software," she said, still sounding a little relieved some five years later. The BEEPstack software was responding to the demand for power by calling on generators to match the load in order of economic merit. If the generator didn't respond, she explained, the program would just assume it had. But there was still a deficiency being sensed by the system. So it would go on to the next unit, then to the next one. "So we were getting these escalating prices for very little response," she said.

At one point on opening night, the price for imbalance energy hit nearly 25 cents per kilowatt-hour, or about two and a half times the average retail price for power. Clearly it was a mistake due to the software glitch, so California ISO staff performed another manual work-around, knocking the price down to a fraction of a penny while the problem was being fixed. That was a price more in keeping with the expected value of the service.

But in a new market, who was to say what the price ought to be?

"That was one of the first questions that Jeff Tranen had asked me," Sheffrin said. "What was ancillary service costing under the old regime? What was the right price? We tried to do some historical studies to see what was the percentage. It ended up being an ongoing indicator that I tracked; what percentage of the energy is ancillary service cost? I had read it was anywhere between 3 and 5 percent in the old regulated utility, so that was the benchmark I was going to be looking for."

That was the first instance of California ISO fixing a price cap on transactions in the real-time market, but it wouldn't be the last. "That one incident explained to me how many things I would have to figure out, which then culminates in one price," Sheffrin said. "I knew I was in for a bumpy ride."

There were several other glitches, major and minor, experienced during those initial weeks of the new market. Issues included making sure that power transactions had all the proper information, what were called "tags" under system reliability rules, to verify the source and destination of the transactions so transmission paths could be scheduled.

Also, there seemed to be a dearth of bidding in the reserve markets, and operators had to rely upon the reliability must-run (RMR) units more than had been expected.

The best news, Tranen told the Electricity Oversight Board later that week, was that the scheduling process that had caused the initial delay was working better than anticipated. California ISO was able to close out its day-ahead schedules by just after 1:00 p.m. Schedulers were handling up to 1,200 schedules each day, he reported.

Overall, though, the new market seemed to be sound. Power Exchange prices were very low from the start, benefiting from an excess of hydroelectricity being imported from the Pacific Northwest and a healthy snowpack in the Sierra Mountains, running about 170 percent of normal. In the first few weeks of PX operations, nighttime prices ranged between zero and 2 cents/KWh, with daytime prices running between 2.3 cents and 2.7 cents/KWh.

Later in the spring, the combination of water and moderate demand for electricity pushed prices to less than zero. George Sladoje, the PX's chief operating officer, said such low overnight numbers had never appeared in the market simulations. "You just don't know what is going to happen until there's money changing hands," he said.[2]

For everyone but the generators, that was welcome news.

Meet the Family

Despite many bumps along the road, the stakeholder board of governors for California ISO was settling into a productive working relationship with management and each other—although it might not have appeared that way to an outside observer.

After six months on the job, communications director Dorinson was getting used to the monthly reality series. "It was always reminding me of Thanksgiving," he joked. "You know, you've got Uncle George, over in the corner, who drinks too much, and Aunt Mary, who talks to herself. But they're all family."

Meetings of the 26-member board, then held at the Hyatt Garden Hotel a little way up Folsom Boulevard from California ISO headquarters, were almost always chaotic affairs.

Stephanie McCorkle remembers the open meetings as "just being loud," with people in the audience talking among themselves and on cell phones regardless of what else was happening. "There was a lot of excitement in the air," she remembered. "People had a hard time sitting still, and not just the board itself but people in the audience. There was so much going on and a lot of cell phones going off, to the point where it just became annoying. Finally, the board came down and said 'We can't talk with all the cell phones going off in the audience!'"

Looking back on his relationship with the stakeholder board, Tranen tactfully admitted, "It was a challenge, sure. It was a pretty large board." But the times were exhilarating, he said, and a sense of common purpose prevailed. "People with pretty different ideologies could work together."

The sentiment was echoed by COO Terry Winter. "The whole structure of the board was for people to do things in their own interests but have the proper balances so you got the right decisions. They were all extremely dedicated to the ISO as an organization because they'd put it together."

Many of the board members had been through every phase of the industry restructuring, from the Blue Book to WEPEX, the trust advisory committees, and the stakeholder board. There was a tremendous proprietary interest in every action that was being brought up for consideration. In time, though, the design

debates had given way to discussions of management proposals, and the deliberations frequently resulted in unanimous votes.

"It was a fabulous board," declared Elena Schmid. "And I've sat on a lot of
boards; it was probably the best." Schmid initially represented the CPUC's Division of Ratepayer Advocates until mid-1999, when newly elected Governor Gray
Davis relieved her of her job as interim director of the consumer unit. Though
she stayed with the CPUC for a few months, Schmid eventually left to work for
the Association of Bay Area Governments, a joint powers agency that was trying
to establish energy-buying pools for its members.

As a consumer representative at large, she was able to remain on the board
until December 1999, when she was hired as California ISO's vice president of
strategic development and communications and became the corporation's liaison
to the board.

With the perspective of time, Schmid believes that the early stakeholder board
was effective because its members were able to set aside their differences when it
mattered. "They understood that they were building something and that they
were creating an institution. When you are given that, there is something that
lifts you up from your myopic perspective. So everybody could sit around the
table and argue about this or that, but they could reach decisions. We listened,
and we learned to listen to each other. I thought there was an amazing amount of
wisdom that came out of that group process that led to decent decisions."

Barbara Barkovich, another veteran of restructuring, also had experience with
nonprofit governance but found the California ISO board to be unique. "The
variation in knowledge base of the board members was significant," she said.
"Some people really felt they could make contributions because they knew things.
I think there were people who really wanted to control everything, who felt they
had to comment on every single thing that came up and be involved because of a
fear of how things would turn out. There were people who just thought this was
the most interesting and most amazing thing in the world and really wanted to be
part of it. There was a lot of individual psychology and circumstance that went
into people's desire to be involved," Barkovich said. "Some board members went
to a lot of stakeholder meetings; some didn't go to any."

One of the most difficult aspects of being on the stakeholder board, she said,
was to "try to figure out whose interests you were representing at a given time
unless you're really conscious about it and say, 'OK, I'm doing this as a board
member. I'm listening to this as a board member. I'm not listening to this as an
industrial consumer representative.' My attitude was that you should separate

those. Other people would disagree. They would say the notion of a stakeholder board is that you represent the interests of your constituency."

The dual roles often conflicted, especially for Smutny-Jones, who was the chair of the board as well as executive director of the Independent Energy Producers. There were times when he had to turn the running of meetings over to vice chair Ken Wiseman so he could stand up for his IEP members' interests on some issue. "I was a very, very strong advocate of the stakeholder board, and I've repented since," Smutny-Jones said. "The intellectual concept behind it was that the people who actually were going to pay for the system or have to live under the rules could be heard and make a decision."

Being the chair of such a disparate group was, in one of his favorite expressions, "like herding cats." He found it similar to trying to bring a unified vision to IEP, which represented everything from small wind generators to huge marketers, including Enron.

"The stakeholder board did a superlative job of getting the ISO up and running," he said. Things changed much later, when the economic consequences of the power crisis introduced politics to the board's every action.

The relationship between board members and California ISO employees appears to be a complex one, different for each participant. Some governors demanded a lot of time and information from staff, while others felt they should serve as resources to the staff, perhaps to influence the way that things should be done. Others tried to keep their distance. Some top managers reciprocated.

General counsel Beth Emery said she faced a quandary in dealing with board members who represented adversaries in the many proceedings and complaints she was shepherding through the Federal Energy Regulatory Commission. Municipal utilities and generators alike had full representation on the board, and Emery sometimes felt that she was giving them ammunition along with her regulatory updates and strategic recommendations.

"I thought I was prepared for a stakeholder board because I'd dealt with co-ops all my life," she said. "But co-op boards are generally made up of farmers and ranchers and small businessmen who don't know a whole lot about the power industry." In contrast, the California ISO board had people who had been involved from the beginnings of restructuring, she said. "Plus, they ran the ISO about four to six months before senior management was really in place. They were making all the little decisions, and I think once you get into that habit, it's hard to let go and focus on the big picture."

More than anyone else, Wiseman pushed for a committee structure that would help professionalize the relationships between the board and staff. Issues would be worked out in committee, then brought to the full board with a recommended action plan. "I've been on over 40 boards, public and private," he said. "That's how it works in corporations."

On the other hand, consumer advocate Mike Florio said he was never really comfortable with the attempt to turn the California ISO board into a corporate-type board "that's supposed to be sitting here very genteel in giving policy advice to management. I felt it was a policy-making entity."

To some, the times when the board met under the most stressful conditions—such as start-up, or in dealing with unexpected market events—brought out the best in the group. "We'd have to have emergency meetings," Schmid pointed out. "We could get it together in nothing flat. You know, it was that sort of commitment that everybody would turn their calendar around for it."

"I liked it when order broke down and people had to roll up their sleeves and work on the issues," Florio admitted. "It was more like solving public-policy issues."

"I do think, in general that the people on the board had good intentions and were trying to do the right thing," observed SoCal Edison's representative John Fielder. "There are no easy solutions when it comes to keeping the lights on."

During the history of the stakeholder board, which formally lasted from mid-1997 to January 2001, there were hundreds of meetings. Though scheduled monthly, there were times when the group met every week, while other sessions became marathons lasting two days. On at least one occasion, observers and California ISO staff ran a betting pool to guess when an interminable meeting would finally end.

The Incredible Expanding FERC Docket

Even after start-up, the workload at California ISO never seemed to diminish for anyone, whether he or she worked in grid operations, market services, information services, administration, communications or the legal and regulatory department. Attorney Roger Smith said he was still a bit shell-shocked after arriving in Folsom just in time for the first day of operations, but he jumped right into the fray alongside his colleague Steve Greenleaf, who had also been a FERC adviser before joining the ISO.

"I wasn't ready for the flood of things," Smith said. "People were overjoyed to have Greenleaf and I there—somebody who knows something about FERC! The problem was everybody was coming to us with problems and you'd have to do triage, but of course, nobody was coming to you with insignificant problems." Everything was urgent.

"This is one way to describe the entire time I was there," Smith said of his four years in Folsom. "You'd have to do triage and the most important things for board meetings, but lo and behold, somebody's low-priority problem two weeks ago or a month ago would all of a sudden turn into a crisis."

The problem mainly stemmed from trying to apply the California ISO's huge volume of tariffs and protocols to operational policies, although there were many areas of conflicting language and interpretation. Whatever California had included in its initial filings was taken as a given, and every proposed change was subject to comment and challenge from market participants. Even when he was an adviser to FERC member Don Santa, Smith said, he "had the sense that FERC really didn't like this design, but California had spent so much time, so many people were involved, that they sort of said OK, we'll try it."

Greenleaf recalled that the original California ISO tariff was filed "for informational purposes only," and FERC wanted to know before the market opened which parts of the tariffs and protocols would be in effect. "The commission applies a rule of reason as far as what needs to be in the tariff, what doesn't need to be in it, and a certain level of detail. You need to make a cut at that," he said. When the attorneys representing California ISO did not do so, probably because of the rush to meet deadlines and the transition to permanent management, FERC, "out of frustration and default," determined that everything would be part of the package, Greenleaf said.

No one anticipated the workload that would result. Even with two regulatory attorneys on staff to back her up, general counsel Emery contracted with the D.C. law firm of Swidler Berlin Shereff Friedman to take on the bulk of representation at FERC beginning in summer 1998.

Principal partner Ed Berlin said that when he negotiated the original contract, "I structured it on a flat-fee basis on the assumption that the workload was fairly predictable. That turned out not to be the case at all, and that arrangement was modified several times over the succeeding years."

Besides a steady flow of tariff amendments needed to reflect any change in operational rules, there came an unprecedented number of complaints from market participants and FERC itself about various aspects of the ISO.

"There was so much more embedded in the ISO's tariff than was true for any other comparable organization," Berlin explained. "That struck us as unfortunate, not because there's a problem with FERC oversight but because it becomes a much more cumbersome process. For years we talked about some form of tariff simplification, but crisis piled upon crisis."

The legal landscape for California ISO was complicated by a number of other factors, Berlin suggested. "One is the presence of very large and entrenched municipal utilities. It's not unique among California munis that they are very insistent that they not cede jurisdiction to the FERC. You had the sense that the munis were viewing every proposal on two different fronts: does it make sense operationally, but even if it does, does it subject us to encroaching federal jurisdiction." That cast a cloud over every filing, he said.

Another complication derived from the expansion of FERC's jurisdiction beyond the interstate transmission function to cover much of the new California marketplace. "When the utilities owned 75 to 80 percent of their capacity, they were not in the wholesale power market," he explained. "FERC did not have jurisdiction over the embedded cost of the commodity. It wasn't the creation of the ISO that changed that. It wasn't the development of spot markets that changed that. It was the decision that was made to have the utilities divest themselves of the bulk of their generation, and therefore, of necessity, to engage in wholesale power transactions in order to be able to be providers of last resort."

The changes coincided with FERC's attempts to replace cost-of-service tariff structures for generators with market-based rates. One of the big battles at FERC would be how to ensure that the new merchant sellers could not exercise market power to dictate prices once they took over the former utility power plants.

Run We Must

In devising the rules for utility generation divestiture, the California Public Utilities Commission had made several conscious policy decisions meant to maximize the potential sale price of the old units. This was largely because regulators wanted to speed up the stranded-cost recovery effort, thereby shortening the transition period to full competition.

The commission had rejected any requirement that the new buyers sign power-sales contracts, called "buyback" contracts, with the utilities. The assumption was that any long-term commitment could limit market opportunities and reduce the selling price. It was also presumed that companies would naturally sell all their power to the PX at prices that barely covered their costs because competition would be fierce when new, more modern power plants came on line.

Instead, the CPUC imposed a two-year transition period during which the existing utility personnel would continue running the units before they were completely turned over to new management. The output from the plants was initially bid directly into the PX daily markets, and operational availability decisions were made under traditional precepts for least-cost dispatch.

Many units were sold as bundled packages by location, in part to accommodate air-quality rules that had allowed the utilities to avoid strict emissions limits on individual facilities while meeting "bubble" or areawide standards. There was also the fact that many of the big utility generators had been built to serve local reliability needs, not network needs, or to avoid siting new transmission facilities.

Taken together, all that meant that particular units in particular places were necessary for reliable grid operations and they could possibly command higher prices for their energy and capacity when system demand peaked.

Early planners of California ISO tried to establish a middle-ground approach to ensuring availability. Based on the work of an outside consultant, the board in 1997 had approved a package of "reliability must-run" for scores of plants located in areas of potential constraint. Essentially, the RMR contracts were like insurance policies, obligating plant owners to make capacity available under specific terms. Most units, in addition, could still sell energy on the open market even if they were collecting capacity payments.

That pricing structure proved to be a bonanza, especially for those units holding "Contract B" options that covered their entire fixed costs of operations. At first, there were 117 power plants granted RMR status, with about 16,300 MW of capacity. Some 80 percent of that capacity was contracted under the B pricing option, with a total price tag of about $850 million in the first year.[3]

With FERC committed to replacing the traditional cost-of-service tariffs with "market-based" rate authority for the new wholesale competitors, there was a greater potential for higher profits. For those analysts most concerned about the potential for generators to exercise "market power"—often defined as the ability to dictate prices above marginal cost levels that economists presumed would derive from full and fair competition—the turning over of control to new operators was a calamity waiting to happen. The companies that bought the old generators had paid premium prices for what was essentially an antiquated fleet of power stations, and so they had every incentive to try to maximize their returns.

Many of the issues described above—problematic ancillary service markets, use of price caps, stakeholder board ideologies and interactions, California ISO's complicated tariff structures, FERC's jurisdiction over the new generators and determining their market power potential—all seemed to collide in a series of incidents during California ISO's first summer.

Measuring Market Power

In retrospect, it seems ironic that the first California entity to win market-based rate authority from FERC was Southern California Edison, allowing it to bid its fossil-fueled generation units into the new PX, and ancillary services to California ISO, although subject to cost-of-service caps.

More critical to the new market, however, was the rush of applications for market-based authority coming from the companies that purchased the utilities' power plants, with the first firm to receive full approval being AES Pacific on June 30, 1998, for three units it had bought from Edison.

Other companies, including Duke Energy, Noram, and Houston Industries (later called Reliant), were also in line for market-based approval, while the Dynegy/NRG joint venture initially was turned down in its request covering the El Segundo power plant. FERC found the companies' filing deficient in its proof that the units did not possess market power.

California ISO was taking a position in the cases that nearly all of the generators had the potential to exercise market power because there were times when the markets for reliability services were too "thin." That is, there was little competition to supply the needed capacity in that area. The grid operator asked FERC to limit prices to $25/MWh, but FERC rejected the argument, stating, "substituting new caps would perpetuate the problem, and approval of market-based rates may improve this situation."

FERC also determined that one of California ISO's categories of ancillary services, replacement reserves, was not defined in Order No. 888, and so it was not being considered by the order.

California ISO feared that without pricing restrictions, there was no limit to what people might bid. In the various cases, California ISO had asked federal regulators to apply new standards for determining market power based on locational constraints, rather than the traditional approach that looked at the whole marketplace. The standard tool used by regulators was called the Herfindahl-Hirschman Index (HHI), a measure of market concentration that was employed by courts, antitrust investigators, and regulators while scrutinizing merger applications in various industries.

Essentially, FERC just added up the installed capacity owned by a company as a percentage of the whole market or region. If the figure was less than 15 percent, there was no market dominance, regulators felt.

There was a growing feeling at California ISO that the HHI was inadequate for assessing potential problems in dynamic electricity markets, said Greenleaf.

"The static HHI test is not a complete analysis because you're looking at hourly markets. Installed capacity isn't really indicative."

But FERC stuck to the traditional approach in granting market-based rates to the new generators.

"I thought FERC was dead wrong," said Berlin. "I thought we put in a series of fairly persuasive arguments that tried to point out there were two phenomena that simply were ignored by the traditional market-power test that FERC historically employed. One was the locational problem, and the second was temporal. I was absolutely shocked that we got a deaf ear in response to that."

Berlin detailed the arguments: "Because of the geographic structure of the California market, with every utility having made a generation-transmission tradeoff on a single utility system basis, there were clearly a large number of units that had locational market power. And you couldn't do a damn thing about that. Secondly, they failed to recognize that at time of peak, there was clearly market power, even by those who had relatively small shares of overall market capacity. FERC didn't accept that at all."

What had been a somewhat obscure debate among industry analysts and economists about potential market-power abuse would soon become front-page news in California.

9

Spikes, Peaks, and Smoking Screwdrivers

THE CALIFORNIA ISO communications department had already planned a news conference on July 9, 1998, to describe just how well things had been going during the first 100 days of grid operations. The actual news revealed during the briefing was very different, however.

The day before, there had been several hours when California ISO had to accept a price bid of $5,000/MWh to obtain replacement reserve capacity; that is, power that could be called upon within an hour, if necessary. Hot weather had caused higher than anticipated demand beginning at 1 p.m., and operators needed to secure an extra 1,000 MW. Some was purchased from the imbalance energy market, but additional reserves had to be secured. Only one plant was available to bid, Tranen told the reporters.

The situation lasted several hours, with the bid price rising from $2,500 to $5,000 once the generator realized it had a corner on a tight market opportunity. California ISO later revealed that the price excursion cost about $1.5 million for services that would normally cost $1,500 under the utility price caps. What the bidder did not know at the time was that it could have entered any price at all, and the California ISO software would have accepted it. Technically, there were no limits on price bids.

"We are very concerned about this," Tranen said.[1]

Media representative McCorkle said she was taken completely by surprise by the revelation. "We did not know about that bid," she said. The staff had prepared an entire set of "talking points" for Tranen so he could describe the general run of operations. Because it was the first media event in three months, there were three TV crews and "a ton of media on the phone," she said. "The spike ended up being the story."

The circumstance repeated itself on Sunday, July 12, with the top price spiking to $9,999/MWh, at a total cost of nearly $5 million. California ISO immediately imposed a bid cap of $500 on its replacement reserves and filed an emergency request with FERC to stay the market-based rate approval for four generation companies. "Although it appeared on July 10 that the market for replacement reserves would self correct, events over the weekend confirm that even when all market participants have uncapped rates the markets are not yet workably competitive in all hours in all zones," California ISO wrote.[2]

The incidents provided the new Market Surveillance Committee (MSC) with its first surveillance opportunity, but members exhibited a variety of sentiments during a July 15 meeting of the California ISO board's Market Operations Committee.

Stanford economist Frank Wolak suggested it was all part of the "necessary growing pains" of the new market. Robert Norhaus bristled at Edison's suggestion that hard price caps be imposed on all plants. "The cost-based caps for individual generators don't make sense, and they're screwing up the market," he said, while endorsing the emergency $500 limit.[3]

Within a week, though, the full California ISO board voted to cap prices for ancillary services and replacement reserves at $250/MWh. The board noted that FERC had accepted its emergency motion for caps, but it did not stay its prior approval of market-based rates. Regulators also directed the market surveillance committees for both California ISO and the PX to conduct investigations of possible market power in their markets.

Although some generator representatives on the board argued against caps, there was a consensus that the incident required action, recalled board chair Smutny-Jones. "I have the dubious distinction of being the first person in California to authorize a price cap," he said.

He had given Tranen a verbal approval for the emergency cap and supported the board measure to reduce it to $250/MWh.

The decision did not sit well with the generator community that Smutny-Jones represented, but something had to be done. "It was very clear to me that someone had just figured out a math game, and a week of that and we're back to being regulated. From the standpoint of someone who is trying to build a market, we can't tolerate that," he said.

Caps and Costs

Over the course of the summer of 1998, the $250/MWh cap would be hit frequently as a spell of hot weather blanketed the West. During the end of July and the first week in August, for instance, bids on the ancillary service markets reached the price limit in 20 percent of the hours, escalating the total cost of energy.

The cap was much higher than the top price being recorded by the Power Exchange. Tranen openly worried that the costs of reliability services alone might equal the commodity costs of energy.

Earlier in the summer, the average cost of ancillary services was a mere $1.20/MWh, or about $100,000 per day. From July 26 through August 6, the average climbed to $21/MWh at a daily cost of $2.65 million, reported operations engineering manager Jim Detmers.[4]

The escalating costs coincided with a period when the demand for electricity in Northern California broke all previous records. Pacific Gas & Electric on August 3 set a new peak of 23,031 MW, more than half of the California ISO's top demand of 44,927 MW. Municipal utilities in the region also set new records. Southern California Edison approached its historic peak but did not set a new record.

For the first time, the grid operator put its system of staged emergencies into effect and needed to call for about 500 MW of voluntary power curtailments from PG&E customers east of San Francisco while the utility scurried to perform maintenance on distribution lines. Edison curtailed power to some agricultural customers and put its air-condition cycling program into effect to help trim demand.

On the PX, hourly prices frequently rose higher than $100/MWh and peaked at a then-record $154/MWh in a single hour.[5]

The situation posed a number of problems for grid operators, not the least of which involved "underscheduling" of load by utilities and "withholding" of bids by generators. "It's an economics game," Detmers explained during an August 7 board meeting to review the volatile market.[6]

For utilities, the goal was to try to avoid paying the top PX price for all energy needed during a particular hour. By posting less demand than would be expected and pushing load into the California ISO markets, the utilities might reduce their overall cost. During the heat wave, as much as 8,000 MW of load shifted from the PX to the California ISO market.

On the other hand, some generators also appeared to be holding back from bidding into the PX, hoping to capture higher prices as California ISO markets approached the $250 cap price.

On August 12, Detmers reported, generators bid 5,000 MW less than was needed for the peak hour in the PX day-ahead market. That meant California ISO operators became responsible for finding 5,000 MW of operational reserves.

It also appeared that bidders were directing their reserves into higher-priced markets, for instance, shunning the regulation capacity market and waiting until California ISO was willing to pay a higher price for replacement energy. Part of the problem was attributed to the software program for dispatching bids, and board member Mike Florio complained that the previous rush to implement systems was coming back to haunt the market. "It is the cost of haste," he said.

As time went on, the weather and the market prices calmed, but the market monitors were growing more concerned about the trends they were discerning from the data. "At least 80 to 90 percent of the hours, an inferior product is selling for a higher price," said MSC economist Wolak in mid-August. The computer program design was preventing California ISO from acting as a "rational buyer" of electricity services and should be fixed, he recommended.

A few weeks later, Anjali Sheffrin reported on her initial findings: bids for ancillary services were hitting the $250/MWh cap far more frequently than anticipated, and this was driving the overall cost of reliability up to about 9 percent of the total energy costs, and in some peak periods up to 15 percent. "Artificial barriers are allowing excess superior services to be let go in favor of inferior ancillary services at a higher cost," she said.[7]

The evidence added up to the need for changes to the ancillary services market, while maintaining the price caps. California ISO technical staff would be directed to start redesigning the reliability markets, while legal staff began preparing amendments to the tariffs.

Meanwhile, the need for RMR units appeared to be growing, with a new report showing that 266 units and 20,000 MW of capacity might be required to meet reliability needs for 1999. Although staff were trying to identify transmission upgrades that would alleviate the need for RMR units in certain locations, only one such replacement project was considered feasible in the next year.

Pattern Recognition

Barely six months into its first year, California ISO was establishing patterns that would be repeated throughout its existence.

From watching the data flow each day, transmission scheduler Pete Garris was able to recognize how different scheduling coordinators were conducting business in the new environment. "You could see that some folks did monthly and quarterly deals, and they were fairly consistent," he said. Movements of peak-period energy under traditional arrangements—16 hours each day, from 6 a.m. to 10 p.m., Monday through Saturday—were called "6 by 16" blocks. Off-peak power deals ran from late evening until 6 a.m. and on Sundays and holidays. Baseload, or round-the-clock power, was called "7 by 24."

"That actually helped us in the scheduling office, being able to identify schedules. You know what to look for and then you can pick out exceptions," Garris said. There were always new wrinkles being introduced by tariff amendments, but the schedulers and market players had advance warning of those kinds of changes.

Schedulers like routine and predictable patterns; they enjoy watching the ebb and flow of electric demand on an hourly, daily, weekly, and seasonal basis.

But they must always be prepared for the unexpected to occur—a transmission-line outage, an unscheduled curtailment at a power plant, or a sudden increase in load because of hot weather—and understand the best ways to respond to the situation or to work around a system constraint.

"If you've been in the business any length of time," Garris said, "you know all the scheduling nuances. This is the rule, and you know it works 99 percent of the time. But you always have that 1 percent that doesn't fit any rule that you create, and you have to deal with it."

The Smoking Screwdriver

Probably the single best example of such an anomalous event occurred on December 8, 1998. At 8:15 a.m., a PG&E repair crew forgot to remove grounding wires before re-energizing the main substation south of San Francisco. Within seconds, the local generation units at Hunters Point and Potrero Hill automatically shut down, and the frequency of the regional transmission network fluctuated upward as a million people in the major business and financial center in Northern California lost electricity for about eight hours.

"Having worked at a substation, I'm not sure how you can miss a set of grounds hanging there," said Deane Lyon, a California ISO control shift manager who previously worked for PG&E.

"In every PG&E switching log, the first item in putting things back together is 'Check that all personnel and grounds are in the clear.'" Lyon shook his head.

"The thought of what happens when you energize into a solid set of three-phase grounds and what it must have felt like for the operator who closed that circuit breaker…. That is one of the worst feelings. I was lucky enough in my career as an operator never to have experienced that, but I sure know how it would have felt."

A phrase used by utility crews to describe such an unfortunate accident is "the smoking screwdriver."

Although the event caused an estimated $1 billion in economic disruption to the city's economy, it had relatively small effect on the overall transmission system, owing to San Francisco being a cul-de-sac in the grid. "It's like breaking a piece of the system off that's not an integral part of the system operating reliably as a whole," Lyon said. "But there was a sudden loss of load—a pretty good chunk of load of about 1,200 MW lost instantaneously—that gives you a significant area control error" (ACE).

"You're oversupplying, pushing all this extra generation into the area. The immediate concern was, first you want to know what happened, but the generation dispatchers are trying to get the ACE back to zero," he explained. That involved ordering some units to back down and soliciting decremental energy bids on short notice.

The job was made harder because the surge knocked out the equipment that sent data from the San Mateo substation to the utility. "Our ability to evaluate the status of the system was quite a bit impaired," Lyon said.

California ISO got a lot of calls from media and officials, who assumed the outage was the system operator's fault. Investigations were launched by both the California ISO and state regulators to determine what caused the outage, and after it was established that the cause was "human error" PG&E paid a fine of $440,000 to California ISO.

Even though the mishap occurred on the utility's distribution system rather than on the transmission lines, it was the first time that the grid operator exercised its authority to penalize a utility or market player for violating reliability criteria.

Riding the Peaks

More common but just as challenging for grid operators is a peak-load day, when hot weather spreads throughout the state and surrounding regions, pushing electricity consumption to seasonal or all-time records. California ISO had established its first significant peak in August 1998. Although summer 1999 featured milder temperatures on average, the prior pinnacle was surpassed on July 12, when California ISO's load hit 45,884 MW, and most Northern California utilities also set new records.

For Pacific Gas & Electric, the new daily energy delivery record set that day was less significant that it might have been when utility employees were marshalling the transmission and generation resources needed to meet load.

In Folsom, though, there was a sense of accomplishment and elation among the schedulers and dispatchers, Garris remembered. "I think the group felt pretty proud of the fact that California had a new all-time peak record. Maybe that is part of the old world that hasn't changed. When you're the grid operator, and you manage a new all-time peak with basically no news to report, you feel pretty good about that."

Energy prices spiked briefly as temperatures exceeded 110 degrees in Northern California. At the PX, there were a few hours when the clearing price on the hour-ahead market hit $200/MWh, and congestion on transmission lines from the Pacific Northwest and on Path 15 caused an uptick in imbalance energy prices while California ISO staff secured an additional 1,000 MW to balance loads.

But aside from the normal generation snafus that accompany stressful days, such as loss of hydroelectric units and boiler-tube leaks at old fossil-fuel generators, the day did not require advancing beyond a Stage One Alert.[8]

"If we'd had something occur when we were in a Stage One, lost a big generating unit like Diablo Canyon, it could very possibly have put us into a Stage Three," said Lyon. Stage Three is triggered when operating reserves fall to dangerously low levels and power curtailments might have to be effected to ensure system stability.

Nothing like that happened, however, and the warning system to alert utilities of a potential resource deficiency and impose a "no touch" day so generators would defer maintenance went smoothly. "There was some additional generation available; there was some additional energy available from outside the control area," Lyon said while reviewing logs from that July day to discern exactly why things went so right on the way to a new peak-load record.

He recalled the sensation of watching the load curve crest at a new plateau, knowing that the system had made it through intact. "Seeing that load curve turn and flatten out and start to go down. It's like, 'Yeah, we made it again!' It's amazing on days like that how things just seem to hold together."

For the operators, it all added up to a successful day, Garris said. "We did everything we could as far as the normal processes, and when we had to go the extra mile or take the extra step to make sure the grid operated reliably, we did that."

On September 30, the focus shifted to Southern California, where another burst of extremely hot weather in combination with a variety of system events presented new challenges to operators. Fires near the Pacific AC Intertie had reduced the ability to import energy from the Northwest at the same time that Path 15 was undergoing extensive maintenance. The 1,110 MW nuclear unit at PG&E's Diablo Canyon had problems, and a 750 MW steam unit at the Navajo Station in Nevada tripped. In all, 4,600 MW of generation or transmission was unavailable.

While the peak demand of more than 40,000 MW was not a record, it was still running about 2,500 MW higher than forecasts. Stage One quickly escalated to Stage Two as reserves fell below 4 percent, and utilities were asked to curtail about 1,100 MW from customers who had signed interruptible power contracts. The situation was so fluid that California ISO did not even have time to issue a media alert about the Stage Two before it was scaled back an hour later in response to the voluntary load curtailments.

The next day, problems continued as two key transmission lines were taken out of service because of smoke damage. But while the operational side of things stabilized, the prices on California ISO's transmission market jumped to $690/MWh for four hours. That day, the price caps of $250/MWh had expired and a new cap of $750/MWh took its place. The difference in total cost amounted to about $9 million.[9]

A New Picture Emerges

Absent such singular events as peak-load days or system outages, schedulers and dispatchers remain vigilant for unusual load patterns; for instance, if a particular line or path becomes congested for no known reason.

One of the new patterns that emerged with the new market, Garris observed, was that generators appeared to be basing decisions on their ability to maximize income. "I think what you could see is that folks were driven more by the dollars," he said, referring to the way that new owners of the power plants divested from the utilities were scheduling and bidding. "You could see that the new owners were driven more by the bottom line."

Both the grid operator and the Power Exchange soon uncovered instances of companies trying to take advantage of system congestion, by scheduling too much energy on a particular line, for instance, then seeking payments for decreasing the load.

One of the most infamous cases, which actually proved unsuccessful, occurred in May 1999. Traders at Enron Power Marketing tried to schedule 2,900 MW per hour across the Silver Peak transmission line, a minor intertie with Nevada's Sierra Pacific Power utility that could accommodate only 15 MW. The attempt was immediately detected by PX and ISO monitors, and the exchange fined Enron $25,000.[10]

While the Silver Peak incident became part of the folklore of market manipulation, it wasn't until much later that Enron was revealed as the culprit. Market monitors were trying to balance confidentiality concerns against the need to enforce rules, and protocols did not favor revealing identities of market miscreants.

Garris believes that suspicious actions that later formed the basis for the state's accusations of market manipulation against generators and traders were already being tried out during the first two summers of the new market.

"I think we all knew there were folks playing games out there. In some cases, they were clearly illegal, and in other places it was a matter of testing the rules to see how things would perform with the different rules," he said. "My main concern was the scheduling process and how to best make things work. I suspect a lot of folks were in that mode: how do we make this thing work and that should take care of some of these problems."

Surveillance and Sanctions

Just as the schedulers and grid operators watched for market anomalies on a real-time basis, Sheffrin and the Department of Market Analysis monitored the flow of data to make certain that scheduling coordinators were not taking unfair advantage of flaws in the system.

Having lost a series of battles at the Federal Energy Regulatory Commission to limit market-based pricing for the new owners of divested utility generation units, California ISO tried other ways to limit the potential exercise of market power. The market surveillance committee in summer 1998 had issued a report concluding that the RMR units were most likely to be able to take advantage of stressful periods by withholding their capacity, and terms of the RMR contracts did little to prevent the problem. Several months of negotiations led to changes to the contracts in June 1999 to eliminate incentives for withholding.

From July 1998 through December 1999, California ISO made more than a dozen filings at FERC that were specifically intended to identify and correct various problems in the reliability markets and put teeth into enforcement of rules. A common thread of the filings was to try to use market-based tools to correct system design flaws. For instance, the grid operator asked to be able to purchase ancillary services from outside the control area to counter instances of market power.[11]

In December 1998, two tariff amendments were filed to extend California ISO's ability to impose price caps on energy bids and to rescind payments to generators that deviated from their schedules or ignored dispatch instructions.[12] Sometimes, California ISO declared new policies that it felt did not require FERC approval, such as issuing a market notice determining that all interzonal congestion where there were fewer than three generation alternatives was noncompetitive and subject to mitigation by employing RMR units.[13]

The FERC cases were always contentious and results were mixed or disappointing to California ISO. When California ISO asked for the ability to mitigate the exercise of locational market power in November 1999, FERC turned down the proposal and instead ordered a redesign of congestion-management practices.[14]

It all translated into a burgeoning workload for the regulatory and legal department and frustration for market monitors, who felt they could identify problems but had little authority to prevent them or penalize any who took advantage.

"We knew that marketplace profit-maximization behavior is the driver, so we try to study all of its implications," Sheffrin said. "I don't think the people who designed the market before did that type of study. What you call fundamental assumptions didn't pan out. People are going to do whatever it takes to maximize their profits."

One of the big issues in the market was whether generators would withhold their capacity in order to wait for prices to move higher and what exactly were the rules governing such behavior. "I was constantly back at FERC," Sheffrin said, promoting a greater ability for California ISO to impose sanctions and penalties, just as commodities exchanges can punish bad actors. "They were very reluctant. They said, 'No, we're the ultimate regulator of rates. We'll keep that authority.'"

She complained that it felt like she was dealing with "sleepy regulators."

10

Balancing Acts

AFTER A YEAR on the job as California ISO general counsel, Beth Emery was still struggling to find the right balance between work and family. She recounted an occasion in late 1998 when she was supposed to meet her family for dinner at a restaurant to celebrate their first year of living in California. Some urgent matter intervened just as she was getting ready to go home, and CEO Jeff Tranen called a meeting of the California ISO officers.

"I got out of his office at 7:00 and I'm driving back to Granite Bay," she recalled. "I realized that I don't know where I'm supposed to meet them. They're not answering at home, which means they're already there, and I'm calling [my husband] Lee's cell phone. He's not picking up. It's now 7:30; I'm at home try-ing to figure out what I'm going to do. Finally, he called my cell phone. They were at Red Lobster, so I went over there and said, 'Oh, I'm so sorry.' And my son said, 'But Mom, this is perfect. You're never around. You show up late, and you completely forget where you're supposed to be.'

"Nobody had a life," she sighed. "Even though, you know, we all tried to."

The need for a better balance in life was beginning to wear on Tranen and his family as well. The California lifestyle really did not suit him or his spouse. Part of it related to his wife's health, which was complicated by chronic diabetes and a necessary kidney transplant, with Tranen himself supplying the replacement organ. Part of it was the fact that their only daughter was at Harvard, not at the much closer Stanford Business School as they had anticipated when he agreed to move to Folsom in 1997. When an offer came from Sithe Energies in New York, Tranen decided to take the job as president and chief operating officer of the company's newly formed power-generation affiliate, beginning March 1999.

The announcement was a surprise and a shock to California ISO staff, espe-cially to the top managers who had grown accustomed to Tranen's energy and leadership during those daily morning meetings. "We always knew he would leave, but we all thought he would stay at least for two full years," Emery said. "It was just a matter of time before they were going to move back to the East Coast. He got an offer he couldn't refuse, and it turned out to be great for him, but there was a lot of unfinished business."

Tranen later dismissed the notion that he was simply job-hopping from one creative opportunity to another. "It wasn't like the Lone Ranger, job done, off to do something else," he said. "My job was to get it running, identify the flaws and get them fixed," he recalled.

There were still many bugs in the system and too many of them, in his opinion, derived from political decisions made before the California ISO was formed or its employees hired. "My presumption was that when things settled down, I'd be able to start building a political constituency for changes that had to be made."

Ironically, the apparent success of the market meant that Tranen was unable to get much interest from lawmakers in coming up with new policies that might smooth out some of the kinks in the system. "While I was there, we had a pretty good result, with 2- or 3-cent power," he noted. "You can't build political support for change when things are working."

Terry Winter was quickly named CEO, adding a new layer of job responsibilities to his supervision of operations. He admitted that the organization was somewhat overwhelmed by everything it had in the works: an ancillary market redesign, discord between scheduling coordinators and dispatchers, trying to renegotiate the terms of the reliability must-run contracts, completing the delayed auction process for firm transmission rights, and ensuring that the grid operator's systems were prepared for any problems related to the so-called Y2K bug.

Now he also had to deal more directly with the politics of the corporation and, in particular, governance issues in the wake of the Federal Energy Regulatory Commission's rejection of some powers that state lawmakers had granted to the Electricity Oversight Board.

"I'll have to do a good job of prioritizing," Winter said.[1]

The California ISO board of directors for months had been caught in a quandary by FERC's firm rejection of the EOB's ability to set a state residency requirement for governors or to decide on any appeals of board decisions. For instance, in September the board had voted to amend its bylaws to extend its members' terms for three months in hopes of a resolution of the jurisdiction issues, but it made the changes without EOB approval. "It is not in the public interest to have either board reperpetuate itself over and over again without consideration of other qualified people," argued EOB general counsel Erik Saltmarsh.[2]

As New Year 1999 dawned, California ISO governors and their counterparts at the Power Exchange made additional changes that edged the corporation further into FERC's camp: deleting the California residency clause; removing EOB as the selector of new governors, but giving it an opportunity to narrow any list of prospects and make recommendations; limiting EOB's ability to hear appeals to the issues of reliability and transmission maintenance; and eliminating the oversight board's power to approve the bylaw changes.

Significantly, the California ISO board also revised its rules to allow for eventual inclusion of other states by easing restrictions for out-of-state agencies and municipal utilities to participate as voting members.

The establishment of regional transmission organizations (RTOs) was a policy actively promoted by FERC. Both the outgoing and incoming California ISO CEOs supported an eventual evolution of the corporation into a role as central player in a Western RTO. "I thought it made sense for us to be a Western RTO as the technology became available," Tranen later explained. "Electricity doesn't honor state borders."

Winter also expected that California ISO would grow beyond its legislated territory, but at the moment he had more pressing concerns.

Design and Redesign

As early as the first few months of operations, California ISO staff had begun seeing deficiencies in its ability to effectively deal with some of the problems that were popping up.

While the overall market price appeared stable, there was a lot of variation in the reliability markets, noted Kellan Fluckiger. "We started with a redesign of ancillary service markets almost from the minute we started operations," he said.

As director of operations and engineering, Fluckiger was in charge of what seemed a never-ending process of change. "There was a lot of work, a lot of fast changes, a lot of reactions," he said. "As soon as that was done, we started the next one. What market redesign is next? What do stakeholders need and/or want?"

The major redesign of ancillary service markets involved altering software or creating new programs to allow automated scheduling of bids from dozens of smaller generators in order to meet last-minute load requirements, rather than relying on the same backup resources again and again.

During the summer market excursions, scheduling coordinators complained about California ISO dispatch policies, claiming the operators were inconsistent in their calls for additional power and prone to ignore their bids in favor of "out-of-market" purchases.

"You hear a lot about us skipping the bids," Winter explained. "Well, if you're sitting there and you've got 10 guys that can give you 5 MW each, or you can go to this one guy, make one telephone call, and he can give you the full 50 MW," the choice became clear. "We could not make enough telephone calls to keep the system operational," he said. "We came in and automated all of these phone calls, so that people could put in their bids, and I didn't care whether they were 5 MW, 1 MW, or 500 MW. The operator can just look down the list and say, 'I need 600 MW,' and you hit a button and it automatically sent an e-mail to all the generators. They had 60 seconds to respond, and all they had to do was hit a button to respond. If we didn't get an acceptance from them, we went down to the next on the list."

The new automated dispatch system made a big difference. "We just couldn't handle it in 1998," he said. "We put the systems in in '99, and we were able to handle the problem. But it all relied on having enough capacity out there," Winter said.

The "inc/dec" bidding problem in imbalance energy markets was something else that had plagued operators from the very start.

"We always had the inc/dec problem," Winter said. "Units are going up, we've got to have them go up, then somebody brings in another unit, now we've got to bring them down and we get a price disconnect. What that allowed people to do was they could play the game, they can overgenerate for awhile, force you to dec, then get a high price for that, then run it down and go the other way. And so that's when market monitoring started getting more involved, we started looking at new software programs."

One of the reasons generators could benefit from ramping up and down was that the California ISO's main imbalance market was scheduled on an hour-by-hour basis. At the start, there had been plans to monitor dispatch status every 5 minutes, but that proved impossible to set up under the urgent deadline for market operations. Now the grid operators began planning for a 10-minute market, but they were finding resistance from generators and utilities in the adjoining states.

The market redesigns and information system improvements put into effect in 1999 cost nearly $40 million but were responsible for cost savings estimated at $300 million.[3]

Besides the significant cost savings, the changes were meant to align actual market performance with the costs being incurred and payments made. Besides moving to charging for service on the basis of metered demand rather than scheduled load, California ISO also instituted a controversial "no-pay" system. Simply put, if scheduling coordinators did not operate when they said they would, or if they did not follow dispatch instructions, they would not be paid. That went hand in hand with corrections to the billing settlements process that had provided incentives for players in the real-time market to ignore dispatch orders.

The "rational buyer" program allowed California ISO to secure higher-value ancillary services at a lesser or equal cost to lower value services, and a greater emphasis was put on buying replacement reserves to avoid costly out-of-market purchases.

Probably the change with the most financial impact, though, was reaching a settlement of costs associated with the reliability must-run (RMR) units. Instead of paying the full fixed costs for these standby generators, a new formula brought the payments down to about 50 percent for a majority of plants. Meanwhile, California ISO and utilities were pursuing about $250 million worth of transmission upgrades that would alleviate the need for RMR in certain locations.

The RMR settlements had been "tortuous, tortuous negotiations," said attorney Ed Berlin. Although not all the generators were happy with the outcome, the result was a reduction in RMR costs by about $250 million in 1999 compared to 1998.[4]

Although the computer changes needed to fix these various problems were costing tens of millions of dollars, Winter said they led to savings that were ten times the cost. Nonetheless, the monetary expense paled in comparison to the cost in market ill will.

Elena Schmid recalled that the 10-minute dispatch market as a "solution to a very real problem" of scheduling coordinators not following dispatch rules. The so-called "uninstructed deviations" were becoming rampant in ancillary markets. "But it was a solution that was an ISO solution," Schmid said. "It had zero support from the stakeholders. It had zero support from outside California, and it was absolutely rammed through. Years later, we are still living with the repercussions."

The FERC tariff-amendment cases became battlegrounds, not only over the cost of revised systems but about California ISO dictating new ways of doing business to its neighbors. "The rest of the world at the ties, where you had historical means of doing business, were all up in arms," recalled attorney Roger Smith. "The rest of the West was up in arms."

It was reminiscent of the early market-design wars, when the new California system tried to impose a seven-day trading and scheduling routine on Western markets, which traditionally operated five days per week, prescheduling for weekends and holidays.

A Confluence of Cultures

The constant attempts to fix the market designs also contributed to the continuing imbalance in people's personal lives. "It was busy, frantic, frenetic," Fluckiger said. "People were still working 60-70-80 hours a week. [There was] a constant discussion about 'We're going to burn people out. We can't keep working like this.'"

That became another priority for the organization after Winter took over as CEO, getting a handle on making a transition from being a start-up enterprise to settling into the hopefully less frantic pace of an ongoing operation.

Randy Abernathy was especially concerned about the cultural implications of having such a driven workforce. "It was tough, because you've got these competitive folks. At first it was a competition about who could stay later. We kept pushing to say, 'People, you've got to find your own balance. Just because so-and-so is staying until 10:30 at night does not mean that you have to.'"

He had seen the "big macho ego trip" plenty of times in the Silicon Valley high-tech culture and tried to encourage California ISO employees to focus on getting the job done while maintaining their sanity. "One of the things I've learned about this process is that people have different balance levels. When you say work, life, family, balance, that's not 40 hours a week for some of these guys. For some of these guys, balanced is 80 hours. That's where they feel good, that's where they're in their zone."

The dilemma was a complex one, as California ISO had been consciously staffed with Type A individuals—bright, ambitious, and certain of their expertise. There were tensions between the operators, who lived in a real-time environment, and those in planning functions, who had to look beyond the immediate needs. There were tensions between those who came out of the utility culture and those working in information services. There were even tensions among former utility employees from different organizations, which had always exhibited different styles of conducting business.

"We had a couple of different cultures here," noted Schmid, who late in 1999 was hired to be vice president of corporate strategy and communications. One of the big differences she found was between operations and information services. "They think differently. They react differently. They analyze problems differently. I wouldn't say they were warring camps. It was much more a different way of looking at problems."

The same held true for transmission planners and operators, agreed Armie Perez, director of grid planning. "The environment between a planner and an operator by nature has to be a little controversial. If you let an operator plan a system, you're going to have a lot more transmission lines than you need, because he wants to be assured that he can take care of any problem, anywhere, anytime. A planner wants to make sure he has a transmission system that complies with a prescribed reliability criteria and goes no further," he said. "It's a healthy difference, the two talk to each other and try to come up with a transmission plan they can agree with, they're happy."

"You're bringing in all these different cultures," noted California ISO board chair Jan Smutny-Jones. "There were people who had radically different ways of doing things, of interacting with people. That in and of itself led to the need to smooth out the rough edges."

Ken Wiseman, who had the most experience with corporate cultures among the board members, said he was initially taken aback by the differences among the people who had come from the utilities. Not just the differences between those with a public-power background and those from IOUs, but between individuals from within the regulated sector.

"You have these three separate and divergent cultures: San Diego, Edison, and PG&E. It was like three different planets," he said. "And you didn't just have three cultures. Within that, you had a power engineer and you had techies. So you had what would be a clash between two types if you were in any one company, and then you laid on three companies. And you picked the best and the brightest and the ones who came because they saw this as something exciting," Wiseman observed.

Surprisingly, some of the expected points of conflict in the new organization did not prove to be especially problematic. The generational splits among the individuals who had come of age in the middle part of the century, those of the "baby boom" years and the more technology-oriented "Generation X'ers," did not seem as much of a problem at the California ISO as they were becoming in many corporate environments.

Nor was the overwhelmingly male population of employees a problem for someone like Anjali Sheffrin, who said she had always been one of the few women in her college economics classes or in the utility departments she'd worked in before joining California ISO. "I was a manager of 45 individuals at SMUD; I would say 80 percent of them were men," she said. "I'm used to working with men. What surprised me was how everyone here was a Type A personality and wanted to push because they thought they knew the answer. I tend to sort of sit back and say, 'Well, shouldn't we *think* about it first before we just plow down a path?'"

To a large degree, the common goals of getting the organization off the ground and being part of an entirely new energy business obviated the disparities of age, gender, or different utility cultures. The question was how to keep people together under changed circumstances.

"There was an energy there that we were able to capture," Wiseman said, but it required nurturing and outside help to bridge the obvious gaps in communications among disparate individuals.

The Hay Group Surveys

Another initiative that Winter launched during this time was a "benchmarking" survey of employees, conducted by the Hay Group, a consulting firm that helps organizations identify and achieve strategic goals. The company does a lot of work with *Fortune 500* firms and compiles an annual listing of "Most Admired Companies" for *Fortune* magazine.

One of Winter's tasks while at San Diego Gas & Electric was to oversee a cultural transformation among utility staff and its customer service representatives, "to make the utility see that it actually had customers" and not just the regulators as its main clients. "And then I came up here, watched the entrepreneurial thing, which was kind of every man for himself dedicated to what they were trying to do. That's how you get people to work 80 hours a week," he said. What he wanted to do was survey the employees to discover their attitudes about California ISO and to benchmark the results against the best companies in the world.

"We came up with 90 percent of the employees thought this was the greatest place to work you could imagine," he boasted. "They would tell their friends about it, they would recommend the place to them." In a typical utility, he suggested, you might get positive ratings from half the workers, who were driven more by job security than passion for their work.

The figures from the Hay survey were astonishingly positive, with 90 percent of the employees saying they were proud to work for California ISO, and 89 percent believing that their work made a real contribution to the success of the organization.

Compared with the nation's top 25 companies, California ISO scored well in employee loyalty, organizational flexibility, and timeliness of response to solving problems but much lower on certain measures of organizational structure. "We didn't have enough structure, but you know, a year-and-a-half-old company, we probably shouldn't be that structured," Winter observed.

A clear deficiency, although not uncommon for a new corporation, was process. "We didn't have enough processes. We're a brand-new start-up company, the processes haven't been put in place yet." Also, California ISO staff were constantly battling some of the outside vendors, such as ABB, so the scores for working with outside groups were lower than average.

The overall rating was very favorable, with above-average scores in 28 out of 41 areas surveyed, compared to the top companies. Lower averages were recorded in 4 or 5 areas, including internal communications, process and working with various constituencies.

"I put together a plan, here's how we're going to correct some of these things. We've got to get a little more organization, got to have more process. And we did that for about three years," Winter said.

A reorganization of the corporation was instituted that elevated a layer of managers to director status. The timing for change seemed opportune, as several of the original top managers and executives decided to leave shortly after Tranen's departure. There had already been a key departure during Tranen's tenure, when chief financial officer Charles Smart left as a result of a personality clash with the CEO. Bill Regan, who came from the New Orleans utility company Entergy, replaced him in June of 1999.

Susan Schneider vacated the client-relations position in May; Zora Lazic, who had previously represented the Canadian marketer PowerEx on the California ISO board, would eventually fill it.

Beth Emery decided to return to private practice in Washington in November 1999. "The general counsel's position is really the most personal with the CEO, and Terry really wanted a different kind of general counsel," she said. "Not really a FERC warrior but more of an administrator. I finished the RMR negotiations and settlement, which was a really big thing, so it was a good time to go." Roger Smith would fill in for a few months until Charlie Robinson was hired as general counsel in early 2000.

Some of the original employees retired or moved on to other challenges. Jack Allen, for instance, became a systems consultant for other ISOs and utility pools around the world.

Over time, Winter expected to build a new team that fit the evolving needs of the organization. "Jeff wanted people to be like him," he observed about Tranen. "He wanted people who he could give a list of things to do, they go do the list;

they would give their subordinates a list of things to do, they would go do it. And I think there's a place for that. Especially with operating types. Strategic planners? You want them thinking broader. So as I went out, number one, I wanted very bright, competent people. Number two, I wanted people who were very dedicated to what we were trying to do here. But more than that, I wanted people with different strengths."

Winter said he likes using the interplay of different personalities to achieve balanced decisions. "I don't see my job as being the smartest guy in the world. You move organizations forward because you get people to work together and you capitalize on their attitudes and their ideas," he said.

Meanwhile, the California ISO staff kept growing, especially the information services division, as expensive consulting contractors were transformed into staff positions. More and more, it seemed, the solutions to market problems required system and software changes. That added up to a lot of hours being invoiced by consultants.

"Why am I paying $300,000 for a consultant when I can convert them to an ISO employee and get them for $120,000 to $150,000?" Winter reasoned. "So we had a real migration from contractors to full-time employees, but while I increased the manpower, I've actually brought my costs down."

I'm OK, You're OK, Y2K

For communications director Patrick Dorinson, returning to California had been the first step in restoring balance in his personal life after a divorce. The political lifestyle in Washington had become unhealthy, he realized. "When I came back from Washington, I was actually about 30 pounds overweight. My blood pressure was up, so I started working out. I got a trainer [and] lost all kinds of weight."

He didn't mind the long hours occasionally required at California ISO and enjoyed the sense of community he was finding in Folsom. "I love small towns," he said. "I'd been looking for a small town to settle in all my life."

When his regular trainer took ill, the six-week replacement, Carol, turned out to be someone who would play a far more permanent role in his life. They were married in September 1999 at Folsom's Lake Natoma Inn. Dorinson wore the traditional kilt of his Scottish ancestry while a Celtic harpist provided the music. For the first time in years, he was enjoying life and felt that work at the ISO and living in Folsom with Carol were bringing him back into balance.

"I spent my first New Year's Eve with her at the ISO," he laughed. About 170 other California ISO employees who had signed up for Y2K watch joined them.

Chief information officer Dennis Fishback had led his information services crew and consultants through a nearly 18-month-long process to make sure there were no computer system failures that would ripple through the grid as 1999 transitioned to 2000. It was widely asserted that computer software programs from the 1960s and 1970s would be unable to recognize the new century, and corporations across the country had been scared into spending hundreds of millions of dollars to upgrade their systems.

Despite the near paranoia over a potentially catastrophic systems collapse that some media outlets seemed to be promulgating, Fishback had always been confident that the new California ISO systems would not exhibit problems. While there was a possibility that some older systems at power generators might foul up the flow of data to the central grid operators, Fishback saw little real risk. "It's more a case of a funky date on an invoice instead of things being hosed up," he told a reporter.

Still, the grid operator undertook a Y2K readiness program, with staff and consultants logging almost 15,000 hours to review nearly 400 computer systems and products to ascertain reliability and certify that "mission critical" systems were in shape. Some problems had been uncovered, but they had been resolved more than six months before New Year's Eve.

As the date drew nearer, officials took precautions against another concern—that consumers would try to sever their power connections to the grid, causing an undesirable fluctuation in loads and frequency.

The communications department broadcast public-service announcements urging business as usual. "California's electric system works best when the flow of electricity is predictable," intoned one radio PSA.

The Y2K watch in Folsom was both determined and lighthearted, Dorinson said. Extra security patrols had been scheduled on the grounds, and controllers were prepared for any eventuality. "Auckland, New Zealand, is the first major city that switched. I get in, Auckland's already done, they're partying down there and there are lights on. Now we're moving across to Asia, Horn of Africa, and Russia even. As you start going across time zones, you know nothing's going to happen. I'm holding press briefings every half hour. 'The grid is fine, nothing has happened. Thank you very much.'"

There was only one power-loss incident to report, he said. A transmission tower in Oregon was knocked over. The anxious reporters were asking, "Was it terrorism?" Dorinson checked with a member of the control-room team who was familiar with the transmission system and quickly identified the problem as occurring next to an Indian reservation. Every year somebody hops the fence and cuts a guide wire on a tower and removes the bolts, he was told. Wind must have knocked down the tower.

"It's their way of protesting," Dorinson said.

11

A Bridge Too Far?

BY WORKING on improving internal communications and trying to understand the evolving corporate culture, California ISO's vice president of corporate strategy Elena Schmid realized how to get a better grasp on the organization's future. Schmid launched a process to develop a new vision for the corporation. In so doing, she hoped that solutions to many of the other complexities would make themselves more apparent.

The start-up culture had accomplished its mission, and it had defined the character of the corporation. "It meant that if there was a problem, you went after the solution to that problem. You did exactly what was in front of you. You did it fast and you did it however you could," she explained. "We had a lot of unintended consequences because we didn't think through how all these different problems fit together, how the solutions to these problems fit together. And so we were layering problems."

To help define a new vision, she decided to review the historical roots of the organization and then create a map of where things might be heading. Schmid enlisted the services of David Sibbitt, a San Francisco–based "graphic facilitator," who listened to people describing a company or a situation and then illustrated it in the form of a pictorial narrative that unfolded over time. The result was both a timeline of significant events and a portrait of the way California ISO saw itself.

As the graphic story unfurled in time from left to right across the page, Sibbitt drew a bridge that served as a metaphor of potential future directions for California ISO. Beyond the span was the sunrise of a new day dawning on a Western grid operator. Clearly, the people in the organization expected that FERC's promotion of regional transmission operators would influence the California organization's future role.

Something else that appeared on the other side of the bridge was a permanent headquarters building for California ISO. As employment levels at the organization kept climbing, space became a problem. Additional offices were rented in another building on Blue Ravine Road, and many of the staff members had to accept a downsizing of the cubicles to four feet by six feet in order to make room for everyone. "That is just so small, people can't even turn around in their desks," Terry Winter said.

Winter wanted a new building that would be constructed with specific security protections to house the California ISO control room and backup facility and to consolidate all the other offices.

He didn't want a return to the bunker-style control operations, but something with a campus setting and a secure fence. "People could jump over it," he said. "But if you see someone jumping over a fence, that's a pretty good indication you've got a problem." Another consideration was that the lease costs for the Blue Ravine Road facilities were more expensive than constructing a new site, especially if the costs of communicating with the Alhambra backup site could be eliminated. "So the economics were very, very favorable to building the new building," he said.

With the approval of the board, California ISO purchased 30 acres at Iron Point, near the Intel Corporation facility. Winter told his people, "Hang in there, next year we'll have a new building."

But there was still that bridge to cross.

The Guardian and the Grid

Graphic artist Sibbitt contributed more than a picture of the California ISO's mission. He recommended that Schmid and the other officers read a book by Jane Jacobs called *Systems of Survival.* Jacobs was best known for her work on the economic life of cities and nations, but this book was billed as "a dialogue on the moral foundations of commerce and politics."

The main thesis, as hashed out by a salon group of intellectually curious characters, was that human civilization had developed two distinct moral codes, or syndromes—Trade and Guardian. Trade morality relied on business contracts and openness in dealings with a wide variety of cultures, because that broadened the base of potential customers. "The occupations associated with it overwhelmingly concerned commerce and production of goods or services for commerce; and in addition, most scientific work." The other syndrome comprised "armed forces and police, aristocracies and landed gentries, government ministries and their bureaucracies, commercial monopolies...law courts, legislatures, religions and especially state religions." [1]

According to the reasoning of Jacobs' characters, the two distinct moral codes were frequently at odds with each other; only rarely could an individual, corporation or culture mix the two successfully. The messy, contentious, bargaining nature of trade and commerce, indeed of democracy, is constrained by the rigid uniformity of the guardian. Commerce needs rules, of course, but they are contractual in nature.

And yet, that was exactly what California ISO was trying to do, to be a market-based corporation encouraging trade among disparate elements of the energy sector while at the same time serving as the creator and enforcer of market rules.

The metaphor most frequently used to describe California ISO, an air-traffic controller for the electric transmission system, was adequate only to explain its role as grid operator and dispatcher of electrons. The job of ensuring system reliability was clearly an outgrowth of the guardian ways inherited from the monopoly utilities, and California ISO was certainly the "guardian of the grid."

But it was also attempting to conduct transactions, in essence to *be* a marketplace for the reliability services and energy purchases necessary to maintain voltage stability. To the extent that its employees still carried a cultural identification with their utility backgrounds, the guardian instincts were strong in them. Those who came from outside the utility cultures, particularly those in information technology and market services functions, had a different way of looking at the world. The two were engaged in a nearly constant tug of war between making and enforcing rules for reliability's sake and coming up with innovations that would help break down the rigid barriers of past practices.

For Schmid and other California ISO corporate officers, the insights provided by Jacobs' explorations of moral structures did not necessarily resolve the multiple cultural conflicts that they saw within the organization. But it helped them to understand the conflicts a little better and to realize that part of their challenge in moving the organization forward was to find a proper balance, a workable equilibrium, between the two poles.

Human resources director Jerry Fry put it this way: "I think the markets tend to appeal more to the entrepreneurial and the creative, while the guardians tend to appeal more to the security minded. 'Protect mine,' as opposed to 'Let's create something new.' I think it takes a balance of the two. I'm concerned with seeing it tilt either way."

Although he was long gone by the time California ISO underwent this cultural self-examination, former CEO Jeff Tranen seemed to understand the need for balance and a clear definition of roles and rules. "The ISO has a role to play as quasi-regulator, but not to be the judge and the jury," he said. The quandary for controllers was to maintain a system under which markets could thrive without allowing people to take unfair advantage.

For that, Tranen said, you need good, flexible rules and an understanding of market mechanics. "High prices don't necessarily mean market power. It could also mean scarcity," he observed. "I would argue that it's inappropriate for the ISO to be an investigator and assign penalties. That really is the role of the regulator."

What was most important, Tranen said, was that the corporation maintains its independence. "We had to be perceived as neutral and not having biases in favor of the transmission companies as opposed to generators or munis. We really had to be independent."

Even though the market fluctuations of 1998 and 1999 were requiring that a little more of the guardianship needed to be built into California ISO's market systems, Terry Winter held the line against perceiving the corporation as the enforcer.

"Never wanted to enforce," he said. "I always wanted to identify for the regulator. You ought to think of us as a utility, not a regulator. To me the ISO ought to be 'the policeman.' Which means I give out tickets. If you don't like that and you want to contest it, then you go to FERC or whatever regulatory body you decide is going to be the adjudicator. But not me."

The search for the guardian/trade balance and the corresponding need to retain independence were issues that would always be part of California ISO's cultural heritage.

The Stakeholder Report

Pleased with the outcome of Sibbitt's work on the vision process, Schmid enlisted him to try to understand another nagging problem, the adversarial relationship with scheduling coordinators, who were the "customers" of California ISO.

"My thing was always, what's the history, what's the context," she explained. "So we did a big mapping of what the stakeholder process had been up to this point in order to figure out what it means going forward."

The resulting document is a concise, multilayered history of the entire restructuring process, revealing in a picture the story of how national and state policies evolved during the 1990s to result in AB 1890 and the formation of California ISO.

"What the picture says is that the development of the ISO, the development of the structures that carried out deregulation was done by the stakeholders,"

Schmid explained. "Tremendous involvement. Decision-making. Absolutely listened to. And then it stopped. Institutions took over, and the stakeholders were left high and dry. The decision power was taken away from them."

Even though key constituencies found an institutionalized role on the board of governors, their fiduciary duties necessarily took precedence over the economic interests of the firms or groups they represented. This had direct consequences for the broader field of stakeholders and transmission system users.

"Their input was at a different level. They no longer had the direct input that went into a direct decision that affected them. They now had a body, if not two bodies, that stepped in and said, 'Now, we're going to start deciding for you,'" Schmid observed. "Any time you have a representative form of government, the balance of power is different than the balance of power in a direct form of voting."

On one hand, that was a positive aspect of governance; on the other, it meant the commercial interests needed to find another way of expressing their needs.

One venue was through membership in the Western Power Trading Forum, whose founder, Gary Ackerman, became a kind of gadfly at California ISO. Using his sharp wit and "loyal opposition" status, Ackerman regularly skewered California ISO decisions and promoted the interests of scheduling coordinators. When he worked for energy marketer Mock Resources, Ackerman had participated in the restructuring process and was a member of the trust advisory committee for the Power Exchange. He knew all the players and personnel.

Each week, Ackerman broadcast his analysis of events along with humorous observations of the California ISO process in an e-mail memo to clients and others that he called the "Friday Burrito."

From Ackerman's perspective, the breakdown in the stakeholder process was apparent from the start and had to do with the need for the control operator to also be in control of information systems. "It was adversarial from the get-go," he said.

The sheer complexity of the new market and its rules was a major problem, he said.

"The ISO's design went way too far way too fast and didn't consider the fact that simplicity would have allowed for some gradual development of things on a more normal, orderly timeframe." People "couldn't understand why the ISO was spending such an enormous effort and time creating an ancillary services market," he said. "It made no sense to them."

While he constantly argued for creating "a simple energy market," Ackerman felt that Tranen had committed to the "Reliability Through Markets" mantra mainly because ancillary services had been part of the design that the CEO was handed when he arrived.

There was no time to change course. "That, in my opinion, made it too top heavy, led to a bloated ISO, and was really unnecessary. But that was the track we found ourselves on."

Minimal Oversight

One result of the federal assertion of authority over the governance of California ISO and the Power Exchange was that the Electricity Oversight Board fell into a kind of limbo during 1999. The members of the board were essentially volunteering their services, and meetings were few because there was rarely a quorum. Staff members who had been loaned from the California Energy Commission, Gary Heath and Erik Saltmarsh, helped keep the EOB involved in FERC proceedings and pursued the appeal to federal court, but otherwise there was little to be done.

In January 2000, Governor Gray Davis asked attorney Michael Kahn to become chair of the EOB and to try to revive the panel. Bruce Willison, the dean of the Anderson Graduate School of Business at UCLA, was also appointed to the board. The nonvoting legislative members were Senator Debra Bowen (D-Redondo Beach) and Assemblymember Rod Wright (D-Los Angeles). Both lawmakers chaired the energy policy committees in their respective houses of the Legislature, and they took their role with the EOB seriously. They attended "every minute of every meeting," Kahn said.

Kahn, a senior partner with the San Francisco firm of Folger, Levin & Kahn, had only the most cursory knowledge of restructuring and energy-policy matters and was glad for any assistance from the lawmakers. He had once successfully represented a wind-power developer in a case against Pacific Gas & Electric, but otherwise he expressed no expertise in electricity matters. "I had not even heard of the Electricity Oversight Board," Kahn said. "I called the former chair and he didn't call me back. I called him three times and finally I gave up trying to talk with him."

Kahn began a process of "due diligence" about his new assignment, meeting with staff, visiting the Power Exchange in Alhambra and California ISO in Folsom. "From my perspective, it was tabula rasa," he said, a blank slate. "There were no prior meetings, there were no minutes. Nothing."

He recalled that Wright introduced legislation to grant the EOB $300 million to try to get municipal utilities to join the ISO. Otherwise Kahn remained unclear as to exactly what the function of the EOB was. "It seemed to me that the ISO reported to this thing called FERC and it basically called the shots. I wasn't entirely sure what difference it even made at that point in time."

About the only person who seemed concerned about California ISO was Senator Steve Peace, who sometimes attended the EOB meetings. "Anytime Steve wanted to come, he was welcome to come to any part of the meeting and say anything he wanted to," Kahn said.

"And he seemed very exercised about the lack of acquiescence of the ISO. I think none of us really fully understood what Steve was upset about."

Within about two months of his intensive self-tutorial, Kahn believed he understood what Peace was getting at whenever he talked about California ISO bowing to FERC. "What I figured out very quickly is that we didn't deregulate. We federalized," Kahn explained. "Unlike deregulation, where you could then reregulate, it seemed to me that it wasn't so easy for the state to reregulate because it divested itself of jurisdiction and placed the jurisdiction somewhere else."

Was that likely to be a problem? At the time it didn't appear to be. "I probably talked with 50 people in the first 45 days," Kahn said. "Not one single person said we had an energy crisis or an energy shortage."

Clouds on the Horizon but Little Rain

As autumn of 1999 turned to winter, grid engineering director Jim Detmers grew increasingly worried about the future. It wasn't the Y2K problem and it wasn't the market side of California ISO operations that troubled him. They were somebody else's problems.

What he was seeing was the lack of rain in the Pacific Northwest and a big increase in power demand throughout the region—two issues that could boomerang on California during the next summer.

He began expressing his concerns to anyone who would listen, including communications director Patrick Dorinson. "We're walking down the hall near the control room," Dorinson said. "Detmers came to me, I'll never forget it. He said, 'We've got problems coming. We don't have enough water and the load's creeping up. We're not going to make it.'"

Detmers wasn't talking about that day or even that season; he was looking ahead to the coming summer resource situation with increasing dismay.

He wasn't the only one.

Earlier in 1999, the California Energy Commission had compiled an assessment of how the state's power system might fare during an extended period of hot weather spread across the entire West. There had been five separate periods of hot weather during the summer of 1998, the report noted, and the Independent System Operator on several occasions had to declare Stage Two alerts, when reserve margins fell below 5 percent.

"The coincidence of high temperatures and electricity demand over most of the western half of the country strained the electricity supply and transmission system to its limits," declared the document. The report asked the question "Was the summer of 1998 a truly unique event...or was it an indication that electricity supplies have not kept pace with demand growth?"[2]

There was evidence to suggest that because of the state's return to economic health and the growth of the Internet, energy consumption was indeed climbing faster than anticipated. And it didn't take much deep research to conclude that few power plants had been built in California in the previous decade. There was a several-year lag in the siting process for any new facilities, and the low energy prices that resulted from the new competitive market did not seem to be encouraging new investment.

CEC analysis had shown that given the average energy prices clearing the Power Exchange, even a brand-new, efficient generator would not be profitable. Without new generation, California would become increasingly reliant on hydroelectricity imports from the Northwest.

The worst-case scenario, a 1-in-40 occurrence of extended high temperatures throughout the West, would certainly cause problems for the state, the report said, and it would require enactment of extensive power curtailments. A more likely 1-in-5-year event would be manageable.

The CEC report did not foresee immediate problems with meeting peak load, but there was a possibility of strains in the 2002–2004 time frame, said deputy director of energy information and analysis Daniel Nix. That would coincide with the elimination of the rate freeze put into effect by AB 1890, and it "might lead to spiking price problems or actions to reduce demand," he suggested.[3]

Few outside the energy industry took immediate notice of the CEC's "heat storm" report. A *San Francisco Chronicle* reporter, Rebecca Smith, had obtained a draft of the report and wrote a detailed analysis that suggested, "Electric Users Could Be in for a Jolt." The story appeared just two weeks after California ISO had set its new peak record on July 12, and Smith correlated the volatility of Power Exchange prices with cautions about the potential for rolling blackouts if power supplies could not match demand. She quoted CEC analyst Richard Grix as saying, "Our ability to reliably meet the summer peaks is becoming shaky," and alluded to the heat-storm report.[4]

Curiously, the CEC tried to downplay the worst-case scenario, deferring public release of the report. When Smith saw the final version, she felt the agency had watered down some of the conclusions that had appeared in the draft.[5]

California ISO management was taking the potential for problems seriously and late in 1999 began a series of workshops around the state to discuss the future resource assessment.

There was a particular concern about the San Diego area, where there was an inadequate resource base and a boom in population. Another complicating factor was that San Diego Gas & Electric had declared that it had captured all of its stranded costs—largely because of the sale of its power plants at premium prices—and it would remove the rate freeze. Consumer advocate Michael Shames of the Utility Consumers' Action Network saw the possibility of a 20 percent increase in consumers' electricity bills, although SDG&E disclaimed the potential.

San Diego Union-Tribune reporter Craig Rose started following the story closely, especially after the CPUC held a workshop in January to assess potential problems in San Diego. When California ISO vice president of operations Kellan Fluckiger pointed out that power demand was outstripping forecasts and that problems were on the horizon, Rose took notice.

"My working theory was that deregulation would look good in times of surplus, but it would never look good when things got tight," Rose later said. "It's Economics 101. Essentially, when you have a commodity in short supply, the price goes up." Rose headlined his story "Energy Market Headed for Failure, Experts Say."[6]

Fluckiger said he had been harboring concerns about the impending situation, but the January 2000 workshop in San Diego was the first time he had publicly sounded alarms. "I painted a very concerning picture about the upcoming summer and said we'd need to put 5,000 MW of capacity on line every year as fast as we could for the next three or four years," he said. "I said we didn't have a lot of time, we don't have a lot of excess capacity, and we need to move."

12

Preparation, Precautions, and Politics

THERE ARE ONLY TWO effective ways to face an impending crisis: prepare for the expected impacts and do whatever is possible to prevent the worst. Denial, the first resort of the unprepared, is always a counterproductive strategy for dealing with the inevitable.

While individuals within California ISO actively began planning ways to prepare for and try to prevent a difficult summer in 2000, there was plenty of denial to go around in the state.

The Legislature tentatively approached the question of electricity undersupply during hearings in February and March convened by the Senate Energy, Utilities and Communications Committee. While the first session did not seem to lead to specific ideas for legislative action, the March 14 meeting concentrated on establishing new conservation and demand-response programs in time for the summer.

Demand-responsiveness had always been a topic of interest at the California Public Utilities Commission forums on restructuring policies, but aside from reliance on the existing system of interruptible-rate contracts, there was little progress in developing new demand-side programs.

Newly appointed CPUC president Loretta Lynch told lawmakers that structuring payments to consumers to reduce their energy consumption was problematic. She endorsed real-time metering, even though the markets for such meters had been stymied by the retail rate freeze.

About the best the CPUC could do at the present was to work with other agencies to put together a public-awareness campaign that could encourage conservation in advance of peak-power days, Lynch said.

The California Energy Commission was eager to promote public awareness, and its chair Bill Keese estimated that as much as 2,000 MW could be saved by altering consumers' demand on high-temperature days. Keese said the CEC was also actively working on efficiency projects at state facilities, and he encouraged particular attention to air-conditioning cycling programs, as residential air-cooling demand amounted to about 28 percent of summer peak energy use. But it was the CPUC's job to approve utility rate structures for any such programs.

California ISO representatives introduced two initiatives they hoped to have in place by mid-June, a demand-reduction program for large industrial customers and a pilot to encourage smaller commercial customers to join resources to bid into the ancillary services markets for operating reserves.

A fee from all transmission users, perhaps $50 million in aggregate, could be used to buy down as much as 1,000 MW of industrial load, suggested communications director Patrick Dorinson. Some participants might agree to an up-front payment in return for giving the ISO control over curtailing their load when reserve margins approached emergency levels. "It gives us more flexibility if load starts creeping up," Dorinson told the committee.[1]

Kellan Fluckiger also described a pilot project for aggregated-load bidding in the ancillary services markets in optimistic terms, with a potential for 800 MW.

California ISO also pledged to join in developing a public-awareness campaign. Dorinson later said that it soon became apparent that his office would have to take on the job by itself as other state agencies disappeared from the plan.

An initial meeting brought together representatives of the Electricity Oversight Board, the Resources Agency, the CEC, and California ISO, Dorinson said, but no CPUC staff attended. "Where's the PUC?" he asked. "They're the only ones with any money to do any kind of public-awareness campaign." A second meeting was called, but again no CPUC. The agency representatives discussed a variety of information strategies, including getting Governor Davis to appear on a public service announcement.

Soon afterward, however, the EOB cancelled any further meetings on the plan. "We're just going in a different direction," Dorinson said he was told. Later a representative from the governor's office explained that a decision had been made not to "expose the governor" to the issue of a potentially problematic summer.

"That's when I knew we were truly on our own," Dorinson said. "Right away, we knew the public-awareness campaign was not going to happen," Dorinson said. "*We've* got to do something."

With Stephanie McCorkle and the rest of the communications staff, he developed the idea for a "Power Watch 2000" program, akin to the "Spare the Air" smog-day alerts issued by air-quality regulators. They put together a list of television meteorologists and radio weather announcers and formally announced the program in early May.

If California ISO expected help from the competitive market, it would also be disappointed by the results. Increasingly concerned about potential gaps in resources around the state, the ISO hurriedly put together a request for bids (RFB) for emergency peaking power. Its main areas of concern were San Diego and San Francisco, but utility officials at San Diego Gas & Electric claimed there would be no problem that summer because they had paid for some transmission upgrades to ensure reliability of service.

The rushed RFB for San Francisco elicited little response but a lot of criticism. Prospective bidders complained that there was no way they could get a new project sited and certified by air-quality agencies in the Bay Area by that summer. Only one bid came in from an 80 MW unit offered by Sempra Resources, which later withdrew from the solicitation after California ISO determined the bid price of $35 million was too high.

Similarly, the 1,000 MW "demand-relief" solicitation was truncated because the response was too little and too costly. Only 180 MW of valid load-shedding bids were received, at an expected cost of $26 million. About 67 other proposals for 250 MW of demand reduction had been rejected as infeasible. The statewide small-load aggregation solicitation was more successful, with more than 150 MW of bids for non-spinning reserves and almost 500 MW for replacement reserves and imbalance energy resources.[2]

Spikes and Caps

As early as March, electricity traders and utility schedulers began to notice an upward creep in prices for the coming summer. Although trading in futures contracts was thin on the New York Mercantile Exchange for California/Oregon Border (COB) and Palo Verde (PV) hubs, there was an obvious increase in prices compared to those seen on the daily spot markets. By late April, the differences were more pronounced. Clearly, someone thought it was going a hot summer.

The high-temperature trend began in the Southwest early that spring and by mid-May, PV futures prices for August were shooting up to nearly $100/MWh, dragging daily prices along for the ride.

Several factors were at play besides the early arrival of summer-like weather in the desert Southwest.

Natural-gas prices were approximately double what they had been the year before, and there was a noticeable spread between what it cost to purchase gas at the producing basins in New Mexico and Texas and the delivered price at the Southern California Border. To avoid the higher prices, big utilities were using gas that was supposed to be put into storage for later in the year.

Concerns about precipitation in the Pacific Northwest were adding to the market fears. Although rainfall was about average, there was less runoff coming into the reservoirs. Water managers at federal dams in the Northwest had to choose between generating energy and trying to fill their storage as much as possible for summer. Cutbacks in generation forced the Bonneville Power Administration deeper into purchasing energy for daily needs, helping to put upward pressure on spot prices.

There were two large nuclear facilities off line for scheduled refueling outages, and some traders were betting on delays in their return to service.

On May 22, record-breaking temperatures throughout Southern California and the Southwest brought the situation to a boil. Prices spiked at the California Power Exchange to the highest levels ever seen—$863/MWh in the late-afternoon hour-ahead market. The hourly price was above $300/MWh for 17 consecutive hours. Prior to that day, the hour-ahead price had never exceeded $200/MWh.

The day-ahead market proved volatile as well, with clearing prices averaging $325/MWh for the peak period on May 23. The high price for a single hour was almost $470, a record, and there were five hours above $400/MWh that day.

In trading outside of California, prescheduled prices averaged over $200/MW, while real-time emergency power in the Southwest hit $750/MWh, traders reported.

California ISO found itself resource-deficient by 6,000 MW from the combination of lost generation, limited imports, and unanticipated demand. As load climbed toward 40,000 MW, California ISO moved into a Stage Two Emergency for the first time in 2000. The afternoon peak crested at 39,808 MW, but utilities had managed to shed 1,040 MW of load from voluntary customer cutbacks and their curtailment contracts. The imbalance energy market price began hitting the $750/MWh cap at noon and just stayed there.[3]

The upcoming Memorial Day weekend managed to throw a little cold water on the superheated market, and prices edged back down to earth. The price-spike scenario, however, would repeat several times over the next few weeks, and emergency declarations from California ISO became commonplace events.

Whatever price records had been set at the Power Exchange were eclipsed on June 14, as the heat wave moved into Northern California and the daytime PX average rocketed to $464/MWh, with a high single-hour price of $663/MWh.

Although California ISO enacted a Stage One for the entire state, the situation was far more critical in San Francisco, where the average temperature reached an unheard-of 103 degrees F. As Pacific Gas & Electric moved closer to a new all-time record of 23,400 MW, grid operators called upon the giant utility and its neighboring municipal utilities to cut firm power in order to maintain transmission stability. At the worst point, power was cut to 97,000 PG&E customers.[4]

The need to enact staged emergencies became routine during the summer of 2000. When another three-day heat wave struck on June 26-28, California ISO was able to meet load only by declaring Stage Two Emergencies to elicit up to 1,000 MW of non-firm load curtailments.

Prices in the various markets rose and fell as if on a rollercoaster ride, and clearing prices that previously would have been unimaginable were now an everyday occurrence.

For the electric utilities that still operated under the retail rate freeze, the commodity cost of electricity was eating into their collections for other components of the energy cost and eliminated their ability to transfer funds into the stranded-cost recovery accounts.

In June, for instance, the average price of wholesale electricity for Pacific Gas & Electric and Southern California Edison was nearly $170/MWh. That translated to 17 cents/KWh, while the amount the utilities could collect from customers was somewhere between 5.4 cents and 6.2 cents/KWh.[5]

San Diego Gas & Electric faced an entirely different situation. Because it had ended its rate freeze, the higher cost of electricity was being passed through directly to consumers. Beginning with the monthly billing statements in late June, the cost of electricity was between 30 percent and 40 percent higher than it had been during the spring.

As summer progressed, those bills would double or triple. Consumers, especially small-business owners, began to contact their local officials to express their shock and outrage.

The politician in the center spotlight was Steve Peace, the state senator from San Diego whom people considered most responsible for California's restructuring program.

Supply and Demand Out of Balance

One of the curious aspects of California's energy market design was that while daily electricity prices were established at the Power Exchange, most of the concerns about price volatility and the demand for strict price caps played out at California ISO. Everyone believed that price limits in the California ISO imbalance energy markets would serve as de facto caps for PX prices.

The reason was simple. As prices moved higher at the PX, the electric utilities would "underschedule" their load; that is, move a portion of their expected needs into ISO's real-time energy market.

There was a strong economic incentive to do so. Under the "market clearing price" set up at the PX, the cost of the last supply bid accepted to meet load would establish the price paid to all the rest of the generation that was being dispatched that hour. The utilities reasoned that even if a portion of their load was being met by high-cost energy procured at the last minute by California ISO, the overall expense would be lower because the bulk of demand was clearing at a lower price in the PX markets.

If the California ISO prices were limited, many people believed, there would be no incentive for this kind of underscheduling.

The possibility of manipulating load to reduce prices had been raised during the discussions about market structure and market power in California, but influential economists downplayed the potential harm.

Severin Borenstein, a professor of economics at the Energy Institute on the Berkeley campus of the University of California, for instance, argued that such behavior by buyers would be self-defeating. Power sellers would quickly realize the game and would either raise their prices at lower demand levels or hold back on bidding in the PX's day-ahead market, pushing even more load into the real-time market, where higher prices would result. Such tactics "will ultimately fail," Borenstein had argued when the Market Surveillance Committee examined the issue in 1999.[6]

And yet, that seemed to be exactly what was happening. California ISO's market analysts had documented instances of underscheduling of load by utilities during previous summer periods of high demand. Now it appeared that whenever PX loads crossed the 30,000 MW mark, bid prices rocketed higher, partly because older, less efficient units were submitting bids and partly because sellers could capture "scarcity" payments if they deferred bidding resources into the day-ahead market. At 35,000 MW, the total amount of both load and generation would plateau, with the result being that more and more of the demand was pushed into California ISO's real-time market.

During the extremely hot days, when peak-hour demand could reach 40,000 MW, the level of underscheduling exceeded 20 percent of the demand. That meant California ISO's operators had to secure 8,000 MW or more each hour.

When system loads peaked at 43,447 MW on June 16, the Department of Market Analysis reported, "total loads exceeded final Hour-Ahead schedules by 9,064 MW, or about 21 percent of total system load."[7]

Operators faced the additional problem that there were few spare generators that could be called upon. May and June are traditionally periods of mild temperatures and moderate loads in California, and many power plant owners use the late spring to schedule maintenance so their units will be ready for summer.

During the May 22-23 heat wave, for instance, more than 20 percent of the 17,000 MW of capacity at power units that had been sold off by the utilities was unavailable because of scheduled or unplanned outages. Although availability was better during June, at least 10 percent of the capacity was out of service when the subsequent peak days hit.[8]

As a result of all this, the prices being paid for real-time energy frequently hit the $750/MWh cap. Whenever the California ISO had to resort to out-of-market purchases to maintain reliability, the prices paid could potentially exceed the cap.

During the first three weeks of June, CEO Terry Winter reported, the cost of purchasing power via the ISO's markets was nearly $2 billion, and May's cost was about $1 billion.[9]

The California market was missing two elements that could have helped alleviate the situation, price responsiveness by consumers and "hedging" contracts by the utilities. While one of the underlying precepts of supply and demand is that higher prices tend to cause people to use less of something, that did not hold true for electricity, in part because it is an essential service but more importantly because consumers, except those in San Diego, were not exposed to the higher prices.

The market rules established by the CPUC required utilities to buy all of their energy through the Power Exchange. Although the PX had begun offering "block forward" contracts, similar to the NYMEX futures contracts, the CPUC had limited how much could be procured under these contracts.

The utilities were not even using their full potential. According to California ISO's analysts, PG&E had only about 1,100 MW of block forward contracts out of its 3,000 MW to 3,500 MW limitation, while Edison has taken 1,750 MW of its 2,200 MW limit in June and less than 3,500 MW of its 5,000 MW limit for later months of the summer.[10]

Taken together, everything in the market pointed to an over-reliance on spot power purchases at an increasingly uncomfortable price.

Peace at War

Senator Peace on June 22 sent a letter to the California ISO board of governors demanding a reduction in the price cap from $750 to $250/MWh. The market "is not workably competitive," he wrote. "Sadly, last week's market performance confirmed my worst fears. Electricity prices and electricity costs reached grossly unreasonable levels considering that, from a statewide perspective, there were ample supplies."

In addition, the new limits should be made retroactive to May 1, so that San Diego consumers could be spared the pain of recent price excursions, Peace urged.[11]

The California ISO board took up the controversial issue during an emergency meeting June 28 that coincided with the third heat wave in a month. Senator Peace addressed the board and introduced letters from various legislators and state agencies that he said "present a united, unambiguous policy" of the state, asking that the price caps be reduced to $250/MWh.

The debate raged for hours, with opinions ranging widely across the board. California ISO staff preferred a $500/MWh cap. They were unsure whether adequate resources could be obtained in an emergency at the lower price, Fluckiger said.

CEO Terry Winter concurred. He reminded the governors that the original motion was to have been $500/MWh and that a $250 price might not be sufficient because of the increase in natural-gas prices. A tight cap could mean that operators would be unable to purchase energy that was flowing to other markets where prices were higher, he said, and that would necessitate enacting curtailments and rotating outages on a regular basis. "When I go to the governor's office and tell him I'm dropping 4,000 MW, I want back-up," Winter said. "Either that or we'll be facing this every day."[12]

Out of deference to Peace, the board initially considered a $250/MWh limit, but the vote deadlocked at 12-12.

The measure was reintroduced with a $500 cap, and on a vote of 16-4 (with 4 abstentions), the governors decided to reduce the price cap for imbalance energy, reliability, and transmission congestion from $750 to $500/MWh. Replacement reserve bids were capped at $100/MWh. As part of the measure, owners of generation were urged to make all their resources available to the market whenever loads reached 38,000 MW, but California ISO recognized it had no power to enforce the request.

Peace was livid and stormed out of the meeting when it became clear the board would not pass his proposed cap. The next day, he appeared before the Electricity Oversight Board to rail against the decision. "The California ISO board is a cabal of insiders," he claimed, promising to bring in the state auditor general and the federal Department of Justice for antitrust investigations.

Peace's energy adviser John Rosza interrogated Winter about the price-cap vote, alleging that Winter had steered the board into accepting the $500/MWh level even though generators would have accepted $250/MWh. He also criticized the lack of limits on out-of-market purchases, accusing Winter of establishing "carte blanche" for making OMM purchases at any price.[13]

Divided Loyalties

While these events and statements were being played out in the venues of public meetings of California ISO and the EOB, Peace was exerting just as much pressure behind the scenes. One person who bore much of the brunt of his anger was Robin Larson, who had been Peace's legislative aide during the AB 1890 period but later joined the regulatory affairs team at California ISO.

As principal architect of the restructuring law, Peace was one of the few state lawmakers who paid much attention to California ISO, and for the first two years of operations, he seemed pleased with the way the organization had performed. "We had a pretty good relationship until the market prices went up," Larson said. "I think we were looked at as an entity that did a fine job, a top-quality organization to take care of reliability."

When the FERC orders came out rejecting the EOB's governance provisions, Peace had worked out a compromise with the federal regulators to maintain partial state oversight ability as long as the new market entities operated within state borders. The deal was enacted in Peace's Senate Bill 96, one of the few pieces of legislation meant to fix problems with AB 1890. It declared the state's intent to provide for "the evolution of the ISO and the PX into organizations that would serve the Western regional market and would be governed by members selected by participating states."

The 1999 bill statutorily endorsed the changes in corporation bylaws made by the California ISO board earlier in the year that restricted the EOB's confirmation powers to appointments of customer representatives on the governing boards and limited its authority to serve as an appeals board for ISO decisions to matters that were exclusively within the jurisdiction of the state.[14]

Although Peace had been willing to compromise on the governance issue, Larson said cooperation disappeared after the June 28 price-cap vote. "It was an extremely stressful time, and I think it eventually led to the disintegration of my relationship with Steve," she recalled. "I'm having these screaming matches on the phone with Steve. That's not new, but these were serious." Although Larson said, "I felt very comfortable with what I was told to do and the positions I needed to advocate," there was no longer any middle ground in dealing with Peace.

"Our mission is to make sure the lights stay on," she reminded him. "I remember having a conversation with him, 'If you want to put something in legislation that at $250 we shut the lights out, OK; that gives us a new mission.'"

Larson believes that Peace acted out of two motivations, the impacts of the price spikes on San Diego consumers and the sense that an agency he created was defying him. "Part of it is 'You're putting my constituents in jeopardy.' Part of it is 'You're defying me.' So there's a lot of deep resentment," she said.

The political pressure mounted on all fronts. Peace was said to be demanding that Winter be fired and that the consumer representatives who voted against the $250 cap be replaced by the EOB.

Marcie Edwards, the representative from the Los Angeles Department of Water & Power, who had attended the meeting via telephone, declared that she had misunderstood the original vote. Bill Carnahan, head of a consortium of Southern California munis, also professed confusion as he listened to the debate on a cell phone. Dick Ferreira of SMUD and Jack McNally of the utility union joined Edwards and Carnahan in asking that the $250 cap be reconsidered during a special meeting on July 6.

Many people presumed that Edwards was being pressured to change her vote.

Camden Collins submitted a letter of resignation from the board, containing a thinly veiled reference to Senator Peace. "The very idea that one person could take down the whole board and the chief executive officer over a difference of opinion on the appropriate wholesale price cap is truly stunning," she wrote. "It saddens me that I continue to hear reports of verbal abuse, browbeating and being whipped and excoriated stemming from the same source."[15]

Even though the motion to reconsider Peace's lower price level failed on a 12-9-1 vote at the July 6 meeting, the issue would come up repeatedly during the summer. During the August 1 meeting, San Diego elected officials pleaded with the board to reconsider the $250 cap. Mayor Susan Golding said that senior citizens were turning off their air conditioners and refrigerators because they could not afford to pay their power bills.

Governor Davis had begun pressuring his appointees to act on containing power costs. Earlier in the day, the EOB passed a very strongly worded resolution urging a new vote. After another long debate, the reduced price cap was approved 15-6-2.[16]

Still the issue never went away, and various motions to reconsider, remove, or further tighten the California ISO price caps dominated every board meeting through October.

A last-ditch effort to enact a "load differentiated" price cap raised by TURN's Mike Florio was adopted despite protests that reducing prices as demand went up turned economics on its head. The plan never was put into effect, as FERC came out with an order asserting its jurisdiction over the California market situation a week later.

The October 25 meeting proved to be the last hurrah for the stakeholder board.

By that time, the panel had fallen into serious dysfunction, and price caps seemed to be at the root of increased animosity among members. Dave Freeman, general manager at LADWP, removed Edwards from the board because she had voted for one of the measures to eliminate caps after the summer emergencies seemed to lessen.

"I was very strong for reducing the cap, and I blew a fuse when I found out Marcie had voted with the crowd," Freeman said. "Frankly, I just removed her from the board and attended the last meeting of the board before it was disbanded. I'd been in vicious verbal combat with Ken Lay [Enron's CEO] on the phone about price caps. I was the guy who rounded up all the muni votes to reduce the cap. Marcie just made a mistake."

Edwards, who has gone on to be the general manager of the Anaheim municipal utility, declined to talk about the price-cap votes.

The price-cap issue was "a dramatic turning point" for the California ISO board, said chair Jan Smutny-Jones. "It made everybody behave differently. People were voting against their own better judgment but for their employer's interests. We had people resigning, people making emotional statements. At the same time, the agencies were beginning to be attacked from outside. Up until that point, there was a relative immunity, but then you had Steve Peace declaring he was going to terminate the ISO."

Peace also pressed the State Auditor to undertake an investigation of ISO and Power Exchange operations, with an particular focus on how effective the market surveillance units were in detecting and remedying problems in suppliers' bidding.

The Backlash Begins

Shortly after the June 14 outage incident in San Francisco, Governor Davis wrote a letter to Loretta Lynch at the CPUC and Michael Kahn at the EOB, asking them to investigate the situation, "including the reasons for the generation maintenance and transmission problems and related impact on electricity prices and advise me on actions that can be taken to avoid recurrence of this situation." The governor asked for findings and recommendations by August 1.[17]

What Davis received was a declaration of war against competitive power markets and a diatribe against the federalization of electricity. The document declared California's power market to be dysfunctional and out of control and suggested that the cause of the problem was that the California Independent System Operator and the Power Exchange had "no duty to protect the public."

While the report acknowledged that "Hot weather, aging power plant and transmission infrastructure, and dysfunctional bidding behavior in the wholesale market combined to drive prices up and to create inadequate electricity supplies in the Bay Area," it strongly implied that the outages called by California ISO were unnecessary. "Changes in power system governance resulted in PG&E being ordered to black-out over 100,000 of its customers—without an ability for the State to weigh in on that decision."

The report to the Democratic administration alleged that "decisionmakers in previous administrations traded away" the state's ability "to project, plan for and act to control electricity supply shortages and wholesale market run ups." The power over markets had shifted to the federal government. "Washington, D.C. now controls pricing decisions directly at the wholesale level and indirectly at the retail level…Washington, D.C. now affects California's ability to attract new investment in power plants."

Plainly, the report was all about control and how the state could regain control over the entities that had been created to oversee the new markets. Rather than fixing the market, the regulators proceeded from the assumption that the system was irreparable and out of control.

The report alleged the PX and ISO had been taken captive by generators—"governed by boards whose members can have serious conflicts of interest. Some of these board members or their companies financially benefit from higher prices in electricity markets. Neither of these private organizations is accountable to the State or its consumers, and neither is charged with the task of keeping electricity prices reasonable for consumers and businesses."[18]

Nowhere did the report mention the state's purposeful policy of balancing interests of various stakeholders on the governing boards, or the fact that restructuring legislation had been a bipartisan effort.

Most of the 30 recommendations listed in the report were noncontroversial; indeed, many were commonsense approaches to preparing for electricity emergencies. But the text of the document hinted of illegal behavior by market players and potential collusion by staff at the California ISO and the PX. It complained that the corporations were refusing to provide data and "failed to detect manipulation and gaming on several fronts."

The situation needs to be investigated, stated the report. "We recommend that the California Attorney General immediately subpoena relevant records and data to determine the pricing and offering behavior of market participants, and the actions of the ISO and its board members, and the actions of generators in supplying California's energy needs."

If there had even been a chance to cooperatively assess the problems in the market, the Lynch/Kahn report effectively dispelled the opportunity. Even before the report became public, the CPUC and Oversight Board issued subpoenas against California ISO and its board. Attorney General Bill Lockyer said his office was looking into whether there were antitrust violations.

California ISO board chair Smutny-Jones revealed that deputy attorney general Lindsay Bower had outright accused him of "colluding" with Dynegy representative Greg Blue and Enron's David Parquette on the price-cap votes. Smutny-Jones pointed to the minutes of the board meeting to show that he had voted for the $500/MWh cap, but the other two had abstained.

"It's intimidation," Smutny-Jones declared. "It's Nixonian."[19]

In retrospect, Kahn acknowledged that none of the investigations of the California ISO board or Smutny-Jones' actions ever uncovered anything illegal or improper. But at the time, he said, the entire structure of the stakeholder board seemed like a big mistake.

"It was impossible for the governor and I to get our minds around the notion that the decision of price caps was being made by a board on which this guy was the chair," Kahn said. "People talk about foxes in chicken coops, and generally that's a metaphor. This was literal, not figurative. And it was disorienting; it seemed so preposterous to us. We were just astonished at the idea that 'Well, let me see, you're going to vote whether to cap the prices you get to charge?'"

13

Thirty-Five Rabbits

JIM MCINTOSH WAITED a couple of years before finally joining the team in Folsom in early 2000 for what he anticipated would be a relatively easy gig before entering full retirement. "Just in time for things to go sideways," he said.

Over the course of three decades, McIntosh had worked through just about every job in operations and dispatch at Pacific Gas & Electric—as a journeyman electrician, substation engineer, hydroelectric operator, steam-plant operator; then after a few years, it was into the control room, where he moved up the ladder to supervisor of power operations.

He had been one of PG&E's representatives to the WEPEX development group and had been on the informal committee that selected the Folsom site for California ISO headquarters. "When they started hiring for the ISO, a lot of the folks I was working with decided to come over originally. My family wasn't ready to do that, so I was actually given a bonus to stay [at PG&E] rather than a bonus to leave."

Prepared to do just about anything that was asked of him, the job that McIntosh least expected was that of television celebrity. After he took over as director of grid operations, he became one of the "faces" of California ISO for millions of Californians during the power crisis of 2000/01.

The California ISO communications staff kept reporters informed of the latest information, but frequently they turned to the control-room experts, including McIntosh, Ed Riley, and Jim Detmers, to explain to the public exactly what was going on.

When it was all over, McIntosh could laugh about having been named one of the "sexiest men of California's power crisis" in a late-night TV show skit. For most of that yearlong emergency, however, the situation was no laughing matter.

Indeed, by August 2000, the problems in the electricity market had become front-page news throughout the state. Even a few national newspapers were writing about the continuing price spikes, the consumer revolt in San Diego, and the

Stage One and Stage Two Emergencies that The California ISO was enacting just about every day.

The June episode of rotating outages in San Francisco had put a spotlight on problems with the energy system, and the continuing electricity price volatility had moved San Diego residents to take their complaints to the California Public Utilities Commission in San Francisco and to the state Legislature in Sacramento.

Armed with a report from his regulatory agency appointees that alleged a market out of control, Governor Gray Davis on August 2 issued a series of emergency declarations to limit power consumption at state facilities and to order every state agency involved in the permitting of new power supplies to streamline their approval processes.

"Electricity prices in a deregulated market are largely the function of supply and demand," Davis stated. "California agencies should work faster to increase supply." He also established an Energy Reliability Task Force to coordinate actions by energy agencies, something that had been recommended in the Kahn/Lynch report.[1]

California ISO personnel couldn't wait around for new power plants to be built, however expedited the process. They needed additional supplies immediately. With the accelerating problems of utilities underscheduling their load and some generators waiting for prices to rise before offering supplies, McIntosh's main occupation was helping the transmission operators identify and secure last-minute resources in order to keep the power flowing and the lights on.

He had long suspected that "the failure was imminent," he said. During those years with PG&E, he noted, "We'd had some really close calls, supply-wise. We quit building generation. Load continued to grow at the rate of 1,500 MW a year. The thing that saved everybody's bacon was that up to that point we were really lucky with the weather."

The diversity of weather patterns in the West also meant that California could usually depend on excess energy being available from the Northwest or the Southwest.

But those regions were growing in population and energy consumption even faster than California. When the high temperatures spread throughout the West in late June, he said, "We made the request outside the region to get power and there was nothing available."

Meeting load increasingly meant calling on every possible generator to squeeze out a few more megawatts, leaning on utilities that owed him favors, and sometimes rerouting energy around the system to get past the transmission bottlenecks that prevented power from getting where it was needed. "I used to have a list of 35 things I could do when I first got here. I had what they used to call 'rabbits in my hat,'" McIntosh said. "I knew everybody in the industry. I knew where the energy was."

As the summer wore on, each of those rabbits got pulled out of the hat, some many times over. One of the tricks that became standard practice was to use the DC Intertie as a transmission detour around the near constant bottlenecks on Path 15.

The DC line, owned and operated by Los Angeles and the Bonneville Power Administration, connects the BPA system in Oregon to L.A. at the Sylmar substation. Though used primarily to import power from the Northwest, ISO operators entered arrangements to ship power from Southern California north, where it could be transferred to the Pacific AC lines and sent back into Northern California.

Despite a significant loss of energy—nearly 10 percent—that happens when DC current is converted to AC, the strategy successfully allowed system operators to move power where it was most needed.

Another ploy was the heavy reliance on pumped-storage units. There are three large pumped-storage reservoirs in California: PG&E's Helms, Edison's Big Creek and LADWP's Castaic. Instead of letting water run down the riverbeds after it flows through hydroelectric turbines, engineers built lower reservoirs to collect the stream. At night, when power is less costly and load is low, the water is pumped up to a higher reservoir for recirculation the next time it is needed. Again, it is a costly strategy, as it requires more energy to pump the water to higher elevation than is generated, but it makes power available at peak times.

There were occasions when California ISO relied so much on the pumped-storage systems to meet demand that the upper reservoirs were almost completely drained. A utility worker would stand on the lip of the dam to let operators know when they needed to shut the gates and cease flows.

The code phrase they used was "We're sucking mud."

The Stage Two Emergencies and associated voluntary load curtailments that had only rarely been declared during the first two years of operations became routine. From May 22 though the end of September, California ISO entered Stage Two nearly every time daily peak load exceeded 42,000 MW—17 times in all.

Sometimes it was not necessary to cut power to the interruptible customers, but on other days, California ISO needed every unit of demand reduction possible. During a four-day period of consecutive Stage Twos during the week of July 28, for instance, customer cutbacks helped trim the peaks by between 1,775 MW and 2,200 MW—with just about every program participant shutting off their lights and closing shop between noon and 6:00 p.m.[2]

The emergency situation was so much a part of the routine of people in the utility business that everyone kept their pagers and cell phones ready for the afternoon call. Utility customer representatives would quietly excuse themselves from whatever meeting they were in, head out into hallways and work though their lists of telephone notifications to make sure that large customers knew about the Stage Two and tally up how much conservation could be counted on that day.

California ISO's policy of keeping the control room open to media paid off again and again, said Stephanie McCorkle. Although operators had initially balked at giving the press access to the inner sanctum, they began looking forward to seeing the TV crews standing in the area known as the "blue box."

At one point during the crisis, someone estimated that each camera tripod on hand when an emergency was declared led to 100 MW of customer conservation. "Before noon, they'd do a live shot with Patrick [Dorinson] or one of the guys, talking about the afternoon peak and how we need to conserve," recalled Ed Riley. "We could see that load come up and just level off before it should have, and it was a really good thing."

Another positive to having reporters on hand was that it gave the public a picture of how things worked, of professionals doing their best under difficult circumstances, Riley added. "I think what changed was the knowledge and perception of the outside people, the real-world people, that we're trying to do a good job. We *are* doing the job, and we're being as open as we can be about it."

For those who knew how to gauge the control-room mood, the summer emergencies brought an entirely new vibe, noticed shift supervisor Deane Lyon. "There was a whole different atmosphere from start-up. It wasn't a lot of excitement. It was tense, waiting to see if something was going to happen. The activity was trying to find additional energy, making phone calls, trying to do energy deals."

Remarkably enough, despite 17 Stage Two declarations and 32 Stage One alerts, California ISO staff kept pulling rabbits out of the hat to avoid a repeat of the firm-load curtailment episode of June 14.

After the last 40,000 MW day of the summer passed on September 20 without the need to curtail interruptible customers, everyone hoped that the worst of the crisis was over.

That was not to be the case.

The Tip of the Arrow

The fluctuation of electricity prices that summer had focused utilities' and customers' attention on the need to enter contracts for secure supplies at predictable prices. The problem was that no one could predict what prices would be, making it difficult to enter agreements with any sort of certainty.

Prior to May 2000, the wholesale index prices derived from Power Exchange trading gave market participants a false sense of stability and a belief that the electricity commodity portion of retail rates had found a niche in the 2.5 cents to 3 cents/KWh range. When power marketers tried to sign customers to longer-term contracts at 4 cents or 5 cents, they found no takers. Everyone was "going short" in the market; that is, they relied on the low near-term price signals to try to achieve the best deal.

So the price run-ups came as a major shock to both the utilities and to direct-access customers. Marketers that had promised energy deliveries at a certain cost found they could not buy power that cheaply, and they began throwing customers back to utility default service.

The direct-access market in California peaked in June 2000, with about 224,000 customers taking non-utility supplies. That figure represented only 2.2 percent of all customers but 16 percent of the electricity delivered by the three regulated utilities. Household participation barely reached 2 percent of accounts, with the highest participation rate reported at about 165,000 residential customers.[3]

Each month thereafter saw accelerating attrition among participants, particularly among the industrial segment that had previously been the main proponent of customer choice. At the peak of program participation one out of five large commercial/industrial customers had a direct-access contract, accounting for about one-third of energy consumption for the class. By the end of summer, only two-thirds of that group was still in the program.

The added load being shifted back to utilities meant even more pressure to sign secure contracts. San Diego Gas & Electric hosted a "summit" in July with generators and power marketers to try to arrange deals.

While in San Diego, California ISO chair Jan Smutny-Jones even investigated the possibility of hooking three U.S. Navy aircraft carriers in the harbor to SDG&E's system to capture 30 MW of power from the ships' on-board generators. Earlier, there had been plans to float a diesel power plant on a barge up from South America into San Francisco Bay to help bolster the vulnerable system. Any source of energy seemed fair game, despite environmental objections or cost.

Utility executives and marketer representatives left the San Diego meeting with optimism, but no long-term deals were signed as a result—even though insiders claimed there were at least 20 offers made in the weeks after the meeting. Part of the problem was that the CPUC continued to insist that all arrangements flow through the PX market, in the form of block forward contracts, but regulators also withheld giving a blanket determination of "reasonableness."

That meant the utility might have to justify the deals in the future and possibly be at risk for rate disallowances if market prices fell below the contracted price.

Meanwhile, the market price kept escalating.

Within the California ISO, there was an internal debate about what to do about the situation. More and more of the problems in the market were falling into California ISO's lap and the imbalance-energy market and ancillary service markets were becoming a greater percentage of the entire energy market than the system had been designed for. But there was substantial disagreement as to whether the grid operator had the responsibility to do more than maintain system reliability.

In some ways, it was a debate between the two cultures, guardian and market, though the lines were not so clear-cut as Jane Jacobs' *Systems of Survival* categories might suggest. In this instance, the guardian mentality took the form of a "command and control" argument, to do whatever was necessary to ensure adequate supplies, including entering long-term contracts and signing up peaking power units for backup supplies. More cautious voices on the executive team felt that went beyond the organization's mission.

There was a parallel argument about what the California ISO could do to ensure that generators were not purposely withholding supplies from the market. The Department of Market Analysis had uncovered evidence that operators at some Southern California power plants had extended a maintenance outage with the intent of seeing whether it would raise market prices.

DMA was also looking into whether the ISO had been forced into making block purchases for more energy than was necessary. Anjali Sheffrin began investigating the situations, but it would take months to determine whether rules had been broken. The market monitors in July also felt compelled to issue a notice to all scheduling coordinators forbidding a form of gaming in the transmission congestion market.

Chief of operations Kellan Fluckiger increasingly took the position that California ISO needed to respond to circumstances more forcefully. "The ISO in its initial year developed a culture and an ability to respond quickly to fix things and to make things happen," he explained. "After the markets started, that continued for awhile. We responded to anomalies that we saw. We put caps on when we saw the $10,000 [bid]; we did a fast dance to keep up with things. We then stopped."

He recalled a phrase used during officers' meetings: "We want to be the feathers on the arrow, not the tip." The feathers are to guide market actions, but the tip is where the action is, he explained. "I was a tip guy. I was not a feathers guy."

As an organization, Fluckiger said, California ISO had "moved from the point to the feathers, and whether or not it was the ISO's responsibility to do any particular thing—in my mind at least—wasn't very important. If it really needed to get done and it wasn't getting done, you either have to do it, or you have to change something. You can't just stand around.

"I think [the ISO] could have been a lot more aggressive and done some stuff. I think they could have been the catalyst for others doing things as well. The PUC should have been moving aggressively to have the utilities tie up contracts and power supply; they did not."

Fluckiger's tendency toward aggressive market corrections put him at odds with Terry Winter. "You know, we think we can do just about everything," the CEO said. "There are very, very bright people here. They look out and say, 'God, we've got to have some peaking units.' Well, no, we shouldn't do it. Demand programs, why am I in demand programs? All I should do is set up a market that allows people to bid load in, but I shouldn't be in demand programs. But people came in and said we've got to have demand programs."

It was a case of trying to be the savior of the market, and clearly not part of the organization's mission, Winter said. "But we have a tendency to say, 'OK, we can solve this problem,' and really go beyond what is our authority to do."

The tension was apparent in Winter's August 10 testimony to the state Legislature, in which he laid out a 10-point action plan to accelerate generation, transmission, and demand response.

A number of the proposed priorities went beyond California ISO's statutory and tariff authority, while others recommended actions for other agencies—such as more contracting by utilities to alleviate the burden on real-time markets, or expedited siting of power plants in line at the California Energy Commission and transmission facilities at the CPUC. Though California ISO recommended enhancing its own existing demand-bidding programs, it also endorsed establishing real-time price signals.

These were things California ISO could not do by itself, Winter acknowledged. "I had asked our people here, 'What do we need to do and what do I need to put on the plate at the Legislature?' They were the basic things: encourage more generation, make sure the transmission runs more economically, have long-term contracts to stabilize the market." While he thought that the lawmakers would take the plan and run with it, little happened. "I couldn't get any traction," he said.

California ISO lobbyist Robin Larson believes that the report was received poorly because California ISO had already been identified as "evil" by the Lynch/Kahn report and because the board had resisted Senator Peace's price-cap recommendations. "People just didn't want to take it seriously," she said of Winter's action plan. "It got shelved."

In some areas where the ISO tried to take action, it met resistance. In August 2000, the board approved a solicitation for contracts with peaking power units that would provide emergency backup insurance. Although more than 2,000 MW of peakers were willing to sign deals, the CPUC and EOB objected to the price tag and opposed the ISO's foray into contracting. The peaking contracts eventually were deferred to the Department of Water Resources.

Meanwhile, the market outlook was worsening. An explosion on the El Paso Pipeline Company system in mid-August took out one of three lines serving California, further pushing gas prices higher. The utilities were beginning to have difficulties securing gas supplies for their customers, and in a highly usual incident, SDG&E curtailed gas deliveries to its industrial customers, including two power generators that were forced to burn oil instead of gas. Throughout California, generators were butting up against their air-quality limits, while others that had deferred maintenance were taking their units out of service for an extended period once summer was over.

The financial problems of Pacific Gas & Electric and Southern California Edison worsened. The utilities had filed emergency applications at the CPUC for rate relief but were met instead with an investigation of what they had done with the money previously collected in the stranded-cost accounts. The *Wall Street Journal* had reported that Edison was "technically insolvent," and financial analysts openly raised the possibility of a bankruptcy filing by one or both of California's largest utilities.[4]

The resource crisis of the summer had evolved into a financial crisis, without ever resolving the underlying market problems. Prices for fuel and power once again began climbing. On November 13, California ISO was forced to declare a Stage Two Emergency and secure 1,800 MW of load shedding from increasingly reluctant interruptible customers.

The day's peak load was just 34,384 MW. The need for emergency declarations to effect load shedding repeated itself the next day, and the next, then returned two weeks later. If the summer had been difficult, all the evidence now indicated that winter would be a disaster.

14

The Festival of Darkness

AS THE YEAR 2000 unfolded, everything was unraveling, especially the relationship between the state of California and the federal government.

California's elected officials continually pressed the federal regulators to step into the crisis, to declare that the market was not working, to enforce limits on power prices, and to order refunds of exorbitant market prices. San Diego Gas & Electric in August filed a formal complaint against all power sellers in the West, asking FERC to impose price caps at the Power Exchange and California ISO.[1]

The SDG&E case became a battlefield, and more than 50 parties immediately responded to the petition. Ratepayer advocates, who were generally shut out of federal proceedings, sided with the utility. "What is happening in California is not competition," argued TURN executive director Nettie Hoge. "It is price gouging, pure and simple." California ISO, however, called a widespread cap "premature" while its board was still dealing with the issue. It urged the commission to distinguish between "true market defects and strategic choices made in a competitive environment."[2]

Besides lining up against the SDG&E complaint, power marketers responded with petitions to eliminate the price caps altogether and asked regulators to launch an investigation into whether the California ISO board's autonomy was undermined by politics. Williams Company CEO Keith Bailey told FERC, "Williams is concerned that system reliability is being threatened as a result of a process that is overly influenced by political pressure."[3] Marketers also turned to FERC to recoup what they considered losses from California ISO decisions to recall power slated for export during times of emergencies.[4]

Municipal utilities, meanwhile, urged FERC to dismantle California ISO entirely and replace it with a publicly owned nonprofit transmission organization and strict cost-of-service rates.[5]

Given such disparate positions, it's no wonder that no one was completely pleased with FERC's action when it finally entered a November 1 order declaring

California's market "seriously flawed." The agency detailed a dozen factors and flaws in the system that combined to produce "unjust and unreasonable" power costs, but said it could not under federal law order retroactive refunds as had been demanded by California officials.

Among remedies set in the order, FERC proposed eliminating the so-called "buy/sell mandate" that limited utility transactions to the Power Exchange, and it required the utilities to schedule 95 percent of their power needs in the day-ahead market or face substantial penalties. FERC also determined that hard price caps would weaken California ISO's ability to secure adequate supplies. Instead it ordered a "soft cap" system to take effect within 60 days, establishing $150/MWh as a benchmark price for reasonableness. Sellers could be paid more than that price, but they would have to prove their costs, and payments would be subject to refund if they were not justified.

Additionally, FERC ordered the boards of California ISO and the PX to be dismantled within three months, with the multi-headed stakeholder panels replaced by seven-member boards made up of the CEO of each corporation plus six people who had expertise in the industry but were not representatives of particular interests.[6]

The issues of federal versus state jurisdiction ran throughout the order, establishing potential confrontations about federal rate structures, the ability to order refunds from marketers, and the governance of the corporations. "It is unclear how much power is left to the state," complained Governor Gray Davis. "FERC seems to be saying, 'Not much.' As governor of this state, I want to assert as much authority as I possibly can."[7]

Though unhappy that refunds were not ordered, Senator Steve Peace declared, "I will take particular satisfaction in the conversion of the discredited ISO and PX stakeholder boards into non-stakeholder boards."[8]

If state politicians were upset about the outcome, they became even more incensed as FERC members began explaining their positions, seeming to blame the state for its own problems.

"Essentially, what we're dealing with are the failures of the old system," said FERC chair James Hoecker. "It's very easy for people to blame competition or deregulation or the machinations of new market players." Hoecker suggested that FERC had been too deferential to California's market system. "That's one of those things we let go on too long," he continued. "The California Legislature was trying to predetermine the nature not only of the retail market in California, but the way the bulk power market in the West was going to operate. That doesn't work, and what happened in San Diego is a graphic example of why that doesn't work."[9]

Hoecker was a Democratic appointee of President Bill Clinton. Shortly after the November election, George W. Bush appointed Mississippi Republican Curtis Hèbert, an even more vociferous proponent of open markets in electricity, to take over as the chair of FERC. Hèbert would have a rocky and ultimately short-lived tenure, marked by constant fighting with Governor Davis and other state representatives over FERC's handling of the California crisis.

On the Sleeve

December marked a significant turning point in the history of California ISO and the troubled California marketplace. Despite any actions that might have been taking place as a result of the FERC order, the market situation had deteriorated substantially since Thanksgiving. By the first week of December, there was nothing short of a panic.

The Edison utility had ceased paying for energy in mid-November, causing many of the independent power producers in its territory to cut back production because they could not afford to operate. PG&E was making minimal payments and its gas suppliers were demanding cash, up front.

"The definition of really crazy is the California market," said one natural gas buyer, citing delivered prices at the border of over $54/MMBtu—almost 20 times what people normally expected to pay for the fuel.

A blast of subfreezing Arctic air spread into the Pacific Northwest, and electricity prices for the rest of the month shot up to $1,200/MWh. Although the $250/MWh price cap was in place in California, it masked the true costs of energy being bought. Loads on the PX dropped precipitously as utilities pushed more demand into the California ISO real-time markets.

At one point, California ISO had to pay over $1,000/MWh for power from British Columbia, and rumormongers hinted that some deals were ten times that price. The Dow Jones NewsWires reported that the California ISO paid B.C. Hydro's marketing unit PowerEx $10 million for 1,000 MW—a price that elicited disbelief from other marketers.[10]

The state had entered another nonstop emergency, with California ISO declaring Stage Two events every day from December 4 through December 14, then again from December 18 through December 23.

A huge issue was that without the utilities to guarantee payment for power purchases, California ISO had to find someone else to buy the energy. Beginning in November, the grid operator started relying mainly on the Los Angeles Department of Water & Power and the Sacramento Municipal Utility District to "sleeve" transactions for it.

A sleeve transaction is necessary when a provider of energy is unwilling to sell to a particular entity because of insufficient credit or other concerns, but it will sell to a third party. That third party, in turn, agrees to resell the energy to the buyer.

Under emergency circumstances, the sleeve deal is done with little or no profit for the middle entity.

Transcripts of telephone conversations between California ISO controllers and marketers around the West show how these deals worked and the amount of cooperation and cajoling that they required. For instance, on December 7, an ISO buyer called on LADWP for help in purchasing 1,000 MW:

California ISO:	OK, we want to try to pick up a thousand with B.C. Hydro.
LADWP:	A thousand with B.C. Hydro?
California ISO:	Yeah, yeah.
LADWP:	You know you're always going to be able to pick up a couple hundred from me. You still have me here on the side, don't forget.
California ISO:	I know, but I've got to pick it up at Malin.
LADWP:	You do whatever you need to do. I'm still here.

Less than a week later, the atmosphere had changed dramatically, as illustrated in this conversation from December 10:

California ISO:	Hey, I was wondering if I could get any of that stuff from the north, from B.C. Hydro.
LADWP:	It looks like the next hour we're going to have to be out. We've got to get clarification, from our management, how many times, how much we can do. Because it's already at a million dollars for us.
California ISO:	Uh-huh.
LADWP:	That's all I can do for one day, and we'll have to start again tomorrow.

The well was running dry, as evidenced by this December 9 conversation between California ISO and a Washington Water Power (Avista) marketer:

California ISO:	I heard a rumor you have 50 megawatts available energy you could send me but didn't have transmission to get it here.
WWP:	That's not a true rumor. I've got 50 MW plus tranny. But I can't sell it to you.
California ISO:	But you can't sell it to me. Oh.
WWP:	You guys, you know, you're bad risks. You think I'm kidding.
California ISO:	We're a bad risk? What Santa's not been nice?
WWP:	That's not the point. No, you guys are playing games with your cap.
California ISO:	What, with the soft cap?
WWP:	And we've been told by our risk manager we're not allowed to sell to you because of it.
California ISO:	So we need to find a marketer for it?
WWP:	That would be the case.
California ISO:	My manager said SMUD will bring it in.
WWP:	What's your price going to be?
California ISO:	(conversation off phone) Around 500.
WWP:	That works for me.

The deal was made, but with each hour it was getting harder, and power was more costly. Marketers were wary that whatever price they quoted would later be undercut by FERC, but California ISO was increasingly desperate.

At one point, a California ISO buyer confessed to an LADWP marketer, "I'm essentially not negotiating anymore. I'm saying, 'What is your price?' And if we need the energy, we'll probably say yes and they'll worry about it later." [11]

The First Stage Three and the Last Hard Cap

On the evening of December 5, Governor Davis stood before the Capitol building, with the state's 56-foot-tall Christmas tree in the background. At 7:00 p.m., he flipped the switch to light the gigantic tree, but his mood was anything but celebratory.

"I wish it didn't have to be this way," he told the crowd. The lights would stay on for half an hour, then power would be cut to conserve energy. He promised to send a picture of the dimmed tree to federal regulators, whom he blamed for not responding sufficiently to the state's energy crisis.[12]

The next day, California Public Utilities Commission president Loretta Lynch ordered employees to conduct surprise inspections at a dozen power plants located throughout the state that had reported their units unavailable because of unscheduled maintenance.

As much as 11,000 MW of power was not available during the emergency week, with 7,000 MW of that unplanned. "Why aren't the plants running?" Lynch said "We need to evaluate why the plants are down."[13]

The situation was reaching a critical point at California ISO. Even though the afternoon peak load for December 7 was expected to stay below 32,000 MW, there was simply not enough power available in the state to meet the peak. For the first time ever, California ISO declared a Stage Three Emergency beginning at 5:20 p.m. The emergency declaration enabled grid operators to call on the federal marketers at the Western Area Power Administration to send 50 MW, while the state water project turned off its pumps to divert 200 MW to California ISO.

In addition, 250 MW of power that had been scheduled for export from the state was pulled back. Together, the actions enabled California ISO to keep the lights on without cutting firm load, although Californians were urged to conserve as much as possible during the holiday season.

For Terry Winter, the underlying dilemma was that price caps in California were inhibiting his operators' ability to secure energy because sellers could get more in other markets, where there were no caps.

No one was bidding into the California ISO imbalance energy market. The only recourse was to purchase power under "out-of-market" (OOM) authority, but that required making telephones calls every hour to find available energy and negotiate a price. "No way could I keep the system running with all those phone calls," Winter said. "So I had to get things back in the BEEPstack, and the way to do that was to allow people to bid and compete with the Northwest."

The FERC soft cap was not scheduled to take effect until the beginning of January, but in an emergency filing on December 8, California ISO told FERC it was implementing a similar system. Beginning at 3 p.m. that day, California ISO's computers would no longer automatically reject bids above the $250/ MWh cap but would evaluate them in merit order.

"The ISO will no longer negotiate prices in real time," stated a news release describing its emergency Tariff Amendment No. 33. To the extent that bids exceeded the cap, "market participants will be required to submit cost documentation to the FERC, with informational filings to the ISO and the state, supporting any energy payments prices in excess of the soft cap." If the costs could not be verified, they would be subject to refund.

Costs of the emergency purchases would be allocated to scheduling coordinators that were relying on California ISO's imbalance-energy market rather than scheduling their load in forward markets. The amendment also declared California ISO's intent to impose penalties on generators that failed to comply with dispatch instructions.

California ISO attorney Roger Smith was amazed at the FERC response. "They approved us in an afternoon. Unprecedented. We filed something and they approved it in an afternoon. That order got us 3,000 MW into our BEEP-stack instantly."

Outside counsel Ed Berlin agreed that the action was unprecedented. "But it was an unprecedented situation," he said. "I think just as the ISO management felt that it would be a dereliction of that responsibility if it did not take every step it could take to forestall the crisis that was imminent, it didn't surprise me at all that FERC would have responded as it did."

The problem was that the bids were comparable to uncapped power prices throughout the region—in the case of the Pacific Northwest, those prices were escalating to as much as $5,000/MWh in anticipation of another cold weather front.

Once FERC approved Tariff No. 33, all limits were off at the Power Exchange. Daytime prices moved from the $250 cap to $650 on Monday, $988 on Tuesday, and finally an all-time high of $1,400/MWh for Wednesday, December 15.

"The governor was just apoplectic," said Michael Kahn, chair of the Electricity Oversight Board.

On the day that California ISO made its filing to FERC, Kahn recounted, the governor's staff was actively working out a deal with Edison to get money flowing again and arranging with the state water project to divert its power to California ISO.

"We were turning off pumping, and we were turning off electricity, and we were cobbling together megawatts for Terry Winter's system so he could run it. While he was, unbeknownst to us, about to do something that was 100 percent contrary to our views. It was a horrific breach of faith and, of course, it was morally wrong. I don't care if they thought we were all going to die; it's irrelevant. They had the obligation to us. We didn't learn [about the filing] until everything was done."

The action was particularly galling, Kahn said, because "This FERC, who took nine months to say hello to us, was rubber stamping this horrific action. And then, of course, all hell broke loose. It all turned out terribly as we expected it to, actually made things worse."

Winter, nonetheless, remains unrepentant. "I'll never admit that December 8th was the wrong thing to do. I look at what came out of it and see it did exactly what I thought it would do," he said. "Did prices go up? You're damn right. But they were already up, and what I did was merely to put it in the open and give FERC the ability to come in and give refunds if we proved those prices were wrong," he added.

"In the meantime, I kept the lights on by doing it."

The D.C. Summit

Removing the lid on power prices was still not the solution to the crisis, and California ISO was pressing the U.S. Department of Energy for an emergency order to require generators to sell into the market. That order came, reluctantly, from DOE on December 14. The question was whether there was any chance that the new Bush administration would allow the order to continue into 2001.

There was also a last-ditch effort by members of the lame-duck Clinton administration to bring all the sides together for a summit meeting in Washington late in December. Secretary of the Treasury Larry Sumners and Energy Secretary Bill Richardson hosted a series of meetings, but little came of them. Governor Davis and CPUC president Lynch fixated on blaming FERC for not ordering refunds. Few other parties seemed to be able to move off their positions of self-interest. Generators appeared willing to enter long-term contracts, but no one could agree on a suitable price.

"And so everybody agreed that no agreement could be made," Winter explained. "That's when I said, 'This is going to be completely out of control.'"

15

Full Impacts

WITNESSES said the 18-wheeler circled the streets around the Capitol, steadily gaining momentum before jumping the curb to crash into the south entrance at 70 miles per hour. The explosion and fire that consumed the big rig was caused not by the cargo inside the trailer—investigators later determined the mysterious white powdery substance to be evaporated-milk products—but by the sheer force of the collision.

The driver, eventually identified from dental records, was 37-year-old Michael Bowers.

No one ever fully understood why Bowers decided to drive the 15-ton diesel-fueled missile into the side of the Capitol. Some speculated that the ex-convict was making a protest against abuses in the state prison system; others suggested he had simply turned delusional after being in solitary confinement for a year at Corcoran State Prison during a six-year term for parole violations.[1]

Everyone would agree that it was a tragic coincidence that at the moment Bowers chose to make his suicide run, shortly before 9:30 p.m. on Tuesday, January 16, 2001, members of the state Assembly were in emergency conference in the other wing of the building, debating how to deal with the ever-worsening electricity situation. The explosion outside their doorway was completely unrelated, but the fiery picture that ran on the front page of just about every newspaper the next morning became a kind of visual metaphor for the full impact of the power crisis slamming into legislators' attention.

One measure under discussion, ABx-1, introduced by Santa Cruz Democrat Fred Keeley, proposed giving the California Department of Water Resources the authority to enter contracts for the purchase of power for use by customers of the nearly bankrupt utilities. The bill allocated almost $500 million from the state's general fund for that purpose and allowed DWR to issue debt to reimburse the state.

Although it took two weeks for an amended version to win final approval in both the Assembly and the Senate, Keeley's bill was the most significant response of lawmakers to the power crisis since they had reimposed a retail rate cap for San Diego consumers the previous August.[2]

During the two-week interim from the introduction of ABx-1 to Governor Gray Davis signing the new law on January 31, the crisis deepened.

On the Edge

The California Independent System Operator on January 17 found that it simply could not meet the day's demand for electricity without cutting power to firm-load customers of the utilities.

Jim McIntosh and his crew in the Folsom control room had finally run out of rabbits and options to stave off the need to initiate rotating outages. From about 11:50 a.m. to 2:00 p.m., Pacific Gas & Electric cut 500 MW in the unprecedented block outages, while other utilities helped chip in nearly 850 MW of non-firm curtailments that lasted until 9 p.m.

"We don't have enough generation to meet the load," said CEO Terry Winter. "We're right on the edge."[3]

In reality, the state had been on the edge almost continuously since the New Year began. Stage One and Stage Two notifications were a daily routine. Stage Three Emergencies had been declared three times during the preceding week, and even though daily load projections were barely 30,000 MW, the supply of power had all but evaporated. Repeatedly, the California ISO dispatchers went up to the precipice, relying on DWR to shut its water pumps and praying for residents to conserve.

Possibly the worst day up to that point was on Thursday, January 11, when a combination of adversities piled up overnight to send system reserve margins down to 1.9 percent by 9 a.m., Winter told reporters that day. Power plant outages remained "extraordinary" after an 800 MW generation facility reported fuel problems, another 800 MW steam plant developed tube leaks, and turbines at a smaller plant began vibrating excessively. In all, about 15,000 MW of in-state resources were not available for service.

Northwest imports had disappeared, and congestion on Path 15 meant any excess energy from Southern California could not be moved northward. Equipment failures at Sylmar limited use of the DC Intertie by 350 MW.

Then things got worse. Winter storms brought 20-foot swells in the Pacific Ocean, forcing the Diablo Canyon nuclear units to reduce output by 80 percent.

Some utility power schedulers openly joked about hoping the storms would bring down local distribution lines to cut service. "It's cheaper than buying power," one said.

Despite the federal emergency order to make all resources available to the market, sellers were increasingly wary of sending supplies into California. "Am I gonna get paid?" was a refrain heard from power marketers across the West. No one was bidding into the California Power Exchange, and daily transaction volumes had dropped to a quarter of their norm, made up mainly of utility nuclear generation and the contracted power that was bid in at a zero price by the utilities. Still, the average price for the week was $450/MWh.

One measure of how bad things had become was that the clearing price on the PX hour-ahead market topped $1,000/MW for one peak-period hour, but it elicited only 70 MW of bids. Every other transaction was going through the ISO's real-time markets.

The grid operators were preparing for "significant and serious interruptions of power" to as many as one million utility customers.

"Anytime we're looking at interrupting firm load, that's a significant problem for customers," Winter admitted to the 196 reporters that had logged onto the teleconference and the dozens of others who had set up camp at the Folsom headquarters.

Miraculously, the system held together that day, largely as a result of emergency deliveries running between 500 MW and 1,000 MW each hour from the Bonneville Power Administration. BPA was violating its own rules by generating power during periods of minimum flows on the Columbia River system, putting protected species of salmon at risk at the cost of millions of dollars.

The next day looked almost as bad, but managers were able to count on nearly 2,000 MW of customer conservation and emergency purchases by DWR for 1,200 MW, along with another 1,000 MW per hour from BPA sent under an exchange agreement. That energy was supposed to be paid back two-for-one within 48 hours, but at least that would be over the weekend.

"Today was a successful day," said an exhausted Jim Detmers at the late-Friday-afternoon news conference on January 12—the third that day that the ISO controllers had scheduled. Detmers, the director of operations, reported, "We were able to avoid firm load shedding."[4]

Communications director Patrick Dorinson began answering the telephone every day at about 5:00 a.m., as media inquiries came in from all over the world. He liked to do the morning radio programs, informing the early drive-time audience of the daily situation and urging them to conserve power at work and when they got home that evening. "Conservation is a way of life," he repeated.

Stephanie McCorkle took on the hordes of TV reporters, each needing a few moments of face time with an expert, and oversaw other journalists' access to the control room. Staff members Lorie O'Donley and Kristina Werst grabbed the constantly ringing phones and filled in the gaps for print media. The message heard round the world was that the threat of rotating outages was now part of everyday life in California.

Customer conservation was proving to be one bright spot in the otherwise dismal daily story. Operators began looking forward to seeing the television cameras already set up in the "blue box" area when they arrived before sunrise, knowing that their pleas for demand reduction would have an almost immediate impact. "I actually saw a public reaction," said director of grid operations Jim McIntosh. "In all my years of making public appeals, I'd never seen that effect. But those particular days, we actually saw load go off."

Eventually, though, McIntosh could find no more rabbits to pull from his hat. "We were getting close, but we'd never blacked anybody out. Everybody around here was doing everything they possibly could to avoid it. And at some point that one day, there wasn't anything left."

"We begged. We borrowed. We tried to steal, but there wasn't anything to steal," added Ed Riley, picking up pieces of the January 17 story. "That was the absolute worst day because I'd never done that before and I had to order it. That's the system operator's worst nightmare, having to shed firm load, because things can happen out there that you really don't want to happen with the lights out."

Up until that point, the controllers had been reserving water at the pumped-storage units and relying on voluntary customer curtailments in the daytime so there would be enough power to keep the lights on after dark. The fear shared by the operators was that somewhere out there in the dark, someone would drive through an intersection that had no working signals, possibly causing a fatal accident.

"The first day we shed firm load, we were in early that day; started about five o'clock in the morning because we knew it was going to be a problem day," Riley recounted. "We pulled out all our resources. We had people calling their friends at other utilities, begging them to send us something."

Except for the desperate phone conversations—short and to the point, then on to the next possibility—the control room was still. "That's the other thing that happens in the control room when it's high pressure," Riley said. "It gets very quiet. Everyone's concentrating, trying not to make a mistake, trying to keep the lights on as long as they can. We had extra people going down our computer screens, looking for people who had capacity but weren't generating at their complete output and calling them. 'Can we get two more megawatts out of you?'"

Some could help; others reported problems with their units.

"We scraped the barrel, squeezed the lemon. I don't know what you want to call it, but we got every drop we could before we pulled the trigger," Riley recalled. "Then we all just stood there kind of shocked. We really did it."

The California ISO had begun 32 consecutive days of a Stage Three Emergency that would last through February 16. There were firm-load curtailments necessary on just three days during that month long crisis, but the continuous Stage Three kept the attention of the media on the situation without yo-yoing between categories and creating needless confusion, Dorinson said. It also ensured that generators would be subject to the "must-offer" rules temporarily extended by the Bush administration's new secretary of energy, Spencer Abraham, and it allowed federal power marketers to justify selling to California despite water-flow restrictions on their hydro systems.

Two other significant events occurred on January 17: PG&E defaulted on $76 million in commercial debt, and Governor Davis declared a state of emergency that would be in effect for the rest of the year. Part of that order authorized DWR to make emergency purchases of electricity on behalf of the ISO and the nearly bankrupt utilities.

Meanwhile, lawmakers were debating dozens of bills—everything from taking over utility hydro and transmission systems in return for a financial bailout, to using $5 billion from the state's budget surplus to send "rate relief" checks to California utility customers. Most never saw passage. Two measures that would take effect with little debate were ABx1-7, authorizing emergency spot-power purchases by DWR, and SBx1-6, to establish a state power authority.[5]

The Electric Coup d'État

The November ruling from the Federal Energy Regulatory Commission called for dismantling the boards of the California ISO and the PX by January 29. Although the stakeholder representatives were supposed to be replaced by industry experts with no direct ties to market participants, and policy control would pass on to ISO management, Governor Davis and the Legislature had other ideas.

They quickly enacted ABx1-5, another measure authored by Assembly member Keeley, which allowed Davis to name the new ISO board members.[6]

On January 24, a new panel composed of five Davis appointees took its place in the Folsom meeting rooms. Much to his surprise, Electricity Oversight Board chair Michael Kahn was named the new ISO board chair. "I was head of the EOB, and it never occurred to me in a million years that I would be asked to head the ISO," Kahn said. "And the next thing I knew, I got a phone call from somebody saying, 'They want to check the press release with you.'"

The rest of the group: Tal Finney, the governor's energy adviser; Maria Contreras-Sweet, secretary of the Business, Transportation and Housing Agency; Carl Guardino, president of the Silicon Valley Manufacturing Group; and Mike Florio, senior attorney for The Utility Reform Network and the only holdover from the stakeholder board.

In another surprise move, each of the members of the existing board had been served a letter by Attorney General Bill Lockyer, demanding they resign within 24 hours or face criminal penalties of $5,000 each. Most were dumbfounded.

John Fielder, senior vice president of Southern California Edison, said the AG's letter based its demand not on California law but on English common law. "It's an old order that kings used to issue to get rid of princes that might be challenging the throne," Fielder explained.

"It was just mind-boggling," said Barbara Barkovich. "As far as I was concerned, if that law had gone through the courts, it would have been unconstitutional. The FERC had approved the original board; it had approved the tariff. The state had no ability to change the tariff through a state law." She joked that she and the other governors might have been "arrested for impersonating a board member."

But the legal issues were serious ones, said ex-chair Jan Smutny-Jones.

The last formal meeting of the stakeholder board occurred January 25. Governance and transition issues were already on the agenda, noted Smutny-Jones. Everyone agreed that the stakeholder board had become too dysfunctional, but the intention was that a more independent board would be selected to take control, as FERC had required.

"We'd retained outside counsel to advise the board on how to make this transition, and I wanted it to be smooth. There were real legal issues. It wasn't at all clear that what the state did was legal. It was awkward because the ISO is a state corporation, founded under state law, and it's a nonprofit, so that gives the AG a significant amount of authority over nonprofits. But it's also a FERC-regulated utility. We were caught between a rock and a hard place."

The legal procedure, Smutny-Jones was told by attorneys, was that as outgoing chair he should write a letter to Kahn, figuratively turning over the keys. "Then I get a call from the *Los Angeles Times* one night about eight o'clock: 'What do you think about the lawsuit that Lockyer just filed against you guys?'"

He was angered by the apparent public relations ploy. "The reality was there wasn't any drama being set up here, there really wasn't. It was very important to us that we transition smoothly, quietly, and let the system operate. We were very concerned about morale at the ISO; we were very concerned about how all the market participants would view this."

Rather than raising a fight, "We all resigned at the same time in the face of this threat from the attorney general," Fielder said.

Changes in D.C.

FERC was not pleased with the action, but it was undergoing a significant change of its own. James Hoecker announced that he was departing from the commission in late-January, leaving the new Republican administration to appoint a new chair.

Although Democrat William Massey spent one day in the chair's seat, President Bush on January 25 appointed Curtis Hèbert to the job. Hèbert was fervent in support of free enterprise in power markets. "I believe it is part of the solution rather than part of the problem for the malfunctioning markets on the West Coast," he said.

In his last statement on California matters, Hoecker predicted a confrontation with Governor Davis over the ISO board. "While stacking the board of a FERC-jurisdictional public utility with state political appointees may not raise ire in California," Hoecker wrote, "it is an unacceptable intrusion into federally regulated power markets."[7]

The change in leadership at state and federal levels left many people expecting one of two things to happen: Either FERC would immediately declare the new California ISO board structure illegal and take over the organization, or the Davis-appointed board would fire Terry Winter and other executives of the ISO at once.

Amazingly, neither occurred. But that didn't mean either Kahn or Davis was pleased with the grid operator's management.

"It was a very hostile beginning," Kahn reflected. "When I became the chair of the ISO, I went and saw Winter and [general counsel Charlie] Robinson. I basically said, 'Look, I think you did a terrible thing that harmed the state of California. You weren't working for me then. You might not have told the old board what was going on, and they didn't discipline you for it. It doesn't seem appropriate to me to come and change the rules, but here's the deal. If you ever do anything, if you ever lie to me, you're fired. If I don't have the votes to fire you, I'll quit.'"

Kahn said he was "very, very explicit" with Winter and Robinson. "I viewed it as a matter of my duty and responsibility to give them one chance…and Winter never told me anything that didn't turn out to be true," he said. "I believe now in retrospect that Charlie and Terry sincerely thought what they were doing was right. I believe that they showed a lack of judgment" about the effects of the soft price cap.

From the vantage point of two years, Kahn explained why the California ISO team was still in their jobs. "They have earned my trust, all of them."

There was, however, no trust between the Davis administration and the federal government. On February 7, the emergency orders from the Department of Energy lapsed for the last time.

Breaking the Banks

"In January of 2000, our market revenues totaled in the neighborhood of $100 million, and our grid management charge revenues were $15 million," California ISO chief financial officer Bill Regan recently recounted. "In January 2001, our GMC revenues were about $16 million. Our market billings, we didn't collect it all, were $1.7 billion."

The difference, Regan pointed out, was that instead of having less than 5 percent of the state's electricity flowing through the ISO's real-time markets, as much as 45 percent of the power was being secured by ISO staff. Power prices were 10 times higher than in the prior year. "These magnitudes were far higher than anything we had previously contemplated," he said. "And this was greatly complicated by the fact that we were sending bills out, but we weren't getting any revenues."

In one of his first presentations to the new board of governors, Regan on February 6 reported on the chain of defaults that left the ISO owing market participants an estimated $3 billion. After Southern California Edison ceased paying the Power Exchange in November, the PX failed to pay the ISO about $666 million. Pacific Gas & Electric had paid only $68.4 million of the $450 million it owed for the month.[8]

No one expected money to flow anytime soon. The PX ceased operations on January 31, after FERC ruled that California's market entities could not loosen their creditworthiness standards to accommodate the electric utilities. California ISO was able to continue collecting its GMC revenues off the top of any money that came in, thereby funding its operations. As the ISO was a pass-through agency, any money owed to power sellers was the liability of the utilities.

Without the IOUs' payments, however, the PX essentially dried up; it would file for Chapter 11 bankruptcy protection in March 2001.

PG&E, too, was on the road to bankruptcy court, and Edison was hanging by a thread of hope that the state would somehow come up with a plan to save it from insolvency. Although the California Public Utilities Commission had finally relented on the IOUs' pleas for a rate increase, the emergency 1 cent per kilowatt-hour surcharge enacted in January was not sufficient to make up for the utilities' past losses or the daily tab.

In order to force generators to continue selling power after the expiration of the DOE's emergency "must offer" rule, the California ISO on February 6 obtained a temporary restraining order against Reliant to prevent the company from refusing to perform its duty to sell power under its participating generator agreement. The injunctions were later extended to Mirant, Dynegy, Williams, and AES.[9]

Even though DWR was now playing banker for everything the ISO needed to buy, the meter was spinning wildly. By the time the enabling legislation actually became law, DWR had already spent its $400 million allocation from the general fund. By February 16, the state had burned through $1.6 billion, and Governor Davis announced that he was seeking another $500 million to fund spot-power purchases through the end of the month.[10]

As the financial statements from 2000 began to come in, it became painfully clear that Californians were expected to pay $20 billion more for energy and reliability services than they had the year before. From an average wholesale price of $32/MWh, or 3.2 cents/KWh, in 1999, the price for power had risen in 2000 to $117/MWh, or 11.7 cents/KWh.[11]

The cost of just the commodity portion of utilities' power deliveries had exceeded the total amount they were collecting from customers. The CPUC enacted another emergency rate increase in March, averaging three cents/KWh, but it was anyone's guess whether that would be sufficient. Because the price run-ups had begun halfway through the prior year, everyone feared that total power in 2001 might easily cost two or three times the 2000 amounts unless the runaway market could be contrained.[12]

Long-term Contracts and Net-Short Positions

The state of California was now fully engaged in the power market in two ways: a new unit of DWR was created, called the California Energy Resources Scheduling (CERS) division to procure energy on a daily basis; and Governor Davis enlisted a group of special consultants to negotiate long-term contracts with power suppliers that responded to the power solicitation that DWR issued in early February.

Both activities were meant to relieve the day-to-day pressures on California ISO dispatchers and move power procurement out of the panic mode that had become a daily nightmare. Federal orders had put the utilities at risk for economic penalties whenever inadequate prescheduling of energy pushed more than 5 percent of the market into the last-minute spot power markets.

Fines were rapidly mounting against the IOUs even though the level of underscheduling gradually decreased.

The state faced mounting criticism for its actions. From the start, the CERS unit was overwhelmed by the task of procuring spot power.

There had been only a handful of trained power traders at DWR, and they mostly dabbled in selling excess energy from the state water project at market prices. Few were versed in negotiating deals under such pressure. Although the state initially clamped down on release of information about market prices, some analyses indicated that the CERS buyers were paying a premium of $50/MWh to $75/MWh over prices otherwise available. The premium appeared to be based almost entirely on the difference in value of last-minute purchases during the continuing supply squeeze.[13]

Pete Garris, the former scheduler at California ISO, returned to DWR and the State Water Project in January 2001. Just nine days later, he said, the state of emergency was declared, and he found himself putting together the CERS unit on extremely short notice.

"We hired folks, we took folks from the State Water Project, we put together a scheduling office, billing, and settlements and created the organization," Garris said—all with no lead time before the job of buying power began.

From the start, there were tensions between California ISO staff and the CERS traders. Although glad to be relieved of the constant search for supplies on a last-minute basis, the ISO dispatchers resented the state's intrusion into the market and felt they were being given less than workable schedules of power purchases.

In addition, the state demanded that CERS be given a place in the ISO control room so that the traders had the best information available about what they needed to buy.

Winter said he resisted allowing CERS to have special access to market data, pointing out to the board that it would amount to a violation of the ISO's tariffs. "They're market participants, they can't be sitting here watching all the data," he said. "Of course, then the Governor stepped in and said you don't have a choice, damn it. So we had some battles and I got in battles with the board."

Right or wrong, Garris said that without close communications and instant access to data, the state traders would not have been able to do their job effectively.

"I don't think we could have managed the bulk of the real-time scheduling without that," he said. "We started out from day one, our schedulers were here [in Sacramento] and the ISO was in Folsom and we tried to schedule and it became clear that minutes in each and every scheduling hour were being lost on the communication process. The ISO made the determination as to how much energy to buy and in what locations, and DWR executed those instructions. The ISO was the grid operator, always has been the grid operator and maintains the reliability. But it became clear from my perspective that you just didn't have a more effective means to communicate what was necessary than to have a presence there at the ISO during the height of the electrical emergency, when the bulk of the transactions were done in real time. There just weren't many alternatives."

Board chair Kahn sided with the governor and CERS on the issue. "There was a constant tension between CERS and the ISO and a constant tension between the ISO being asked to do things by state government or the attorney general's people and the ISO instinctively refusing to do those things. I think this was a real lacking in the ISO, a real failure," he said. "The ISO treated this bureaucratically and institutionally as if it were a situation they have to deal with within the rules: 'We still have market rules. We're governed by FERC. Don't let market people on the floor. Don't do this, don't do that,'" Kahn characterized the reaction.

"I just put my foot down. We had a total failure of the delivery system economically, and the state of California has come in as the buyer—the only buyer—and is propping us up on an emergency basis. It's the only reason it exists. The idea that we're supposed to then use ordinary rules and treat this like an ordinary circumstance is just ridiculous. The analogy would be that to go to the firemen who are putting out a fire in your home and telling them, 'You don't have a permit to gather. You're trespassing. It's illegal to use the hose of that length.' I eventually put my foot down and said, 'Look, you have got to understand that this is an unprecedented time.'"

The other major DWR effort was to try to lock in stable prices and supplies with long-term contracts. Governor Davis asked Dave Freeman, the former ISO/PX trustee who had become general manager of the Los Angeles Department of Water & Power, to head up the negotiations. Joining Freeman were a number of special consultants, including Vikram Budhraja, the former Edison transmission executive who had been so instrumental in the formative stages of WEPEX and the post-AB 1890 market design.

"I was a volunteer, still on the payroll of L.A.," Freeman said. "The mayor and my commission graciously permitted me to accept the governor's invitation to come up here and help in late January. I had one task assigned to me by the governor, to be the negotiator along with Vikram, to negotiate the long-term contracts and to shrink the spot market."

Within six weeks, more than three dozen contracts had been signed, with a total value of $42.5 billion in delivery terms ranging from one summer to 20 years.

The negotiations were not easy, Freeman said, because there was a goal of reducing the average price of power while the daily market prices were over $300/MWh.

The Davis administration had released information that the average price of bids taken in response to DWR's solicitation was about $69/MWh, but Freeman said that wasn't a set figure. In consumer terms, it was the difference between 7 cents/KWh and 30 cents/KWh. "It was the worst time in the world, but we didn't pick the time," he said.

"Vikram and I used all the connections we had in the industry," Freeman recalled. "The deals were pretty straightforward, 'You give us some power right now at about six cents and we give you a long-term deal.' We were kind of begging. We had no bargaining power whatsoever except offering the longer-term contract. We basically bargained for price and term and then just used standard forms."

Critics in the media had a field day with reports that both the prices and contract terms would put the state at a severe economic disadvantage. A legal battle ensued over public disclosure of the contracts, with DWR eventually releasing detailed descriptions of pricing and terms.

Later, a legislative analyst's report faulted the contracts for inflexibility in delivery provisions, for not giving the state termination rights if producers failed to deliver, for exposing the state to fluctuations in natural-gas prices, and in several instances, for the high costs of peaking power. The litany of deficiencies also included the fact that in some instances, the state took on liability risks for generators' environmental compliance fees, scheduling imbalance penalties, and natural-gas imbalance charges.[14]

Almost immediately, there was pressure for renegotiating the contracts, an activity that would take up much of 2002, with Michael Kahn being assigned to lead the effort.

Ironically, there was also dissention at the CPUC, where president Loretta Lynch balked at providing a blanket determination of the reasonableness of DWR contracts and purchases, as was specified in the enabling legislation. The impasse at the CPUC caused more than a year of delay in determining ratepayers' responsibility for the DWR energy costs and in issuing nearly $12 billion in bonds so DWR could repay the general fund and finance the long-term purchase obligations.

Still, Freeman justified the initial results. "I think those long-term contracts not only helped bring prices under control immediately, but they are the basis for the steel that's being built to make sure we don't have a double-dip energy crisis."

He had similar praise for the CERS effort. "The DWR unit came in and played a major role in buying up power in a shrewd way, and they were very instrumental in getting this crazy runaway market under control," Freeman said. "I don't know why they're not getting a gold medal for the job they did do. They didn't invent the crisis. They didn't provoke it. They were called upon to do a nearly impossible job on a very short notice and they got it done."

If the Boot Fits

The regulatory effort at FERC during 2001 was not entirely devoted to meeting the conditions for market stabilization required by the November order, although a proposed market mitigation plan was drafted in early February. Besides promoting long-term contracting, the plan proposed new penalties for participating generators that did not make their full power available when called upon or for disobeying dispatch orders.[15]

But there was another discernible shift in the California ISO's focus at FERC, observed attorney Ed Berlin. "We were no longer focused on how to make the market work. There was no goddamn market. It was completely broken. Now it was a question of recompense for the harms that were perceived to have occurred as a result of that broken market."

Although the change in direction was aligned with the intentions of the Davis administration and the new board of governors, Berlin suggested that it would have occurred even without the appointed board. "I think it was a natural evolutionary step. Who's to say, but I think that the tone of those filings probably would have been the same whether the board had changed or not."

FERC had opened the door to the possibility of refunds as part of the November order, although it limited the appropriate time frame for making such calculations to October 2000. State officials demanded refunds beginning in May, but FERC held that it did not have the authority under federal law to go back that far.

The first indication of California ISO's more assertive policy toward seeking refunds of costs that might be attributed to exercises of market power came in a filing by Anjali Sheffrin's Department of Market Analysis in early March, suggesting that overcharges of some $450 million during December and January should be considered for refunds.

Within a month, a revised analysis put the figure at $6.2 billion and offered what Sheffrin called, "direct evidence that many of the suppliers used bidding strategies that resulted in clearing prices above competitive levels."[16]

The analysis focused on two primary means of driving prices higher: physical withholding of energy by taking units out of service, thereby raising prices for other generation units, and economic withholding from the day-ahead market so that prices reached a desired level in the real-time market. While California ISO calculated withholding to have raised its real-time prices by almost $2 billion, the impacts on the Power Exchange may have been multiples of that figure.

Sheffrin said she was trying to provide an empirical analysis of market power and resulting prices, to determine what could be attributed to market conditions, scarcity of resources or production costs for fuel or air-quality offsets.

"We take the actual price and then we try to break it down by the components and after we've explained all the cost components, we say, what's left over? Could it be market power? And we said yes. Could it be scarcity, though? The other explanation that's been given is that things were so tight that people could name their prices. So then we said of that market power, let's take out whenever reserves fell below 10 percent. No one can say in excess of 10 percent there was a scarcity situation. And we still found significant amounts of market power. So we did go through that quantification because I knew you can't just make an allegation, you have to have quantification, you have to have your methodology, you have to have your assumptions, and that's what we did."

The report, the first of many analyzing the financial impacts of alleged market power, raised a firestorm of controversy that continued for the next two years.

Generators and marketers claimed it was an attempt by the state to get out of paying for power already delivered. Davis and others seized upon it as proof of what they'd been saying for months—that California had been gouged by out-of-state power companies.

The rhetoric of the Davis administration frequently put the blame on Texas companies and alleged a direct connection between Enron Corporation and the Bush administration and FERC in Washington. "If the boot fits...," suggested press secretary Steve Maviglio.[17]

"I think it is unfortunate that somehow it was characterized as just the group of five Texas generators," Sheffrin said. Her analysis identified a much broader set of players, although at the time California ISO did not publicly identify any parties. And while Davis and his advisers alleged a vast conspiracy among players, Sheffrin's staff concentrated exclusively on the empirical analysis unless there was direct evidence of individual misbehavior.

In time, virtually every power seller active in the West would be accused of having inflated prices or manipulating flaws in the market, especially following the release of a report by attorneys for Enron that detailed a variety of gaming strategies that the marketer allegedly used to capture profits from California during the year 2000.

The California ISO's war on alleged overcharges by generators began to pay off with the announcement of a settlement in April 2001 of a complaint the grid operator had filed against the Williams Companies and AES. The companies agreed to pay an $8 million penalty in the case. Telephone transcripts showed the Williams power marketers had directed AES plant operators to purposely extend a maintenance outage in order to put upward pressure on market prices.[18]

For Sheffrin, the case did not offer much vindication of her work to prove that widespread withholding had affected the marketplace. For one thing, the companies admitted no wrongdoing, despite the $8 million fine. For another, an entire year had elapsed since the event, and it would be months before public release of the transcripts of the conversations between plant operators and marketers.

"The AES/Williams problem showed how far we had to go in order to prove an issue," she said. Aside from noticing a pattern of bidding behavior that suggested purposeful withholding, California ISO had also received a tip from a market source. "We did the investigation, and we turned it over to FERC. But FERC was reluctant to act. It's only after FERC subpoenaed the telephone logs and they actually got the smoking gun and then those conversations that were just recently released that then they decided to apply [the fine]. And it wasn't a penalty; it was just give back what you earned. So that's no penalty."

She expressed frustration that FERC itself was limiting how it could punish transgressors. "They sort of have the nuclear bomb and nothing in between. The nuclear bomb being I can revoke your market-based rate authority."

Still, the case signaled a new willingness by FERC to exercise some police powers over the market, even if critics charged it was much too little and much too late.

On the basis of soft-cap pricing benchmarks previously adopted, FERC required downward adjustments to bids in California for several months. In a series of orders based on California ISO claims, FERC required approximately $125 million to be trimmed from generators' invoices since the start of the year.

The biggest single deduction was levied against Duke Energy for entering a bid of more than $3,880/MWh for emergency power for about 2,850 hours during January's power crunch. Duke had tried to justify the high price as a "credit premium" because PG&E and Edison had not paid it for past deliveries.

"We will not tolerate abuse of market power or anticompetitive bidding or behavior," FERC stated. Duke was told to recalculate the cost using the January proxy price, which would drop the delivery price from $11 million to about $775,000.[19]

The order coincided with the appointment of a new member at FERC, after former Texas Public Utilities Commission president Pat Wood III was asked by President Bush to join the commission. Another new member, Nora Mead Brownell, was a former state regulator from Pennsylvania.

California's elected officials welcomed the appointments because they felt Wood and Brownell would be more open to their concerns about the market than Hèbert was. During Congressional hearings on the emergency, Senator Dianne Feinstein directed all her attention to Wood and all but ignored Hèbert. Eventually, Hèbert would leave the commission and Wood was named as its chair.

But the sudden shift in momentum at FERC gave a boost to Governor Davis's claims for $8.9 billion in power cost refunds from marketers. The federal commission said it would expand its investigation of the Western market meltdown, and it required the ISO staff to prepare an analysis of how much money might have been charged by suppliers beyond what would be expected from a competitive market.

Stage Three Redux

Two years later, it remains difficult for the operators and dispatchers at the California ISO to differentiate one day from another during the 2001 power crisis.

"It all just goes together," confessed Jim McIntosh. "I had so many 16-hour days where we just went all day long, all day long, all day long, all weekend long, back Monday, all day long, all day—it all rolls together. I'll be quite honest with you, if you try to pinpoint me on a day, unless it had something memorable happen on it, everything kind of runs together at this point."

And yet, there were two sets of extraordinary events still to hit California ISO during the spring. March 19 and 20 marked the return of Stage Three Emergencies, triggered by an unusually warm front coinciding with the unexpected loss of two generation units at the Mohave steam plant in Nevada, which usually sent more than half of its power into California. A transformer fire knocked out both of the plant's 790 MW units.

Underlying the emergency was the utilities' financial crisis. Because Edison had stopped paying its bills, scores of independent power generators—the QFs and renewable resources that sold to the utilities under long-term contracts—had stopped operating. In addition, that month, the Bonneville Power Administration had cut back on generation to try to restore its nearly depleted reservoirs, eliminating 1,000 MW of peak-period power it had been selling to DWR since winter. "We're getting out of the middle-man business," a BPA spokesperson said.[20]

The problems put California ISO back in the business of declaring rotating outages to keep the system in balance. Both days required extended periods of firm-load curtailments, for six hours each day, affecting something like one million utility customers statewide on March 19 and half a million on March 20.

Those were the most serious and extensive Stage Three episodes to date, but they were not the last. During the week of May 7, the early arrival of summerlike weather pushed spot prices back above $550/MWh throughout the West, and a confluence of market problems—everything from lost transmission to generation outages and renewed reluctance of sellers—caused another Stage Three event over two days.

One lesson of the crisis was that Stage Three events could be triggered by any number of different causes. Indeed, virtually every episode could be attributed to a different "last straw"—whether it was a storm-related nuclear outage, a transformer explosion, a fire near transmission lines, or a sudden increase in air-conditioning demand. Prevention of load shedding boiled down to just two options, more megawatts or more conservation.

Perhaps it was sheer exhaustion and uncertainty that caused McIntosh to declare the May 7 emergency "the worst I've seen in 20 years of operations experience."[21]

Despite best efforts and the financial backing of DWR, everything seemed on the verge of unraveling. "The most humbling telephone call I got was from PowerEx," McIntosh said. "I was sitting in my office and the chief financial officer of PowerEx gives me a call. 'Mac, you owe me $25 million. You're at your credit limit.' Hell, I didn't even know I had a credit limit, and I sure as hell didn't know it was $25 million," he said.

PowerEx, the trading arm of utility British Columbia Hydro, had been the ISO's provider of last resort for months, selling hydroelectricity from the huge Canadian reservoir systems.

"They were a high-priced provider, but it was either black out people or pay the price," McIntosh continued. "This is like nine o'clock in the morning. At one o'clock, they were going to cut us off. And I said, 'Well what do you expect me to do?' They said, 'We want the money. We want it wired.'"

Reliving the moment, McIntosh slumped in his chair.

"Well, I don't have $25 million, but let me make a couple of telephone calls, and I'll see what I can do," he told the marketer's financial guy. "We finally got a reprieve for the day, but essentially [the state] ended up making wire transfers."

Exhaustion and uncertainty seemed to define the marketplace. The interruptible-contracts program that had been California's insurance policy against firm curtailments the previous summer was all but exhausted.

During the March emergencies, the ISO could squeeze only 380 MW of load reduction from those customers, whereas the previous summer it could count on as much as 2,000 MW of voluntary curtailments. The customers had been curtailed so many times they rebelled against participating and refused to pay penalties for noncompliance. The CPUC eventually threw up its hands and eliminated the penalties, but the depletion of the interruptibles program left little dependable margin in the system.

By all accounts, it was going to be an even worse summer season. Even the North American Electric Reliability Council was projecting that Californians would experience up to 15 hours per week of firm-load curtailments during the summer of 2001. NERC president Michehl Gent said, "California electricity users will experience rotating blackouts, much more so than last summer or this past winter."[22]

While dozens of new power stations had signed up for certification, it would take years for most to be built. Although the governor had pledged that 5,000 MW of new resources would be on line by summer, the best estimate by the California Energy Commission foresaw just 1,700 MW of new power by July 1 and 3,670 MW by September 1. There was still much concern that supplies would be short in the near term. One newspaper headline summed it up: "It's bad and it'll get worse."[23]

No one knew what the impacts would be of a new FERC market mitigation plan that was announced in April. Beginning in late May, a new price-limiting mechanism was set to go into effect that was based on a strict formula using current natural-gas prices and other verifiable costs.

Each time California ISO entered a Stage One alert for an hour or more, the new clearing-price limits would kick into effect, reducing the allowed price of power throughout the West.

The previous $150/MWh soft cap would be eliminated, and the then-current fuel prices indicated a new clearing price would be somewhere around $92/MWh, with sellers from outside the state getting an added 10 percent "risk" premium for selling into California.

FERC affirmed its jurisdiction to require all sellers, except federal hydro marketers, to sell into the system whenever emergencies arose, but it also extracted a price from California for the new limits, requiring that the ISO file a plan to join or establish a regional transmission organization.[24]

Comings and Goings

Key people were reaching the point of exhaustion and frustration at California ISO. Communications director Dorinson in early May 2001 announced his resignation to join a media consulting firm. He would later confide that he felt his job had become politicized.

Members of the governor's staff were telling him to "get on the team," he said, and reporters who covered the story most closely noticed a closing of previously open doors to California ISO management. They were questioning whether they were getting the full story from the appointed board of governors.

"You have to leave with your reputation intact," he said of his decision. "You can stay 'til the end and fight, fight, fight. But at some point you just have to retreat and go somewhere else and fight another day."

Stephanie McCorkle stepped into the job with little problem—although she said she quickly established firm limits with state officials to keep the ISO's media outreaches from appearing politicized.

The surprise was that within a few months, Dorinson was back on the energy scene, as director of media relations for Mirant, one of the many power generators that the state had identified as price gougers.

Roger Smith decided to return to Washington, D.C., where he went to work for the law firm Troutman Sanders. "I had just had it. I had been chewed up and spit out," he said of the ISO experience. "If you're somebody who takes pride in what you do, and you want to do a good job, and there was so much work to do—it's my own fault—you know, but I couldn't pull myself away enough to create the type of life that I had [here in D.C.]. I had a whole circle of friends here, a social life here." Though he had many friends who worked for the ISO, they all tended to be married. Of Folsom, he said, "for single persons it was like Death Valley."

Others left for new challenges. Chief information officer Dennis Fishback became an executive at Calpine Corporation, fulfilling his desire to work with a more entrepreneurial company. Calpine was building power plants throughout California and was considered one of the few "good guys" even by the Davis administration.

Kellan Fluckiger gravitated to a consulting position with the state, then helped start the new California Power Authority along with Dave Freeman. Zora Lazik, the vice president of client relations, also left to join the Department of Water Resources.

As always, there was new blood coming into Folsom. Daniel Yee took over the job of chief information officer, bringing the unique qualification of having been in charge of information technologies (IT) at the California Power Exchange after 19 years at PG&E. Yee found the transition to the ISO a relatively easy one for an IT professional, despite the crisis. "Here there's an acknowledgment of how integrated, how important the systems are in carrying out day-to-day functions of the institution," he explained. "At the utility it was viewed as a necessary evil to have IT systems. Here, the systems are so integrated that it is a technology company almost."

Yee would immediately jump into the task of upgrading the ISO's energy-management systems, a continuing task that had been started by Fishback.

16

Recovery and Recriminations

JUST WHEN EVERYONE thought the worst might happen during the summer of 2001, California pulled one last, really big rabbit out of its hat: conservation of electricity.

The California Energy Commission later reported that temperatures in the state were comparable to the averages set during 2000, with both years tied as the 25th hottest seasons in more than a century. Yet energy-consumption patterns were a world apart. With similar summer temperatures, there were 29 days with peak loads above 40,000 MW in the summer of 2000 and only 6 days during the summer of 2001.[1]

Energy analysts from the Lawrence Berkeley Laboratory found that consumers embraced the message of energy efficiency and conservation by reducing peak-hour demand for power by 3,000 MW to 5,000 MW. The report found that six distinct factors worked in combination to bring down energy consumption: increased public awareness of the crisis as a result of media coverage and the "Flex Your Power" public service campaign; concern about price increases; traditional utility efficiency programs and appliance rebates; Governor Davis' 20/20 rebate program; load-management programs run by the utilities and California ISO; and other state or federal programs to encourage conservation.

"Separating the effects of one from another is difficult," admitted Chuck Goldman, a senior researcher at LBL. "The synergies between these various factors were an important reason that customer load reductions were as great as they were."[2]

Joe Eto at the Lab put the savings in the context of avoiding the need for California ISO to declare Stage Three Emergencies. "Our analysis showed that customer load reductions maintained the operating reserve margin over 1.5 percent for between 50 and 160 hours, potentially avoiding rolling blackouts," he said.[3]

The CEC concurred with the LBL analysis, documenting that peak-load reduction in June was about 4,750 MW, while avoided peak use in September was 2,750 MW. In terms of delivered electrons, the CEC reported that actual electricity use in the California ISO control area was down an average 5 percent in the January-September period of 2001 compared with the first nine months of 2000.[4]

The financial implications were positive for consumers in several respects. Not only had wholesale electricity prices dropped to pre-crisis levels by October, the incentives provided by the 20/20 rebate program returned at least $280 million to customers of the three regulated electric utilities. Statewide, roughly one-third of eligible customers managed to capture some of the 20 percent rebate reward by reducing their power use by at least 15 percent compared to 2000 levels in San Diego Gas & Electric's service territory and by 20 percent in Pacific Gas & Electric and Southern California Edison territories.[5]

By averting firm-load curtailments, California also avoided untold billions of dollars in potential economic losses.

Not that there weren't some touch-and-go periods that summer. The first week of July was exceptionally hot, and as loads moved higher, control-room operators at California ISO feared they might need to trigger their first Stage Three since early May. With demand nearing 42,000 MW on July 3, the grid operators declared a Stage Two just 20 minutes after the Stage One designation went into effect at 11:20 a.m.

The call for non-firm load shedding elicited 826 MW, but a crucial factor in avoiding rotating outages was the fact that Calpine Corporation had brought a brand new generation unit on line that week. The 540 MW Sutter power plant moved from testing to commercial operations on July 2, just in time to keep the lid on a Stage Two alert that day following an unexpected outage at the 790 MW Mohave generating station. Calpine and its contractor Bechtel had moved to double shifts of 10 hours each during the last month of construction in order to make their contract deadline and collect a financial incentive under one of Governor Davis' emergency orders to encourage new generation.[6]

After the midweek Independence Day holiday trimmed power use, the resource crunch subsided, and California ISO would not need to declare any more emergencies for the rest of 2001. For the first time in more than a year, system stability appeared to be the norm rather than an elusive goal.

The closest the grid operators came to a critical situation was just before 6:00 a.m. on August 2, but the problem was one of current instability rather than simply a capacity shortage. A multi-unit generation complex failed to come on line just as the morning "ramp-up" began, and a second unit dropped out of service without warning.

The combination of increasing load and less-than-anticipated supply caused system frequency to dip from 60 Hertz to 59.93 Hz.

The problem lasted about 15 minutes, and California ISO dipped into reserves to prevent a possible voltage collapse. "We were short 1,500 MW from where it should be, and it caused a low-frequency event," Jim McIntosh reported at the time.

Because the area control error exceeded California ISO's largest single contingency upon which reserve margins are set—loss of a nuclear reactor unit—the incident "threatens the reliability of the Western Interconnection and cannot be tolerated," the ISO warned generators in an August 8 memo.[7]

McIntosh complained that generators "have little respect" for ISO dispatch orders.

The Other Crisis Continues

Utility insolvency was still dogging the marketplace.

On April 6, PG&E had declared bankruptcy while it was still a solvent debtor, but the financial figures coming out of the case indicated how much damage had been done. The utility owed its 13,000 various creditors more than $13 billion. Power generators filed claims for $8.4 billion, but the utility said most were duplicative and included funds owed by the Power Exchange or SoCal Edison. PG&E recognized $2.3 billion in energy-seller claims as valid, but its repayment plan reserved about $400 million in case the Federal Energy Regulatory Commission ordered refunds of past power costs.[8]

Stabilization of SoCal Edison became a consuming passion at the state Legislature, with on-again, off-again proposals to rescue the financially deteriorating utility.

Governor Davis in April had prematurely announced a deal to purchase the Edison transmission system, but as the summer wore on, that prospect became ever more remote. The utility estimated it required at least $3.5 billion to cover its power debts, and it would be left to a controversial settlement of the utility's "filed-rate doctrine" case in federal court with the California Public Utilities Commission to restore payments to independent power producers and others.[9] Still, Edison would not be able to regain creditworthiness in the eyes of the financial community for many months afterward.

In addition, the investor-owned utilities were amassing substantial penalties for underscheduling loads at the ISO—as much as $1 billion—although FERC eventually forgave the liability.[10]

Meanwhile, the CERS unit of the Department of Water Resources had logged $7.65 billion in energy purchases through the end of June, on its way to a full-year tally of about $10 billion. There was a huge backlog of unpaid invoices sitting in CFO Bill Regan's offices at California ISO in Folsom, estimated at $3.1 billion for imbalance energy and out-of-market purchases made before CERS took over procurement of the utilities' net-short positions.[11]

Although the new market-mitigation plan ordered by FERC in the spring resulted in much lower benchmark price caps for energy transactions beginning in mid-June, it became apparent during the July heat wave that generators would try to charge more for energy than the new cap allowed. However, with sellers on the hook to justify their costs, the high bids by several generators during June and July immediately brought complaints that eventually resulted in FERC orders to rescind any liability for prices above the new benchmark figure in effect at the time.[12]

The Davis administration was still pinning its hopes on winning a determination from federal regulators that the bulk of all past debts to power sellers would never have to be paid and that monies doled out beginning in May 2000 would be refunded to the state.

Exactly how much that might be was the subject of much debate and controversy. The early calculations from California ISO's Department of Market Analysis rose and fell with each refinement of the studies. Counting costs above what DMA considered "competitive levels," the figure was $6.8 billion, reported manager of market monitoring Eric Hildebrandt in April. There was as much as $9.3 billion in total over-market costs, but FERC had ruled that it could not order refunds prior to October 1, knocking $2.5 billion off the table.[13]

A further adjustment made in July to eliminate nonjurisdictional entities and transactions that did not go through the spot market as FERC had defined it brought Hildebrandt's estimate down to $6.1 billion. California ISO staff were trying to downplay any media interpretation that this was a refund demand figure but rather "a potential framework for settlement discussions," Hildebrandt said.[14]

Still, the Davis administration and the California ISO board never let go of the $8.9 billion refund demand.

When the FERC judge launched settlement proceedings in June with acceptance of California ISO's calculation methodology—based on a competitive benchmark price of $92/MWh—a news release on California ISO letterhead hit the wires, declaring: "FERC Settlement Process to Yield Refunds to California."

Board chair Michael Kahn was quoted saying that "California's position has been vindicated" by FERC's chief judge Curtis Wagner. The state's proposed calculation methodology is "sound and will be used," Kahn continued, and California is entitled to refunds. "For the past two weeks, the delegation made an overwhelming factual case to refund $8.9 billion California ratepayers have been bilked out of by power generators and marketers," he stated.

Despite appearances, the release had been issued not by the California ISO communications department, but by Michael Bustamante, an adviser to Governor Davis, who was working "on-loan" to the California ISO board for three months.[15]

California's claim to the contrary, FERC judge Wagner publicly indicated that when the dust settled, the state might owe generators more than the amount it could legitimately claim from offsets. He estimated that the amount suppliers might owe the state was about $2.5 billion. According to some settlement participants, unpaid invoices exceeded that amount by $1 billion or more.[16]

Despite Judge Wagner's efforts to wring a settlement from the parties, the two factions were simply too far apart, and he turned the case over to administrative law judge Bruce Birchman for hearings.

It would take until December 2002 before Birchman issued a proposed ruling that solidified Wagner's initial impression. A strict application of the benchmark formula previously adopted by FERC showed that while generators evidently overcharged California ISO and the Power Exchange by $1.8 billion, they would still be owed $1.2 billion by the state.[17]

And still, the story was far from over. In November 2002, FERC had ruled that because of more recent revelations about market gaming by Enron and allegations of gas-price manipulation, California officials would have an additional 100 days to provide evidence that power sellers abused their market power prior to October 2000. When the state made its revised case on March 3, 2003, it alleged "a vast conspiracy" involving virtually every power seller in the West, including public power utilities large and small. "It's not just Enron, AES/Williams, Duke, Dynegy, Mirant, Reliant—the horsemen of the apocalypse we've talked about numerous times," said Attorney General Bill Lockyer. "There were lots of market bad actors."[18]

The filing to FERC claimed that from May through October 2000, sellers overcharged California consumers by $2.375 billion. "The commission must order the ISO and PX to reprice all sales…and order all sellers to disgorge amounts above the mitigated market-clearing price."[19]

For their part, the generators, marketers and municipal utilities vehemently denied the accusations, claiming that California's case was filled with "half-truths" and "distortions" of the evidence.

In a massive release of information on March 26, 2003, FERC addressed three of the main avenues of its investigations: that Enron-style bidding strategies had tilted the ISO's market; that misreporting of natural-gas prices to published indexes has contributed to higher electricity prices; and that generators in California purposely stayed out of the market.

The final report from FERC staff concluded that much of the problem in California's market stemmed from "supply-demand imbalance, flawed market design and inconsistent rules [that] made possible significant market manipulation...Without underlying market dysfunction, attempts to manipulate the market would not have been successful."[20]

Some surprises in the report included the accusation that Reliant's gas traders had engaged in "large-volume, rapid-fire trading" at the Southern California border that resulted in "substantially higher natural-gas prices" throughout the state. The staff report also declared that Enron's proprietary trading platform, EnronOnline, had provided the company with an information advantage against competitors that was responsible for as much as $500 million in excessive profits.

Declaring that markets for natural gas and electricity are "inextricably linked," FERC staff repeated its recommendation that the benchmark electricity prices used to calculate potential refunds for California should be revised downward to reflect costs at gas-production basins and a standard transportation fee, rather than the published indexes that had been employed. Once again, California ISO analysts would need to rerun thousands of market transactions to derive a new refund figure—although initial estimates were that at least $1 billion would be added to the tally.

In addition, FERC staff held that trading strategies and economic withholding of generation had occurred in violation of ISO tariff provisions and that new proceedings should be launched "to require disgorgement of profits associated with these tariff violations."

While FERC staff also determined that there was insufficient evidence to back up California's claims that generators physically withheld power during times of ISO emergency curtailments, the findings were narrowly applied to specific dates investigated by the CPUC.[21]

Withholding Endorsement

Although the California ISO Department of Market Analysis has promoted full investigation of the impacts of generators' alleged withholding of power to affect market prices, it has not always agreed with the positions or assessments of state officials on the matter.

An example of this is the California Public Utilities Commission's September 2002 report on the consequences of capacity withholding. The commission since at least the autumn of 2000 had argued that the main cause of price volatility was the deliberate withholding of capacity by generators. Most of its evidence had been circumstantial, such as comparisons of plant output before and after the units were sold by the regulated utilities to a half-dozen merchant generators.[22]

The new report, ostensibly based on the agency's investigation of power plant outages during the crisis, went further by accusing five generators—Duke, Dynegy, Reliant, Mirant, and AES/Williams—of causing most of the rotating-outage episodes declared by California ISO. The CPUC said that "between 37 percent and 43 percent of the total generating capacity of the five generators was either not available or not supplied on the 32 statewide blackout and service interruption days" that were examined.

"Had the generators produced the power they had available, most of the statewide blackouts and service interruptions could have been avoided without overloading the transmission lines linking Northern and Southern California," the report found. "For firm service customers, all of the blackouts in Southern California and 65 percent of the blackouts in Northern California could have been avoided."[23]

In its response to the CPUC report, California ISO agreed that generators had not always bid into the market or had declined to provide energy "for inappropriate reasons." But it specifically did not endorse the CPUC's conclusions, because it believed that the way the CPUC analyzed the data "would not answer the critical question of whether any given blackout or load curtailment was avoidable."

Curtailment decisions are made in advance of the hours of the episode, the California ISO response explained, making the after-the-fact analysis difficult to prove because the amount of power availability might not match. In addition, it listed a dozen factors that were not taken into account by the CPUC, including:

The CPUC report appeared to rely on outage data that California ISO warned was not reliable. The report made assumptions about outage data that were inconsistent with actual market operations. The CPUC may have used aggregate data that were "not appropriate for investigation of unit specific behavior" at specific times.

"In other words," the ISO response concluded, "the resulting after-the-fact calculation of available capacity would not answer the ultimate question of whether a curtailment or service interruption could have been avoided had more of the 'available' capacity been produced."[24]

FERC staff would eventually address the CPUC allegations, finding "no evidence that any of the generators had withheld any material amounts of available power" during blackout periods. While physical withholding might have occurred, FERC said, about 90 percent of the power that the CPUC alleged was being kept off the market during the emergencies was unavailable because outages, maintenance curtailments or other identifiable reasons. In some instances, the power was located south of transmission constraints and was not useable, or it was under direct dispatch control of the ISO, which had limited output of the plants to maintain system stability.

In short, FERC staff concluded, the CPUC had "significantly overstated the degree to which generators might have held power out of the market."[25]

Similarly, while state officials have promoted the position that gaming strategies employed by Enron and other power marketers were largely responsible for the price run-ups in the market and contributed to rotating outages, DMA's own analysis found relatively limited financial impacts and no system-reliability impacts.

In a response to analysis from Northwest consultant Robert McCullough, DMA's Hildebrandt could not find that Enron's scheme caused any blackouts in winter 2001. Instead, the problems were due to limited supplies of energy and limited transmission capacity at Path 15, Hildebrandt said.

For all the media attention given to such Enron trading and scheduling strategies as "Death Star," the ISO could attribute less than $22 million in congestion revenues to Enron and 20 other market players. Another possible scheme described by the Enron memos, to sell back ancillary services to the ISO, may have raised about $6 million for Enron and $52 million in all for the marketers—although the ISO report did not allege that such sales were illegal.[26]

Such figures are substantial enough to warrant concern and investigation of possible criminal actions, but they pale in comparison to the estimated $40 billion in increased power costs that resulted from the energy crisis.

The ISO's independent positions on these matters only deepened the rift between it and the state investigators.

DMA head Anjali Sheffrin acknowledged that the ISO sometimes has been accused of promoting one side over another in the withholding and market-gaming debate and of not fully backing the state's effort to win refunds.

"I think we've always tried to advocate a well-run market so people can have confidence and come in and participate," she said. "When a report comes out about something terrible, the ISO comes out and tries to put a more reasonable footing on it. People will do whatever it takes for their own interest. My interest is in having a viable market in the long term."

Customers and Constituents

Even after the replacement of the stakeholder board in early 2001, the management of California ISO continued to be the target of politicians' ire over the market collapse.

While the new board under chair Kahn may have retreated from its prior feeling that "The ISO is the enemy," others retained their hostility toward Terry Winter and the inability to regain control over the market because of FERC jurisdiction over the transmission operator.

Long after the crisis events faded from the headlines, Senator Steve Peace continued to harbor resentment over what he considered California ISO's allegiance to FERC rather than to the state. He never let go of the accusations that the stakeholder board and ISO management were beholden to generators.

Peace's residual ill will rose to the surface during a Senate energy committee hearing in early 2002. "Mr. Winter, let me say this very directly," Peace began. "You better damn well decide who you're going to serve, Mr. Winter. Your organization wasn't created to do the bidding of the sellers and what you euphemistically refer to as your 'customers.'…Now, you didn't have much of a way to fight back when you were beholden to a stakeholder board of directors imposed upon this state by FERC. But you do now, because your board of directors is no longer captive of the economic interests. In the words of FERC, they're no longer independent. FERC talks about independence in the context of economics and believes that not being independent, being appointed by, god forbid, by elected officials, is being not independent. The problem with the predecessor board is that it was economically dependent. This board is politically appointed but economically independent, and it better damn well start redefining the ISO's public face as being willing to fight openly and without apology for consumers. Because that's what your organization was created for."[27]

California ISO's true constituency had been a matter of debate from the very beginnings of the organization. The fact that restructuring law AB 1890 established the ISO as a "public-benefit corporation" was a clear indication that the organization was meant to serve the public interest of California. How that state role was interpreted became entangled in the separation of functions also endorsed by AB 1890 and related deregulatory policies, with the core mission of the corporation defined as that of maintaining system reliability. As the jurisdictional lines were drawn, reliability was seen as a state function, while the operation of the transmission system to accommodate interstate power markets was relegated to FERC's exclusive jurisdiction.

Although early debaters raised the notion that the reliability markets run by the ISO ought to conform with traditional regulatory notions of "least-cost" acquisition, that policy was not put into the words of AB 1890. So long as the costs of the imbalance-energy and ancillary-services markets remained a miniscule portion of the total cost of energy that was not a problem. However, when the market collapsed and prices skyrocketed, any sense of "least-cost" responsibility evaporated along with the bids in California ISO's BEEPstack.

Still, the organization has remained devoted to its sense of responsibility to the public, said Winter, albeit in ways that do not necessarily conform to the expectations of Senator Peace.

"My ultimate customer—first, last and always—has been the people of the state of California," Winter explained. "And that's where I get in a lot of trouble. Because I always keep in my mind that the end goal is to give the customer what he wants. Now, that is very varied in itself. Because I have Silicon Valley who says, 'Reliability is so damn important to me I don't care if it costs a billion dollars. Don't ever let the lights go out.' The residential customer says, 'I'm not home eight hours a day; if the lights go out for 15 minutes, what do I care? Just get the price down because I don't want to pay big bills.' So we've had to mix that while at the same time establishing a market that the generator says, 'This is fair and I'd like to be in it.' The utility comes in and says, 'The generator's ripping me off.'

"What I'm trying to do is make people understand that we have a lot of different customers and we have to at least listen to them," Winter concluded.

That espoused goal of trying to serve a broad constituency equally and fairly had landed both Winter and the ISO staff in hot water many times at the Legislature. They became something of a target of the Senate Select Committee to Investigate Price Manipulation of the Wholesale Energy Market, which held various hearings into the corporation's operations and decisions.

Senator Joe Dunn, an Orange County Democrat who is co-chair of the committee, began looking into power markets in 2001. An initial investigation focused on whether Duke Energy was operating its San Diego–area units differently than they had been run when under utility control. While Northern California suffered blackouts, the committee alleged, Duke's units sat idle.

While raising headlines with the accusations and testimony of three plant workers, Dunn's investigation deflated after Duke and California ISO publicly stated that during the periods in question, the units were run according to dispatch orders from the Folsom control room. Also, the availability of plants so far to the south would not make any difference because of transmission constraints between the regions.

From that point on, it seemed, Dunn's focus turned to the ISO and especially Winter's decision to go to FERC to remove the hard price caps on December 8, 2000.

"There is in our view, at least, a lot of suspicious activities in the few days leading up to the filing of the emergency application on December 8th, that we have been trying to get a handle on because our concern is how much influence did the generator community have on Terry Winter to make that application," Dunn explained.

Dunn's committee issued subpoenas to Winter and 15 ISO employees, ex-employees and past members of the board of governors, requiring they turn over all professional and personal correspondence and e-mails, telephone records, and travel documents from September through December 2000.

When California ISO staff members were called to testify, they told the committee they felt the depositions should be made in public and open to the media. The committee resisted until the first deposition where they learned that Dunn had invited a reporter from the *Orange Country Register* to attend. ISO communications staff alerted other Capitol news media to this development, and reporters from every major newspaper and wire service scrambled to cover the interrogations.

The story that ISO staff told was consistent: Winter had acted without notifying the board or anyone but the few members of the legal department and market-analysis staff who were asked to help prepare the emergency filing.

Winter, appearing before the committee in November, was not contrite. "I did what I did," he told committee attorney Laurence Driven. "I was concerned people would mount opposition to what I was going to do without understanding the operational issues I was facing."

When pressed as to why he did not involve the board in the decision, Winter replied, "You know, the board was dysfunctional at that point."[28]

Dunn said he believes that even if Winter acted alone, it was contrary to the interests of consumers. "He's serving some other master, and it ain't California residents," Dunn said. "Terry openly says he doesn't view his clients as California customers, his clients are the generators. That's who he believes he has to be responsive to because those are the people that provide him the electricity for him to keep the grid working. And that philosophical difference between Terry and me is I believe his number-one obligation is to protect the residents of California."

The investigation turned to other aspects of ISO operations, including the access provided to DWR traders. Generators had complained that the situation provided the state with advantages and undermined the grid operator's independence.

The same complaint was being aired at FERC, which in late November 2001 ruled that the state could not have special access to information or a place in the ISO control room.[29]

Dunn's inquiry focused on a different part of the matter—whether DWR was forcing the ISO to schedule power obtained through the controversial long-term contracts.

"As we all know," the senator explained, "CERS inserted itself into the ISO operation, basically dictated the operations of the ISO and certainly operated to the benefit of the long-term contracts that the Davis administration was signing. We had some concerns that with CERS inserting itself for purposes of ensuring that those long term contracts had power embraced within them that was actually used by ISO despite the fact that they were not next in line in the BEEPstack of power."

Dunn added that his suspicions were aroused by the amount of resistance that the allegations met with from both the ISO and CERS. "The resistance from the ISO folks was at its absolute extreme. They've never been really cooperative, but they became very defensive on that one. CERS and DWR were very, very defensive," Dunn said.

More recently, Dunn has looked into whether ISO controllers' practices to alleviate congestion on portions of the Pacific Intertie contributed to outages in the state. Dunn's committee was also the forum for the release of the CPUC's report on generation withholding and the inquiries into the impacts of Enron's manipulations.

Few knew in advance that Dunn's committee would be airing testimony on the withholding report from Loretta Lynch and other CPUC officials at the September 17, 2002, hearing. On the record, Dunn admitted to California ISO general counsel Charlie Robinson, "We have deliberately excluded the ISO from receiving copies of this."[30] Even the other committee members did not receive copies until two hours before the hearing, co-chair Bill Morrow later complained in a September 20 letter to Lynch detailing dozens of questions about the assumptions and findings of the withholding report.[31]

In interviews with reporters, Dunn makes no bones that his ultimate goal is to force Winter's resignation and to pull the ISO firmly into the state's realm of influence. "If the ISO is going to have to exist—begrudgingly—the ISO has got to be in the control of California," he said.

During the 2003 legislative session, Dunn expressed his feelings in bill form. His Senate Bill 72, introduced in late January, proposed amendments to the restructuring "to remove control of this state's electricity transmission system from the Independent System Operator."[32]

However, the bill was later changed to require that the ISO provide the state with advanced notice of proposed federal tariff amendments and perform a cost-benefit analysis before any alterations in market rules or operations could take effect.

The senator also tried, unsuccessfully, to derail the confirmation hearings for Michael Kahn's reappointment as ISO board chair.

Kahn disavowed any fight with Dunn over his confirmation. "I believe that any California public official should have every right to be upset about the loss of our $40 billion and every right to worry about whether it can happen again. We were the scene of the accident, and I don't begrudge anybody looking into it and investigating it and thinking it through. I also don't begrudge Joe Dunn in expressing his opinion about the personnel. So the dynamic of Dunn investigating, and Dunn pushing, and Dunn probing, I think is perfectly appropriate," he said.

In an interview that took place the week that Kahn's confirmation hearing had been delayed by Dunn, Kahn expressed no interest in a political fight. "I don't want this job. I never wanted this job. I can't wait to get out of it," he said. "There's nothing good about this. It's not good for my past, present or future. I'm doing it purely as public service. I told the governor that I would stay at least until I solved the governance problem so that I could have a transfer—we need a new board so I can turn the organization over in good shape and I can turn everything over to a new board and have a new stable relationship in there for protecting consumers. But I'm not going to fight."

He didn't need to. After the Senate finally held the hearing, members voted 36-1 to confirm the nomination. Dunn had cast the only negative vote.

Winter, on the other hand, declared he would not capitulate to political dictates. "I feel a real responsibility with people" here at the ISO, he said. "Now it would be very hard for me to take another job and just walk away from these folks because they put their heart and soul in it. The only way I walk is when somebody says, 'Look Terry, you've become such a detriment to the corporation because you've stood up to the governor.' If the organization were to take on such an attack, just because I'm here, then I'd be willing to leave. But short of that, I'm here to help these people keep moving forward."

Independence and Governance Revisited

If there has been a single issue that has posed the greatest challenge in resolving the conflict between state and federal authority over the California ISO, it has been governance of the corporation. The makeup of the board and California's demand to maintain oversight raised the earliest FERC objections to California's restructuring plan in an initial ruling on California ISO's tariffs back in 1998.

In July 2002, federal regulators returned to the governance matter. FERC ruled that the board appointed by Governor Davis "will hamper the ability of CAISO to implement [its] market redesign proposal" and interfere with FERC's own jurisdiction over interstate transmission. "This is because the state-controlled governing board…is not capable of operating its interstate transmission facilities on a non-discriminatory basis." In addition, FERC held, "The board as currently constituted does not meet the independence requirement of Order No. 2000 governing regional transmission organizations."[33]

Citing an independent auditors' report of the ISO board and management that found "significant problems regarding the independence of the current board," FERC ordered the California ISO and its management to begin a process for identifying a new nonstakeholder board, plus a six-member stakeholder "advisory" committee and another advisory committee made up of the Electricity Oversight Board.

The new governance structure was to take effect January 1, 2003, but when the state refused to comply, FERC filed suit in federal court to enforce its order.[34]

Once again, California ISO management found themselves caught between the two jurisdictional poles.

For attorney Ed Berlin, the issue turns on how people interpret the word *independent* and what that means for decision making by the board of governors.

"It was intended to mean independence from market participants, pure and simple," Berlin explained. "Now, one could question whether or not the structure of the initial board of 26 members accomplished that. I sat in on probably just about every single board meeting from the summer of '98 through the end of [2001]. Sure, there were people on the board who were there because of their affiliations, but it was reasonably balanced. The constituencies each were well represented, and when it was appropriate for people to rise above their partisan position, they did exactly as they should," he said.

Though not claiming to know exactly what the current FERC has in mind, Berlin offered a suggestion. "It is possible that FERC's attitude on the continuing independence of the board has nothing to do with a distrust for having a state influence over ISO activities, particularly a single state ISO, but rather more relates to the fact that the state of California, as a result of the crisis, became a major player in the markets. That attitude might not exist at all with the current board but for the fact that California is a major player in the energy markets."

Market Design 2002–2004

The design and redesign of the California ISO marketplace is akin to painting the Golden Gate Bridge—as soon as the painters complete the job, another crew begins all over again.

Beginning in autumn 2001, California ISO launched what it called Market Design 2002, or MD02, to address and resolve many of the problems that were encountered during the power crisis. In addition, the process would need to meet new FERC requirements for creating a day-ahead market to replace what was lost when the Power Exchange folded.

Among the initial MD02 proposals unveiled in January 2002 were new requirements that load-serving entities secure the power they need plus a reserve margin so that there would not be an overreliance on real-time power purchases. Other features of the plan were meant to smooth over bumps in the operation of the transmission system.

The process was split into two phases, with Phase I issues devoted to short-term problems of replacing the FERC market-mitigation plan and "must offer" rule when they expired in October 2002. Longer-range proposals, include requiring load-serving entities to cover their available capacity (ACAP) and reserve margin needs and development of locational marginal pricing (LMP) for transmission congestion.

While the MD02 implementation team expected to have a new program in place by September 2002, the difficulties of winning agreement among parties have pushed the timetable back to 2004 for some of the key features, including a new day-ahead market.

Opposition to the program has come from municipal utilities and generators alike. On one hand, munis worry about increased costs under LMP. Generators also believe that the enforcement provisions of the new market design have tipped California ISO into a "command and control" mode. Both groups are wary of the ISO's expanding role in market administration.

Jim Feider, president of the California Municipal Utilities Association, in February 2002 told a Congressional subcommittee, "the independence and credibility of the CAISO is eroded when it is forced to take active roles in markets, either to run the markets or to procure services for others." Increased complexity means increased costs, he said. "CMUA has long held the belief that a minimalist ISO, one that focuses on reliable grid operation and open access to transmission, and stays away from markets and resource procurement, would best serve the requirements of California and the West."[35]

To Gary Ackerman, head of the Western Power Trading Forum, it represents a significant expansion of the grid operator's metaphorical role as an "air traffic controller" for the transmission system. "It's the air traffic administrator and it's also trying to design the color of the seats on some of the airplanes and the prices for when you make a reservation. So it became a reservation as well as a traffic controller, as well as a marketing arm for the airlines," he observed. "It's too broad."

Randy Abernathy, now vice president of market services for California ISO, admits that making the change has been difficult in light of previous market experiences. "We have very real issues in California that we've got to deal with right now, and the current market structure that we have doesn't deal with them," he argued. "We have congestion problems. We have pricing problems. We have resource-adequacy problems that have to be taken care of to maintain reliability of the system."

One of the precepts of LMP is that entities that use congested portions of the system will pay higher wholesale costs so that resources can be devoted to alleviating the transmission constraints. The idea, used by other ISOs around the country and promoted by FERC, flies in the face of munis' historical service entitlements and scheduling coordinators' desires to keep their costs low.

The California municipals expressed particular concerns that the ISO's LMP proposal "would have unfair, noncompetitive and disproportionate impact," on them.

The Northern California Power Agency (NCPA), a consortium of munis, argued in comments to FERC that the ISO proposal might allow PG&E to "subsidize its Bay Area customers by collecting a bit more from customers in other parts of the state," giving the IOU a "competitive advantage" over NCPA members in Alameda and Palo Alto that must use PG&E's lines to access power supplies from the NCPA pool and other sources. "This is particularly unjust where these customers had no say in the decision by PG&E not to build transmission to serve loads without congestion."[36]

Abernathy, though, believes LMP is necessary to bring more efficient operations and rational decisions into the market. "I don't see a real opportunity for anybody to see some of the signals that are going to be necessary to truly make these markets of value. I think until we get some kind of way for the end-use customers to see the impact of their purchasing decisions, a lot of this is going to be suboptimal in terms of its solution."

To some degree, resistance to California ISO's MD02 proposal is tied to the opposition to policies for standardized market design (SMD) being promoted by FERC on a national basis.

Both efforts have been bogged down by fears that they are paving the way to a future of regional transmission organizations that impose national criteria on local systems. In a Christmas Day 2002 op-ed piece, CPUC president Lynch argued that "California must fight FERC's national deregulation plan, which will place our future in the hands of regional, private bodies answerable only to FERC—without any accountability to the public or to the public interest."[37]

The New Guardian/Trade Balance

The power crisis of 2000/01 has caused the California ISO to redefine the way it balances the guardian/market paradigms described in the *Systems of Survival* book.[38]

Clearly, the new equilibrium moves the point of balance closer to the "guardian" side of the equation, as evidenced by new rules to impose steeper penalties against market participants that do not follow dispatch orders or that try to take advantage of system constraints to increase profits.

Adopted in January 2003 by the California ISO board, the "Oversight and Investigation" plan proposed sanctions that could exceed $1,000/MWh against generators that do not comply with dispatch orders and fines of $10,000 per event for companies that file false information about unit outages.

The program specifically prohibits physical or economic withholding of capacity, and it bans gaming and market-manipulation strategies of the sort described in the infamous Enron memos. In addition, the plan called for direct coordination with oversight and enforcement agencies, such as the Attorney General's Office and the Department of Justice.[39]

In approving the new package of enforcement procedures to be filed with FERC, board chair Kahn said, "We are making a strong case that the ISO needs the authority to identify misconduct and swiftly penalize it where appropriate."[40]

While generator groups had criticized the proposals as pushing California ISO too far into the role of market cop and taking on an authority to impose penalties that it does not have, a group of state agencies believed the new rules did not go far enough.

In comments on the initial proposals, the "interagency working group" had argued for much more forceful language and penalties. "The purpose of the proposal should be to ensure that California consumers never again experience the complete failure of enforcement and the resulting harm caused by gaming and manipulation," stated the IWG.[41]

The state group also pressed for publication of the identities of companies that break rules, and it argued, "ISO must have enforcement authority" rather than simply notifying other enforcement agencies. The group also called for specific definitions of withholding actions and a declaration that it "should be defined as anticompetitive behavior."[42]

While California ISO made several revisions to its enforcement plan to reflect the IWG criticisms, it did not accede to all of the demands for control. Instead, according to a response by management, the revised proposal "strikes the proper balance by providing the ISO with substantial authority to impose penalties, while acknowledging the ISO's limited resources, and supporting the proper role of oversight and enforcement agencies."

In presenting the revised plan to the California ISO board, the corporation's management reiterated their desire to find a balance between the extreme poles of guardian and trade functions. "Penalties are no substitute for good market design and appropriate market rules," stated the recommendation for board action.[43]

17

The Never-Ending Business

ON A THURSDAY afternoon in early November 2002, the control room of the California ISO seems quiet and routine. Without a window to the outside world—other than the data on constant display at a dozen or so consoles and on the giant map board—you would not know that the first major rainstorm of the season is about to hit Northern California.

Operators pass along some new information. A large nuclear unit, Diablo Canyon No. 2, is in the process of reducing its generation output to 20 percent because ocean swells have clogged the cooling-water intake ports with kelp and other debris. Unit No. 1 has been out of service for weeks while awaiting installation of a new rotor.

California's other nuclear facility, at San Onofre, has been at half power all week, after a feedwater-regulation pump failed, causing an automatic trip of the 1,125 MW unit. Utility engineers are busy ramping the unit back toward full operation, making up somewhat for the output reduction at Diablo Canyon. One of the Arizona nuclear plants is emerging from a month-long refueling outage, and that morning operators at Palo Verde reported PV No. 1 at 50 percent but rising.

Meanwhile, repairs on the DC Intertie have closed off one of the main electrical transmission highways between the Pacific Northwest and Southern California. With federal marketers at the Bonneville Power Administration looking to sell off some excess energy coming out of the swelling Columbia River system, they are scheduling more power for imports on interties being controlled by the California ISO dispatchers. The paths are relatively uncongested, but a few hourly delivery schedules may need adjustment to maintain a steady flow of current into some parts of the state.

Two years earlier, the combination of windstorms, nuclear outages, and transmission curtailments might have been more than enough to send California into another in the long string of system emergencies it had experienced during the power crisis of 2000/01. But on this day, all the indications are that there will be no problems meeting the daily demand for electricity. Even with the nuclear plants in reduced mode, plenty of generation is available, with the ISO's daily log showing less than 4,000 MW of units out of service for various reasons.

With natural-gas prices sliding and hydroelectric production on the upswing, the apparent market equilibrium is, in fact, pulling prices down from the $40 to $45/MWh range in wholesale trading to below $27 in the Northwest and about $38/MWh in Northern California.

The transmission repairs at Sylmar seem to be keeping a floor under the Southern California power market, though.

In other words, all systems are normal. Everyone gets to go home on time. For the first time in what seems like ages, some will feel secure enough to take the coming weekend off without worry, maybe get to the hardware store to install that insulation stripping at home before the real cold weather rolls in. Some employees even talk about scheduling vacation time with their families over the Christmas and New Year's holidays—something that seemed just a fond dream in recent years.

Rounds and Routines

A uniformed guard making his rounds stops briefly at the front desk to chat with the receptionist, who is printing out a temporary security badge for a visiting journalist. Nothing unusual to report, she smiles. He slips back through the double doors after casting a glance at the media guest, mentally associating him with the red car parked in the space reserved for visitors.

Communications-system contractors are checking out early; they drop off their daily badges at the desk and head out into the rain.

Throughout the main building and in the satellite offices scattered along Blue Ravine Road, California ISO employees follow their own daily routines. For many, that means attending another planning meeting or preparing for the next one.

On this particular day, the LMP working group is in session in the board room, talking about load-aggregation programs and their expected impacts on the scheduling of transmission. Coming up in a month will be a technical workshop at the Federal Energy Regulatory Commission in Washington, D.C., and working-group members offer updates on their efforts to compile all the components of an advanced filing of a stipulation of issues.

FERC has been anxious to see locational marginal pricing become a standard feature in transmission policies around the country, although in California, the concept is still controversial. Despite being wary of the impacts of LMP, an attorney representing municipal power interests has taken a leadership role in drafting the FERC documents, which will help explain the purposes of the group and describe the evolution of work products over the preceding few months.

In another office, members of the client-relations staff prepare for the next day's meeting for the 2004 Stakeholder Process, another evolving development. Rate design is on the agenda, as well as an explanation of how the ISO calculates its grid-management charges. No fireworks are expected, as the 2004 group is still in the formative stages.

About the only point of friction might come during the discussion of the latest market design process. MD02 has hit a snag in meeting federal requirements for starting new day-ahead electricity markets by the new year. Still, FERC will be the forum for any real concerns about the delay in market development. Here, the message will be that the ISO does not want to rush into anything that cannot be fully tested or to install an interim process that will only confuse market participants. That's a message the stakeholders will appreciate, even if FERC staff are unhappy with the news.

Another meeting scheduled Friday will probably be a bit more interesting, as it concerns the ISO's revised proposal for market investigation and enforcement policies. A market-issues forum scheduled for the next week will air the latest version of the plan, and formal comments from scheduling coordinators and other stakeholders are due mid-month.

The compliance staff has been concentrating on meeting the multiple concerns of the Inter-Agency Working Group, in the hope that their recent revisions will find acceptance from the disparate constituency of transmission users and customers. The topic is a sensitive one for generators and regulators alike, with the two sides wanting to pull the ISO in opposite directions along the path of increased enforcement and added authority to impose penalties for market-rule violations.

Finding the right wording for the upcoming presentations will be essential to reaching some level of consensus, so the emphasis rests on the establishment of clear market rules and use of penalties or sanctions only as a backstop. Everyone will need to understand the process for investigations and the mechanisms for nondiscretionary allocation of any penalties that become necessary.

These bulleted items are added to the PowerPoint presentation. Maybe, if the residual wariness of stakeholders is not too great, the proposal will be ready for consideration by the board of governors at its next meeting.

These behind-the-scenes preparations could be taking place at any modern corporation located in Anywhere U.S.A. on this rainy afternoon. Without knowing exactly what enterprise this particular organization pursues, an outside observer passing by the meeting rooms or eavesdropping on an ad-hoc group of young tech-types conferring around a cubical might guess the business at hand to be anything that involves software development, finance, government planning, or corporate strategic development.

In fact, the business of California ISO is "all of the above." What makes this office complex in a Folsom business park unique is the huge master control room behind multiple secure doorways, where the movement of electrons throughout the state is monitored 24-hours per day.

The business never ends, and the process is in a continuous state of evolution.

"I have told everybody that's come into this organization, I can guarantee you two things: What you're doing today is not what you'll be doing six months from now, and that you will never be bored," said Randy Abernathy, the former human resources executive who is currently the ISO's vice president of market services. "I have not yet violated that promise to anybody."

"Every day I come to work is exciting. The ball game changes practically every time I walk in the door," said Jim McIntosh, the director of grid operations. "And us operations junkies get excited by that. I mean that's what you thrive on, figuring out how to make things work when it doesn't look like it should."

The velocity of change has slowed somewhat since the depths of the California power crisis, but at least now, many people who work at the California ISO see the direction of change returning to the positive.

Mission Creep

For some of the employees who left during the crisis era, the sense lingers that the California ISO might have lost its direction as a result of the turmoil and political backlash.

Patrick Dorinson, who shepherded the ISO's public image in the media when he was its communications director, observed that the emergency changed the trajectory of the corporation, and redefined the grid operator's core mission. He used the concept of "mission creep"—a phrase he learned while working at NASA—to explain what he meant.

"Mission creep is you start off with one thing and then you just keep adding stuff on. And before you know it, you can't recognize what the original purpose was. We're supposed to be what?" He cited some examples from government work, mostly, he said, politicians telling technocrats to change what they're working on to fit political purposes.

The metaphor is appropriate for the ISO, he asserted. "You're just going to run the ISO, you're going to operate the system, and you're going to just buy enough reserve to keep it going. Then it turns into, no, no, the utilities are under-scheduling, and now you're buying most of the energy out there. The PX is gone. Then the politicians come in with the new board, and it's like 'You're not looking out for the consumers; you're paying too much.' Oh, I thought we were supposed to keep the lights on. It just morphed to something that I don't even recognize anymore."

Asked about the concept of mission creep, CEO Terry Winter was able to trace a meandering line through many of the events of the power crisis and talked about how they enlarged and redefined the role of the ISO—not always for the better.

"It just became a much bigger job," he said. "It's like buying outside the market. We'd always anticipated we'd have to do that, we just didn't realize it would be 20,000 MW of power instead of three or four hundred. Then after the PX dissolved, all of a sudden the ISO was supposed to take care of everybody's problems. You know, PG&E says, 'We're bankrupt.' Edison says, 'We don't have any money.' CDWR came in, they had absolutely no knowledge at all about how to run things, and they didn't want us to do it because of the state stigma of this federal group that we were perceived as. We would have to do everything behind the scenes. We spent tremendous hours trying to educate them on how to do contracts. Then we got all these contracts that couldn't be scheduled. DWR wasn't scheduling so we were helping them get through all that and again that took a tremendous amount of people and time when we should have been doing other things. We started then having to support the interruptible programs because PG&E and Edison were just saying, well, not our problem anymore. So that's kind of the way things just kept getting bigger and bigger and bigger."

He pointed to the ISO's annual budget as an illustration of how added responsibilities bring added costs. "I'd say, well, it's not our job to really do this. But then people would come back and say, 'Yeah, it is, there's nobody else.'"

The first year's budget was heavily loaded with start-up and infrastructure costs, with repayment of debt adding to the totals. But using operating and maintenance expenses as a yardstick, the $150 million spent in the first full year of operations in 1999 grew to $180 million in 2000 and $205 million in 2001, the full year of crisis.

Such expansion has led to criticism from the scheduling coordinators and lawmakers alike, but chief financial officer Bill Regan defended his most recent budgets on two grounds: expenditures reflect services that the market needs or wants, and the ISO has come in under projections.

"We have put a budget out each year that I've been here that was based on what was required to do the job that the customers wanted," he said. "And every year we've come in under budget."

The original O&M budget for 2002 was about $177 million, Regan said. "Our total O&M expenditures for 2002 will be about $160 million. We have tried like heck to hold costs down. I think we've delivered almost everything we promised in 2002."

The drive to hold down costs and reduce the backlog of infrastructure debt will eventually translate into lower grid-management charges to customers, Regan said.

The New Mission

One of the lasting effects of the power crisis will be that the California ISO can no longer afford the start-up mentality that assumes cost is secondary to achieving the goal—however the goal is defined.

After Michael Kahn and the other appointees of Governor Davis took over the board of governors, one of the things they jettisoned was the original mission statement, "Reliability Through Markets."

Instead, the board amended the ISO's function "to provide safe, reliable electric transmission services to all Californians within its control at the lowest reasonable cost."

The emphasis on least-cost service also appeared in the 2001 annual report, which highlighted "lowest price possible for reliable service."

The changes, though largely symbolic, were criticized in a FERC-sponsored audit, which said it "smacks of a command and control approach more akin to a regulatory body operating in a regulated industry than an independent system operator."[1]

More recently, the mission statement has been changed again, to make it both broader and more specific: "To be the preferred provider of superior transmission services for the benefit of our customers in California and the West."

While not explicitly stated, concern about costs remains in that statement, suggested ISO general counsel Charlie Robinson.

Cost containment and redefining core values are key strategies in matching the ISO's mission to what Robinson sees as the two future trends that will guide the ISO: being more externally focused and realizing that the job of providing grid operations could be a competitive field in the near future.

"In a lot of ways, we are a company that prides itself on being cutting edge in terms of leading others into new electricity markets," Robinson said. "But I don't know that we've quite made the transition in our own thinking about the fact that we also operate in a competitive environment."

Dissatisfaction among transmission owners, customers, stakeholders, and political constituencies could open the door for a rival company, whether PJM, the National Grid Company, TransElect, or a regional transmission organization, Robinson suggested. "We have to be more external, and we have to be more mindful of competition and setting ourselves up to be more competitive."

The new statement implies a regional context for the California ISO, possibly as part of an RTO, as FERC has promoted. That may make sense, Robinson added, but political pressures argue against it happening anytime soon. "It's not simply California policy makers," he said. "To some extent it's policy makers outside of California. It is the economics of cheap power in the Pacific Northwest versus more expensive power in California that results in an averaging across a broader region. There's a lot of politics associated with that kind of cost shifting. It may be inevitable, but it may take us a while to get there."

There's still a lot of uncertainty about the future, Terry Winter admitted, and sometimes that translates into a fear among employees that outside forces are in control of their destiny and the fate of the corporation. For people who call themselves "controllers," that is difficult to rationalize.

Winter said the best way to deal with the uncertainties is to redefine the basic mission of the organization so that employees have a clear sense of their jobs. "Let's go back to the core functions" is the message being conveyed, he said. "What do we do? We operate the grid. We monitor the markets. We make our filings at FERC. We try to make sure we can get power in here. Focus on that."

"And people have done a good job of doing that," he said.

He illustrated his point by citing an unusual system event that occurred on Friday afternoon, March 21. An explosion at Southern California Edison's Vincent substation forced ISO controllers to substantially reduce capacity on Path 26 and curtail about 900 MW of non-firm load. In all, 11 major transmission lines were knocked out by the fire and, for a brief time, Northern and Southern California effectively separated as the system automatically responded to the event by "islanding" utility territories.

Winter called it the most serious system incident since the August 1996 outage. "Everybody jumped on it, and we came up with solutions. The engineers worked on it until late in the night and for the next two days and we kept everything together. We didn't lose any firm load."

If nothing else, the electricity crisis of 2000/01 had prepared California ISO staff to be able to deal with just about anything that comes up, he said.

What has kept people on board has been the real sense of purpose in doing their jobs and the knowledge that no matter how bad things get, they've already been worse than anyone could have imagined—and the corporation survived.

Abernathy recounted a story about a key employee who was offered a new job for a lot more money than what the ISO could pay. After interviewing with the firm, this individual decided to stay in Folsom, and told Abernathy why. "I really want to get this right. I want to do this for the people of California. I want to build something I can be proud of," he said.

"I've had this conversation with a couple of different people," Abernathy concluded. "You've got some of us here who have refused to leave until we get it right. You know, they'll either throw us out or we'll get it right, but until that's done, we're not moving."

APPENDIX A

Jargon, Jokes, and Jingles

EVERY SPECIALIZED INDUSTRY or organization has its own language consisting of acronyms or jargon that are at first puzzling to outsiders. The California Independent System Operator, an offshoot of the utility sector grafted with a high-tech, entrepreneurial spirit, is certainly no exception. For those in the know, a single word or short phrase speaks volumes and doesn't require further explanation to convey complex meaning.

In their pioneering study of "corporate cultures," management consultants Terrence Deal and Allan Kennedy attributed specialized language to the most aggressive elements of the working environment, what they called "this world of high risks and quick feedback" inhabited by police, firefighters, entertainment executives, and venture capitalists. "People in macho cultures like to use words that no one else has ever heard of. They also take common words and make them uncommon."[1]

But a common, specialized language is a manifestation of any culture, according to the later work of Walter Schein, and it can be the key to understanding many of the unwritten rules and jointly held beliefs within any corporate environment. This language, whether spoken or nonverbal, helps new employees "try to figure out how to dress, how to talk to their boss, how to behave in group meetings, how to decipher all the jargon and acronyms that other employees throw around, how assertive to be, how late to stay at work, and so on."[2]

Often, as attorney Roger Smith discovered on his first day at California ISO, the common culture and language have to be learned by trial and error. As a former staff adviser at the Federal Energy Regulatory Commission, Smith had been recruited by Beth Emery to fill out California ISO's skeletal legal and regulatory affairs staff. After driving across the country with all his belongings in the back of truck, Smith showed up in Folsom at a crucial time.

"My first day was the first day of start-up," he said. "Jeff Tranen would have these meetings where everybody is sitting around, and he'd have his little chart and going through all this stuff. You know, BEEPstack does this and CONG does that. These are software programs that do things. Then a problem would come up and they'd say, 'Oh, Ziad does that.' So I thought Ziad was a software program or a computer. I found out a couple of weeks later, no, Ziad is a person!" Ziad Alaywan.

The Regulatory Lexicon

From the very beginnings of California's restructuring efforts, policy wonks seemed to delight in creating new acronyms and phrases, and such shorthand as Blue Book, PoolCo, WEPEX, TAC, PX, direct access, stakeholder board—even California ISO itself—are embedded with rich meanings for those who most actively participated in the process of developing the new market structure.

While generally describing a similar notion of a centralized power pool for electricity transactions, for instance, there are vast differences in the intentions and political ramifications of PoolCo, WEPEX and the Power Exchange as they were played out in the California restructuring saga.

PoolCo derived from the privatization of the electricity industry in Great Britain and explicitly combined the power pool with grid operations. While trying to dispel the pejorative meaning that was attached by PoolCo's opponents, **WEPEX** actually came to represent something worse: an almost imperialistic expansion of the pool and grid control entity throughout the West, with Southern California Edison assuming control. The most vehement promarket voices tended to view the **Power Exchange** as a thinly veiled version of these "quasi-governmental pseudo-markets," but in actuality, the difference between the concepts was that PoolCo and WEPEX were designed to be permanent parts of the firmament of restructuring, while the PX proved limited in scope and evanescent.

The evolution from the traditional term "investor-owned utility" (**IOU**) to common use of "utility distribution company" (**UDC**) might not be distinguishable to the general public, but it implied a huge shift in the monopoly structure of the industry by limiting the scope and business affairs of the utility in question—especially if, as in California, the company had been directed to shed generation facilities and turn over control of transmission assets to the ISO.

Frequently, though, altering the working definition of a term or concept from previously understood meanings can lead to communication failures, misspent energies and lingering ill will.

For instance, when the California utilities made their initial WEPEX applications to FERC in 1996, other interested parties discovered big changes in concepts and how things would play out in the proposed market scheme. Analyst Steven Stoft of the Lawrence Berkeley Laboratory found significantly adverse consequences in some of the shifting concepts: "WEPEX appears to have invented a new definition of the transmission congestion contract (TCC) that is based on actual instead of pre-specified flows" of electricity within the system, he wrote. Ideas like zonal congestion management were ambiguous, he pointed out, and the policies that defined them tended to reward decisions to send power into congested areas of the grid and provided incentives for players to ignore physical congestion.[3]

As it turned out, the policy ambiguities that never fully matched the physical realities of the system caused headaches for system operators long after WEPEX had been disbanded and discarded as an operative vehicle for market change.

Religious Wars and Ancient Tongues

Among the hardest-fought battles in the market-design wars of WEPEX had to do with the difference between **zonal** and **nodal** congestion management, and it would probably take a graduate-level course in economics to really understand the differences between them and a political-science dissertation to explain how and why zonal-based configurations were adopted. But the phrases also became a shorthand way of identifying two opposing camps in the market-structure debates and reflected their conflicting attitudes about almost every aspect of design.

All too frequently in California ISO board discussions, the ancient conflicts were resurrected. Board member Camden Collins employed the phrase **creeping nodalism** to describe how one party might be "hitting old hot buttons" of another.

"It's a religious issue" was a phrase used repeatedly by people to signal that a decision—such as the separation of the ISO from the Power Exchange, or the selection of a particular software contractor or equipment vendor—was so contentious and opinions about it so hardened that the issue was no longer open for discussion.

Barbara Barkovich, a board member who represented industrial customers, said that the entitlements claimed by municipal utilities were akin to religious ideologies. "It was just that the preservation of their rights inherently made the whole system less efficient," she said.

Jan Smutny-Jones pointed to the utilities' demand for full recovery of stranded costs as a sacred belief held by the IOUs. Another religious issue, which went to the very heart of restructuring efforts, was the ongoing debate about whether electricity was a commodity or an essential service, with promarket advocates on one side and proregulation forces on the other.

Consumer advocate Mike Florio, who sat on the boards of both California ISO and the PX, said it was a phrase that effectively truncated any questioning of certain policies. "I constantly ran into the brick wall that this was decided by the great all-knowing ones after an epic battle in history between the forces of evil and the forces of good, and the forces of good prevailed, so why are you raising issues that were brought up by the forces of evil?" Florio said. "It was always very shadowy, like where and when were these battles fought?"

At least in *The Lord of the Rings* there is a detailed chronology of the ancient battles of Middle Earth, and author J.R.R. Tolkien usually attempted to explain the deeper meaning of certain phrases taken from the "elvish tongue." California market players need to invest in, or invent, a FERC/California ISO dictionary.

Federal tariffs and protocols introduced an entirely new set of entries in the restructuring lexicon. Such terms as scheduling coordinator (**SC**), participating transmission owner (**PTO**), and market participant (**MP**) at least had the positive effect of identifying key players in the new market and providing a shared sense of their roles and responsibilities.

Generators may need little explanation, but reliability must-run (**RMR**) units are a specific subset of the utility–divested generation located in areas of transmission constraint that were signed to complex and costly contracts in order to ensure their performance at crucial times.

The Power Exchange tariffs created day ahead (**DA**), hour ahead (**HA**), and eventually **forward markets** for electricity that dictated the ISO's scheduling of transmission delivery. New California ISO **reliability markets** were defined for ancillary services (**AS**), transmission capacity, and, later, firm transmission rights (**FTRs**) and supplemental energy (**imbalance market**). Subcategories of ancillary services were for **spin, non-spin, replacement,** and **reserve** capacity types; generally the terms were derived from engineering terms and inherited from the utility industry. However, these were services that had never before been subject to competitive bidding, or were previously invisible and nonmonetized components of utility generation dispatch decisions.

Ex-post and **ex-ante** described how and when prices were determined, after the fact or before adjustments, and **inc/dec** markets for more supply and/or demand were defined as **incremental** (**inc**) or **decremental** (**dec**) for reductions in supply or demand.

Chief Correspondent

The Energy Overseer

energyoverseer@comcast.net

9 Roscoe Street
San Francisco, CA 94110-5921
415-648-9405 voice
415-401-8957 fax

www.energyoverseer.com

The California ISO protocols added another layer of functions, services and market rules, and people needed to understand such new concepts as **BEEPstack,** or **Bid Energy Ex-Post** (the program used to determine merit-order dispatch of generation), **CONG,** for the congestion market, and **out-of-market,** or **OOM,** purchases (when circumstances or economic opportunity allow for arranged purchases of energy not previously bid into the system, frequently but not necessarily imported energy).

When generators failed to follow through on the schedules they previously submitted, or refused to act on direct orders from California ISO dispatchers, the problem was called **uninstructed deviations.**

For operational staff members, such as Deane Lyon, who was trained in a "command and control" environment at Pacific Gas & Electric, the implication was that what dispatchers ran was no longer a control area but a "recommendation area" or a suggestion area.

Phantom congestion resulted from the existing entitlements of municipal utilities to change schedules up to the last moment and, in some cases, after the hour was in progress.

Then there are the computer systems that keep track of it all: energy management system (**EMS**); meter-data acquisition (**MDAS**); scheduling interface (**SI**); balance of business systems for settlements accounting (**BBS**); scheduling applications (**SA**); and the communication network (**CI**). Obviously, one cannot always guess the appropriate acronym, and ISO staff generally associated the systems with the contractor that developed most of them, **ABB,** a division of Asea Brown Bovari, and **MCI** for the telecommunications network.

Us, Them, and Thus

Sometimes, it took a lot of meetings among the players to figure out exactly what all this really meant. The forum for such interaction went under various names at different times: **stakeholder process, market participant forums, scheduling coordinator users group,** and currently, **MD02** for the Market Design 2002 process.

Gary Ackerman is executive director of the Western Power Trading Forum, an organization representing market participants that evolved from the scheduling coordinator users' group (**SCUG**).

"I remember the first time I ever opened the ISO tariff and I kept seeing the words *scheduling coordinator.* Every page had *scheduling coordinator* at least once, if not two or three or four times. And it was this thick, a couple hundred pages thick," he said, widening the gap between his thumb and forefinger. "And I thought, 'What's a scheduling coordinator?' It was a term of art that we had no idea about."

According to the tariff, a company had to be a certified SC in order to use the transmission system, so the real meaning of what an SC was supposed to be relied on the drafting of the scheduling coordinator agreements with California ISO staff and in determining such practicalities as credit requirements and allocation of the grid-management charges (**GMC**).

It has not always been an easy process of communications, he said, especially at the beginning of the market. Ackerman once described how an "Us against Them" mentality that quickly evolved between market participants and California ISO controllers gave birth to an intermediary group of staff, the client-services branch, which he called **Thus**.

"Us," he told an industry group in 1998, are the market participants, SCs, generators, and other transmission users. At the time, the PX was the biggest SC, accounting for about 90 percent of California ISO scheduling transactions.

"Them" are ISO operators and dispatchers, he said, people who came out of the old utilities and who didn't really understand the needs of "Us" who are just trying to make money, and don't understand why units are not being dispatched according to the BEEPstack or why out-of-market power is being used instead of in-state bidders' power.

"Us ask a lot of questions. Them don't like Us asking questions. Us don't like hearing about all of the things we cannot do or that cannot be explained."

Thus "Thus" was created, he said. "If you have a question, and you are one of Us, ask Thus, who will go to Them, who will get back to Us through Thus. Got it?"

Staged Emergencies

From the very beginning, California ISO had included in its tariffs a process for alerting scheduling coordinators and others about potential problems meeting load, such as notices of **resource deficiency** or **restricted maintenance**, which triggered **no touch** days. The **electrical emergency plan** detailed a series of emergency declarations when reserve margins fell below certain levels:

- **Stage One**: declared when operating reserves fall below 7 percent of expected load.

- **Stage Two:** With reserves less than 5 percent, utilities may be required to curtail service to customers on **interruptible** service contracts.

- **Stage Three:** With reserves falling below 1.5 percent, California ISO may trigger firm-load curtailments, or **rotating outages,** frequently misidentified in general media as **rolling blackouts**.

Not in the Tariff

Though most employees or board members would deny ever having used some of the more colorful jargon heard in and around the California ISO complex during periods of stress—especially before start-up and during the 2000/01 power crisis—some phrases were bluer than Blue Ravine Road. At times when CEO Jeff Tranen used phrases that stirred a surprised reaction from others, he quickly explained them away as "technical terms."

Here are a few such technical terms drawn from various sources:

A boil-the-frog memo—Introducing painful policy changes a little bit at a time, like heating the water after the frog has been immersed in the pot, so it doesn't jump away.

Becoming virgins—What happened when IOUs sold off their generation.

Blue Box—An area within the control room marked off by blue tape that defined where reporters and TV crews were allowed to stand.

Bury your own dead—Originally meant that if a transmission line had been derated, a day-ahead bid had to be rectified with (more expensive) hour-ahead or imbalance-energy buybacks. Later it referred to handling overgeneration situations.

Crisis du jour—What's the current emergency?

Dead cat on the doorstep—A problem no one wants to deal with.

Jam it on the load—Consumer advocates' term for putting residential customers at an economic disadvantage.

Like peanut butter, or peanut buttering—Spreading costs around to all consumers.

Manual workaround—What to do when systems failed; i.e., using the telephone when the communications systems were unavailable, or manually inputting data when an automated system did not work.

Market boomers—A subset of employees who took the job because of attractive salaries or competitive incentive packages.

Moving the finish line—Delaying market start-up from 1/1/98.

Noah's Ark of interests—The 26-member stakeholders board.

Pudding run—A start-up-period phrase for getting schedules in on time, as in "the proof is in the pudding," or when it really counts.

Slapping it in—Creating new systems or making changes to software under urgent deadlines; describes how the California ISO/PX networks were installed.

Sucking mud—Using nearly all of the water at the Helms pumped-storage unit's reservoir to generate electricity on an emergency basis.

Tripods—Television camera crews in the ISO control room.

Undocumented electrons—Energy at the border with no scheduling coordinator.

Rites, Rituals and Ceremonies

"Without expressive events," wrote Deal and Kennedy, "any culture will die."[4]

Looking beyond organizational charts and mission statements, corporate-culture anthropologists find clues about the nature and character of organizations in everything from dress codes (or lack thereof) to the stories that veterans tell to newcomers, and especially in the events that "help the company celebrate heroes, myths and sacred symbols." The creative side of corporate life releases tension and encourages innovation, and humor frequently provides the spark.

There are several examples of expressive events at work in the California ISO culture:

Rituals—The most prominent ritual in the pre-start-up period was Jeff Tranen's daily meeting that began promptly at 7:30 a.m. and featured a round-robin of status reports from managers on all facets of operations. Under CEO Terry Winter, the monthly "all-hands" meeting for employees from all departments is another example.

Rites—These are described as a subset of "recognition rituals" such as a formalized presentation of awards or certificates. At the monthly "all-hands" meetings, for instance, employment anniversaries are announced and applauded by colleagues. In late 2002, the earliest employees that remained with the corporation were presented with "High-Five" certificates to mark their fifth anniversaries.

Ceremonies—These mark special events or corporate anniversaries. During the period prior to the power crisis, several California ISO staff members took special pleasure in devising skits and musical satires of their perpetually stressful situation that they performed on ceremonial occasions.

One example was a "staged" version of *Mary Poppins* put together by Beth Emery and a few others to mark CEO Tranen's departure in March 1999. They called it *"Jeffrey Pops-In,"* the story of how "a struggling start-up company looks for help to find meaning and direction. A CEO mysteriously arrives one day and transforms the organization into a tightly run, professional, spirited 501(c)(3) corporation. Then, having accomplished his task, the CEO vanishes as abruptly as he came…"

Among the songs adapted from the musical film (and some taken from other popular musicals) was this version of "Just a Spoonful of Sugar"[5] that illustrates both the jargon and culture of California ISO:

A Stack Full of Dec Bids

We all once came from companies
 that did exactly what they pleased.
No one to watch us but the P-U-C.
But now we are the I-S-O
 found a different way to go.
They bid! We call! It's clearly plain to see…

(chorus 1)
Just a stack full of dec bids helps the frequency go down,
 the frequency go down, the frequency go down.
Just a stack full of dec bids helps the frequency go down.
 In the California way.

About a year ago they said
 The ISO was nearly dead!
They'll never find a way to make ends meet!
But then we hired a CEO

who found a way to make it go!
Jeff came! Jeff saw! Jeff got us on our feet!

(chorus 2) Just a stack…

And though we may still have some doubts
        and have some bugs still to get worked out,
The ISO is truly here to stay!
Though some stakeholders fear the worst,
        We believe in markets first!
We Beep! We Cong! We inc and dec all day!

Later on, during the power crisis, a California ISO wit adapted the pop song "California Dreamin'"[6] to lay out this gloomy market assessment:

California Dreamin' (The ISO way)

All the bids are gone
And reserves are gray
Out on the floor
They all begin to pray
Down in San Diego
Load is goin' away
California I-SO
On such a winter's day
Fifty units broke
It's a no-touch day
There's a TV crew outside
I thought I heard them say
Seems like record profits
Are headin' for LA
California I-SO
On such a winter's day.

Bids above the cap
That's where they're gonna stay

'Cause the load keeps going up
The system's in decay
When the lights go out
We know who's gonna pay
California I-SO
On such a winter's day.

One note about the above lyrics is that each song uses a different pronunciation of ISO; in the first it is I-S-O and in the second it is I-SO (eye-so). Both are used commonly.

APPENDIX B

Glossary of Electric Industry Terms

Affiliate—A company that is directly or indirectly owned or controlled by another company.

Ancillary services—The services other than energy that are required to maintain reliability.

Baseload—A minimum amount of electric power that a utility or generator must provide.

Bulk power market—Sales and purchases of electricity among utilities; the wholesale market.

Capacity—The rated continuous load-carrying ability, frequently expressed in megawatts (MW), of generation, transmission or other electrical equipment.

Cogeneration—The simultaneous production of two useful forms of energy, usually electricity and steam, from a single fuel source.

Constraints—The physical and operational limitations on the transfer of electrical power through transmission facilities.

Contingency—The disconnection or separation, planned or forced, of one or more components from the electric system.

Control area—An electrical region that regulates its generation in order to balance load and maintain planned interchange schedules with other control areas.

California Public Utilities Commission (CPUC)—a state-level regulator of electric, gas and water utilities.

Curtailable demand—A level of load that can be interrupted at the discretion of the utility or system operator in order to ensure the adequacy of power supplies during peak periods or emergencies.

Day-ahead market—The forward market for the supply of electrical power at least 24 hours before delivery.

Demand—The amount of electricity required by customers.

Deregulation—Reducing government regulation of prices for electrical services, or the elimination of regulatory controls over an industry.

Direct access—The opportunity for retail consumers to purchase electricity or services from non-utility entities, also known as Customer Choice.

Dispatch—The operating control of an integrated electric system to assign generation and other sources of supply to effect the most reliable and economical supply as loads rise or fall; scheduling energy transactions with other interconnected electric utilities.

Distribution system—The distribution assets of utilities used to deliver power to end-users.

Distribution—The local delivery of power by an electric utility.

Divestiture—The sale or transfer of control over such utility assets as power plants or transmission facilities.

Electric utility—A regulated entity that owns or operates facilities for the generation and delivery of electrical energy to customers. Utilities by definition operate in an exclusive territory under license by state and/or federal regulators.

Emergency—Any abnormal system condition that requires immediate manual or automatic action to prevent loss of load, equipment damage or to restore system operations.

Federal Energy Regulatory Commission (FERC)—a federal agency within the U.S. Department of Energy that has jurisdiction over the rates and terms of service for interstate facilities and wholesale markets for electric utilities, non-utility generators and gas pipelines.

Forced outage—Generating units not in operation due to breakdowns, storms or other unplanned circumstances.

Generation—A process for the production of electrical energy, or the output of a power plant, usually expressed in kilowatt-hours (KWh) or megawatt-hours (MWh).

Grid—The network of interconnected power lines used for long-distance transmission and local delivery of electricity.

Grid management charge—A fee charged by the owner or operator of a transmission system as established by federal regulators.

Independent Energy Producers—Non-utility owners and operators of power facilities. A trade association for such companies based in California.

Independent System Operator (ISO)—A not-for-profit corporation or organization established to operate and oversee operations of transmission systems to ensure the reliability and stability of the grid in a non-discriminatory manner.

Kilowatt (KW)—A measure of electricity equal to one thousand watts.

Kilowatt-hour (KWh)—One kilowatt-hour equals one thousand kilowatts delivered or consumed in a 60-minute period.

Load—A device or an end-use customer that receives power from the electric system. Load should not be confused with demand, which is the measure of power that a load requires.

Market clearing price—The price at a location at which supply equals demand; all demand at or above this price has been satisfied, and all supply at or below this price has been purchased

Market power—The ability of a company to establish or affect prices for electricity in a relevant market or under particular circumstances.

Megawatt (MW)—A measure of output or capacity of a power plant equal to one thousand kilowatts, or one million watts, of electricity.

Merchant plant—A power generation facility that operates in wholesale markets without a long-term contractual commitment for its entire output; a power plant not subject to state regulation of rates.

Municipal utility—A publicly owned electric utility subject to the jurisdiction of a municipality, as opposed to state or federal authority.

No-Touch Day—A precautionary restriction, issued to limit routine work or maintenance in an effort to preclude an avoidable loss of resources.

Path—A line or group of lines that have been assigned numbers to differentiate them.

Peak load—The amount of power necessary to meet customer demand during periods of heavy consumption, which can be a particular hour of the day or time of season.

Power marketers—Companies or individuals that buy and sell electricity on a wholesale basis subject to the jurisdiction of federal regulators.

Power pool—Interconnected electrical systems that coordinate operations and/ or provide a centralized spot market for power purchases and sales.

Public Utility Holding Company Act (PUHCA)—A federal law enacted in 1935 to regulate and limit the operations of corporations that own and operate utilities in multiple jurisdictions.

Public Utility Regulatory Policies Act (PURPA)—A federal law passed in 1978 to encourage a diversity of generation resources by requiring electric utilities to purchase power from independent energy producers, especially those operating small-power plants, cogeneration facilities and renewable resources, such as wind, solar and geothermal plants.

Qualifying Facility (QF)—A power plant, as specified under PURPA, that is eligible to sell its output at a price equivalent to what it would otherwise cost the utility to produce or purchase.

Ramping—Changing the loading level of a generator in a constant manner over a fixed time (i.e. ramping up or ramping down).

Regional Transmission Organization (RTO)—The owner or operator of transmission systems covering a broad, multi-state region.

Regulation—Rules and policies established at the state or federal level to control the costs or service offerings by certain companies and entities.

Reliability—Ensuring the adequacy and security of electrical transmission networks and/or generation facilities. Adequacy measures the ability to provide sufficient power to customers at all times; security refers to the ability of the system to withstand unexpected disturbances.

Restructuring—Altering the traditional relationship between utilities, markets and regulatory bodies, which may involve some form of deregulation of utility costs or service offerings, or by subjecting regulated entities to competitive forces.

Retail competition—Allowing providers of electricity and other services to compete directly with utilities to serve customers.

Scheduling coordinator—An entity authorized to submit a balanced generation or demand schedule on behalf of one or more generators, and one or more end-users customers.

Service territory—The geographic area in which a regulated utility operates.

Settlement—A financial process of billing and payments for market transactions.

Spot power—Electricity that is bought or sold on a near-term basis, usually from one hour to one day before delivery.

Supplier—A company or entity that sells electricity to utilities or customers using either its own generation and delivery facilities or those of another company.

Tariff—A document filed with the appropriate regulatory authority specifying lawful rates, charges, rules and conditions under which the utility provides services to parties.

Transition period—The period of time to allow utilities an opportunity to recover costs prior to a loosening of rate regulation or introduction of full competition. Under California restructuring law, this period was defined as January 1, 1998 through December 31, 2001, or until cost recovery was completed.

Transmission—The process of transporting electricity over high-voltage wires from the source of generation to the point of consumption or distribution.

Transmission congestion—Power flows that cannot be physically accommodated by the system.

Transmission owner—An entity owning transmission facilities or having contractual rights to use transmission facilities that are used to transmit and distribute power from suppliers.

Unplanned outages—Unscheduled outages of generation, transmission or distribution facilities.

Wheeling—The use of the transmission facilities of one system to transmit power and energy on another system.

Watt—A standard unit of electricity measured at a particular moment.

APPENDIX C

Chronology of Significant California ISO Events

1978	Passage of Public Utility Regulatory Policies Act (PURPA) mandates utility purchases from non-utility qualifying facilities and small power producers.
1992	National Energy Policy Act requires open-access policies for electricity transmission systems.
April 20, 1994	CPUC introduces "Blue Book" investigation of policy options for a restructured electrical services market *[R94-04-031/I94-04-032]* and suspends resource auction for independent power projects.
December 20, 1995	CPUC adopts "preferred policy" decision for restructuring.
1996	FERC issues Orders No. 888 and 889 setting uniform rates and tariff requirements for transmission access.
August 10, 1996	Westwide power outage affects 11 states and millions of utility customers.
August 1996	CPUC establishes $250 million trust to develop California Independent System Operator and Power Exchange.
September 23, 1996	Governor Pete Wilson signs restructuring bill AB 1890 into law.
October 1996	S. David Freeman appointed trustee for California ISO/PX.
	Folsom selected as location for California ISO headquarters.
December 1996	Consultants hired for start-up plan.
January 1, 1997	Electricity Oversight Board established per AB 1890.
May 5, 1997	California ISO incorporates as public-benefit corporation; board of governors appointed and first employees hired.
June 1997	Computer infrastructure design complete
July 1997	Terry Winter named chief operating officer.

August 1997	Move into Folsom begins.
October 1997	FERC grants operating approval to California ISO; Jeffrey Tranen hired as president and CEO.
December 1997	Market start deferred by computer and software concerns.
March 31, 1998	New power market in California commences with initial operations of California ISO and Power Exchange.
June 30, 1998	Cost-of-service caps lifted from independent generators by FERC.
July 9, 1998	Ancillary services market sees price spike to $4,999/MWh; California ISO suspends next-day purchases and elicits competitive bids for "out of market" sources.
July 13, 1998	Technical limit price of $9,999/MWh recorded on ancillary services market. Price cap of $500/MWh imposed (later reduced to $250/MWh).
March 1, 1999	CEO shift as Tranen resigns and is replaced by Terry Winter.
	California ISO files ancillary services market redesign with FERC.
March 31, 1999	First anniversary of new market structures finds relative price stability but operational challenges.
	Market auction for firm-transmission rights (FTR) raises $42 million from 19 bidders for 9,689 MW of FTRs.
July 1999	City of Pasadena is certified as first municipal utility to join California ISO as a scheduling coordinator and participating generator.
July 12, 1999	Peak record load of 4,884 MW recorded.
September 30, 1999	Day-ahead market price caps raised from $250 to $750/MWh, coinciding with first Stage Two alert of the year.
December 31, 1999	Eighteen-month-long preparations to prevent Y2K problems result in no significant disruptions to computer systems as 170 staff members ride out the transition in all-night vigil.
January 2000	ISO Board approves five-year transmission plan. Staff warns of possible resource squeeze for summer.
February 2000	Board directs $750/MWh price cap through summer.

	Market surveillance committee issues report on competitiveness.
April 2000	Load curtailment bidding approved.
May 22, 2000	Price spikes on PX market coincide with first California ISO emergency declaration of the year.
June 2000	Board alters price cap to $500/MWh.
June 14, 2000	Heat wave triggers Stage Two Emergency and outages in SF area.
June-September	Recurring emergency situations result in 28 Stage One and 16 Stage Two alerts from June 14 to September 30.
August 10, 2000	Terry Winter testifies to Legislature with emergency response action plan recommendations.
September 2000	Market surveillance committee issues report declaring the California market to be not fully competitive.
October 2000	Vernon approved as California ISO member; peaking contracts approved for summer 2001.
November 1, 2000	Initial FERC order on California market.
December 2000	Emergencies return with 18 Stage Two events.
December 7, 2000	First statewide Stage Three declared; involuntary outages averted.
December 8, 2000	FERC approves emergency request to replace $250/MWh cap with a "soft cap."
December 13, 2000	Federal government institutes emergency requirements for generators.
January 15, 2001	Governor Davis says Department of Water Resources will purchase spot power for financially strapped utilities.
January 16, 2001	First of 32 consecutive days of Stage Three Emergencies, with first rotating outage events imposed on Northern California 1/17-18;
	Governor and Legislature declare state of emergency.
January 25, 2001	California ISO board of governors replaced with Davis-appointed group.
January 30, 2001	Power Exchange ceases operations.
February 6, 2001	California ISO sues generators to continue responding to emergency dispatch orders.

February 14, 2001	FERC rejects easing of creditworthiness standards.
March 1, 2001	California ISO makes first claim at FERC for refunds of alleged overcharges amounting to $560 million.
March 19-20, 2001	Statewide power outages ordered.
March 31, 2001	Third anniversary of new market marred by continuing emergencies.
April 6, 2001	Pacific Gas & Electric files for Chapter 11 protection.
April 26, 2001	FERC orders Western market-mitigation plan
April 30, 2001	California ISO complaint leads to $8 million refund order against Williams Energy for alleged market manipulation.
May 7-8, 2001	Final rotating outage events of emergency period.
May 25, 2001	California ISO moves to suspend market-based rate authority for generators at FERC.
May 29, 2001	FERC mitigations for California take effect. Prices begin to slide as rains fall in NW.
June 1, 2001	California ISO files RTO plan with FERC.
June 19, 2001	Market mitigations extended across West by FERC; must-offer requirement imposed for all hours. Refund settlement conference ordered.
July 25, 2001	Blackout-notification program launched.
September 20, 2001	Intermittent resources policy approved by board.
October 11, 2001	Market Design 2002 (MD02) team established.
November 7, 2001	Tariff Amendment 40 rejected; FERC directs ISO to invoice DWR group for purchases; demand-response program OK'd.
November 20, 2001	FERC prohibits California ISO from providing market information to DWR group without release to all participants.
December 6, 2001	DWR begins paying invoices.
December 19, 2001	FERC orders new congestion-management plan by May 2002.
January 2, 2002	New energy-management system on line.
February 27, 2002	Equipment malfunction at San Onofre Nuclear Generating Station causes system disturbance and brief outages.

April 9, 2002	ISO Board approves MD02 comprehensive elements; filed with FERC May 1.
June 18, 2002	Sacramento Municipal Utility District (SMUD) begins control area operations.
June 25, 2002	Next Generation contract approved to replace MCI telecommunications agreement, saving $17 million annually in future years.
July 17, 2002	FERC issues order directing ISO to replace current Board of Governors.
July 31, 2002	FERC releases Standard Market Design (SMD) Notice of Proposed Rulemaking.
August 7, 2002	Governor Gray Davis speaks at ISO Board meeting. Board directs management to not take any action on FERC order regarding governance of ISO.
August 16, 2002	FERC files lawsuit against ISO for non-compliance with governance order.
August 31, 2002	Eleven Northern California municipal utilities sign grid integration agreements.
September 26, 2002	FERC extends west-wide mitigation measures through October 30.
October 30, 2002	Automatic Mitigation Procedure (MD02 Phase 1A) takes effect. Market bids remain below mitigation thresholds.
November 21, 2002	ISO Board accepts applications from four Southern California munis to become Participating Transmission Owners starting January 1, 2003.
	Board authorizes MOU with Seams Working Group-Western Interconnect (SSG-WI) to foster regional markets.
December 31, 2002	Investor-owned utilities resume responsibility for scheduling electricity from California Department of Water Resources; state exits emergency scheduling role. 15 municipalities join ISO grid.

APPENDIX D

Members of ISO Boards and Corporate Officers

The Trust Advisory Committee 1997:

S. David Freeman, Trustee*
Barbara Barkovich, Barkovich & Yap*
Greg Blue, Destec Energy*
Randy Brin, Robinson-Mays Department Stores
Vikram Budhraja, Southern California Edison*
Bill Carnahan, City of Riverside
William Chamberlain, California Energy Commission
Tom Delaney, Bonneville Power Administration*
Marcie Edwards, Los Angeles Department of Water & Power
Richard Ferreira, Sacramento Municipal Utility District
Dan Kirshner, Environmental Defense Fund
E. James Macias, Pacific Gas & Electric*
Karen Mills, California Farm Bureau Federation
Viju Patel, California Department of Water Resources
Steve Ponder, ESI Energy*
Elena Schmid, Office of Ratepayer Advocates
Jan Smutny-Jones, Independent Energy Producers*
Terry Winter, San Diego Gas & Electric*
(* also on PX TAC)

Original California ISO Governing Board May 1997

Transmission Owners:
E. James Macias, Pacific Gas & Electric*
Terry Winter, San Diego Gas & Electric*
Vikram Budhraja, Southern California Edison*
Municipal Utilities:
Marcie Edwards, Los Angeles Department of Water & Power
Bill Carnahan, Southern California Public Power Agency
Richard Ferreira, Sacramento Municipal Utility District
John McGuire, Transmission Agency of Northern California
Government Market Participants:
Stephen Kashiwada, Department of Water Resources
Non-Utility Electric Sellers:
Jan Smutny-Jones, Independent Energy Producers*
Greg Blue, Destec
Buyers & Sellers:
James Feider, Western Area Power Administration
David Parquet, Enron Capital & Trade
End-Users:
Ken Wiseman, Agricultural Energy Consumers Association
Barbara Barkovich, California Large Energy Consumers Association
Randy Britt, Robinsons-May
William Ahern, Consumers Union
Michel Florio, The Utility Reform Network*
Elena Schmid, Office of Ratepayer Advocates
Glenn Sheeren, California Manufacturers Association
Patricia Spangler, Association of Bay Area Governments
Fred John, Sr., Southern California Gas
Public-Interest Groups:
Dan Kirshner, Environmental Defense Fund*
V. John White, Coalition for Energy Efficiency and Renewable Technologies
Non-Market Participants:
Camden Collins, Independent Consultant.
Jack McNally, International Brotherhood of Electrical Workers
(* also on PX board)

ISO Board of Governors as of December 2000

Jan Smutny-Jones, Independent Energy Producers, Chair
Terry Winter, President and CEO, California ISO
Barbara Barkovich, California Large Energy Consumers Association
Greg Blue, Dynegy, Inc.
Bill Carnahan, Southern California Public Power Agency
John Fielder, Southern California Edison
Michel Florio, The Utility Reform Network
David Freeman, Los Angeles Department of Water & Power
Dede Hapner, Pacific Gas & Electric
Tom Ingwars, Sacramento Municipal Utility District
Karen Johansson, League of Women Voters
Carolyn Kehrein, Energy Management Services
Dan Kirshner, Environmental Defense Fund
Jack McNally, International Brotherhood of Electrical Workers
Viju Patel, Department of Water Resources
Steve Ponder, FPL Energy
Jim Pope, Silicon Valley Power
Bill Reed, Sempra Energy
Stacy Roscoe, California Manufacturers Association
Patricia Swanson, Independent Consultant
V. John White, Coalition for Energy Efficiency and Renewable Technologies
Ken Wiseman, Agricultural Energy Consumers Association
Michael Woods, Woods & Daube Law Offices
Eric Woychik, Strategy Integration

ISO Board of Governors Appointed by Governor Davis January 2001

Michael Kahn, Esq., Folger, Levin & Kahn, Chair
Tal Finney, energy advisor to Governor Davis
Michel Florio, TURN
Carl Guardino, Silicon Valley Manufacturing Group
Maria Contreras-Sweet, California Business, Transportation & Housing Agency

ISO Board of Governors Current as of April 2003

Michael Kahn, Chair
Michel Florio, TURN
Carl Guardino, SVMG
Timothy Gage, former state finance director

Original Corporate Officers 1998

Jeff Tranen, President and Chief Executive Officer
Chuck Smart, Chief Financial Officer (left in October 1998)
Beth Emery, Vice President General Counsel
Randy Abernathy, Vice President Human Resources
Susan Schneider, Vice President Client Services
Terry Winter, Chief Operations Officer
Dennis Fishback, Chief Information Officer

Corporate Officers at end of 2000

Terry Winter, President and CEO
Kellan Fluckiger, COO
Dennis Fishback, CIO
Charlie Robinson, Vice President General Counsel
Bill Regan, CFO
Elena Schmid, Vice President Strategic Development and Communications
Randy Abernathy, Vice President Human Resources

Corporate Officers as of April 2003

Terry Winter, President and CEO
Jim Detmers, Vice President Grid Operations
Dan Yee, CIO
Charlie Robinson, Vice President General Counsel
Bill Regan, CFO
Elena Schmid, Vice President Corporate and Strategic Development
Randy Abernathy, Vice President Client Services

Chapter Notes

THE MAJORITY OF QUOTATIONS used in this narrative come from in-person or telephone interviews with the quoted individuals conducted between October 25, 2002, and March 31, 2003. In the many instances where direct quotations from individuals or documents derive from other sources, citations are provided below. Full citations for books and reports are found in the Bibliographic References section.

A great number of these references were drawn from stories and columns published in the *California Energy Markets* newsletter, especially during the period from 1994 to 2001 and before major newspapers and other information services began to cover the California electricity market crisis. Besides the news and opinion columns by this author that were carried in *CEM*, there have been several fine reporters who helped document the rise and fall of the California electricity market over the years as recounted in this story. Special thanks are extended to them all: J.A. Savage, Mathew Trask, Cyril Penn, Shauna O'Donnell, Colleen Turrell, Jason Mihos, Lulu Weinzimer, Elizabeth McCarthy, Ted Rieger, and John Edwards. The reports from these colleagues and friends have proved to be invaluable sources of accurate information, without which this project would have been greatly diminished.

Thanks also to the many professional colleagues from other publications whose work also informed this story directly and indirectly, but most especially: Rebecca Smith, Mark Golden, Jessica Berthold, Jason Leopold, Craig Rose, Carrie Peyton-Dahlberg, Dale Kasler, Jim Puzzanghera, Nancy Vogel, Nancy Rivera Brooks, David Lazarus, and Mike Taugher, among the many, many journalists in print, broadcast and electronic media who have done excellent work covering the California electricity crisis.

The oft-quoted statement that journalism is "history's first draft" has never been truer than in this instance.

Chapter One: The Worst That Can Happen

1. *California Energy Markets*, August 23, 1996, No. 376 [17].

2. *CEM*, August 16, 1996, No. 375 [14].

3. *Los Angeles Times*, December 23, 1982.

4. *San Francisco Chronicle*, December 15, 1995, and December 16, 1995.

Chapter Two: The Deal Breaker

1. California Public Utilities Commission, *California's Electric Services Industry: Perspectives on the Past, Strategies for the Future*, issued February 1993.

2. CPUC, Order Instituting Rulemaking R.94-04-031 and Order Instituting Investigation I.94-04-032, issued April 20, 1994.

3. Energy NewsData, *Restructuring Backlash*, p. 15.

4. *LA Times*, May 8, 1994.

5. *CEM*, September 30, 1994, No. 279 [17].

6. *CEM*, August 5, 1994, No. 271 [16].

7. *Ibid.*

8. *CEM*, July 14, 1995, No. 319 [21].

9. Draft memorandum of understanding, August 15, 1995.

10. Although consumer groups discussed plans for an anti-restructuring referendum throughout this period, a coalition called Californians Against Utility Taxes didn't put Proposition 9 on the ballot until 1998. The measure was defeated.

11. *CEM*, October 6, 1995, No. 331 [17].

12. CPUC, D.95-12-063, December 20, 1995.

13. *CEM*, January 5, 1996, No. 343 [16].

14. *Backlash*, p. 21.

15. Wilson statement, quoted in "Exceptions to the Rule: Bypassing the California Transition Surcharge" in *Public Utilities Fortnightly*, November 15, 1996.

16. *CEM*, February 8, 1996, No. 348 [13.2].

17. *CEM*, September 13, 1997, No. 379 [16].

18. *CEM,* May 6, 1996, No. 360 [14], and June 7, 1996, No. 365 [15].

19. CPUC, D.96-08-038, August 2, 1996.

20. Fessler, Concurring Opinion in R.94-04-031/I.94-04-032, April 20, 1994.

21. *Holland Sentinel*, November 16, 1997.

22. Hirsh, *Power Loss*, pp. 84-86.

23. *Ibid.,* p. 243.

24. Hesse, in keynote remarks to Energy NewsData's "Transmission West V" conference, San Francisco, October 13, 1995.

25. Moler, in FERC news release, April 26, 1996.

26. Hesse, *supra.*

Chapter Three: In Dave Freeman We Trust

1. For an excellent overview of the Rancho Seco vote and its meaning for Sacramento, see Smeloff and Asmus, *Reinventing Electric Utilities*, pp. 25-74.

2. Ford Foundation Energy Policy Project, *A Time to Choose*, Ballinger Publishing, 1974.

3. *CEM*, March 25, 1994, No. 252 [17].

4. CPUC, D.96-10-044, October 15, 1996.

5. "ISO Scope of Work Tasks," document provided by Duke Engineering & Services, February 14, 1997.

6. See Appendix D for listing of TAC members.

7. "Resources Necessary for Forming an ISO," technical presentation by Jack Allen, July 7, 2000, found at *www.electrikgrid.com*.

8. *Electricity Daily*, April 2, 1997.

9. *CEM*, March 20, 1997, No. 405 [16].

10. *Ibid.*

11. FERC dockets EC96-19-003 and ER96-1663-003.

12. *Electricity Daily*, April 2, 1997.

Chapter Four: The People Movers

1. See Appendix D for list of board of governors.

2. *CEM*, September 5, 1997, No. 429 [15].

Chapter Five: Folsom and the Birth of the Electric Grid

1. Folsom History Museum brochure.

2. Williams, *Energy and the Making of Modern California*, p. 93.

3. Folsom Historical Society, *Images of America, Folsom, California*, p. 39.

4. Williams, *supra*, pp. 176-177.

5. Hughes, *Networks of Power*, p. 270.

6. Quoted in Williams, *supra*, p. 177.

7. Coleman, *PG&E of California*, pp. 75-97.

8. *Electrical Journal,* December 1899, quoted in *Electrical West, 75th Anniversary Issue, 1887–1962,* published by McGraw-Hill Company, 1962.

9. Hughes, *supra*, pp. 283-284.

10. *Ibid.*, p. 465.

Chapter Six: Countdown to a New Market

1. *CEM*, October 10, 1997, No. 434 [12].

Chapter Seven: The Hour Ending 01

1. *CEM*, January 9, 1998, No. 446 [14].

2. *CEM*, January 2, 1998, No. 445 [11.2] and [13].

3. CPUC monthly reports on direct-access service requests, as reported in *CEM*, January 23, 1998, No. 448 [17.2].

4. *CEM*, January 2, 1998, No. 445 [13].

5. *CEM*, March 13, 1998, No. 455 [14] and [14.1].

Chapter Eight: Money Changes Hands

1. *CEM*, April 3, 1998, No. 458 [16].

2. *CEM*, April 3, 1998, No. 458 [15].

3. *CEM*, September 4, 1998, No. 480 [17].

Chapter Nine: Pattern Recognition

1. *CEM*, July 10, 1998, No. 472 [12].

2. *CEM*, July 17, 1998, No. 473 [16].

3. *CEM, ibid.,* [16.1].

4. *CEM*, August 14, 1998, No. 477 [14].

5. *CEM*, August 7, 1998, No. 476 [12].

6. *CEM*, August 14, 1998, No. 477 [14] and [14.1].

7. *CEM*, September 4, 1998, No. 480 [17].

8. Energy NewsData, Western Price Survey, July 16, 1999.

9. *CEM*, October 14, 1999, No. 536 [16].

10. *Highlights of ISO Actions with Regard to Gaming and/or Market Power*, filed as exhibit to testimony of Terry Winter to Senate Select Committee to Investigate Price Manipulation of the Wholesale Energy Market, January 29, 2003.

11. FERC docket EC96-19-035, conditionally accepted July 31, 1998, 84 FERC ¶ 61,121.

12. Tariff Amendment No. 12 in ER99-826, rejected January 27, 1999, in 86 FERC ¶ 61,059, and Tariff Amendment No. 13 in ER99-896, accepted with modification in February 1999, in 86 FERC ¶ 61,122.

13. California ISO market notice, March 1999.

14. FERC ER00-555, partially accepted in January 7, 2000, in 90 FERC ¶ 61,006; rehearing denied April 12, 2000, in 91 FERC ¶ 61,026.

Chapter Ten: Balancing Acts

1. *CEM*, February 12, 1999, No. 502 [17].

2. *CEM*, January 8, 1999, No. 497 [19].

3. California ISO annual report 1999, p. 30.

4. *Ibid.*

Chapter Eleven: A Bridge Too Far?

1. Jacobs, *Systems of Survival*, p. 28.

2. California Energy Commission, *High Temperatures and Electricity Demand, an Assessment of Supply Adequacy in California*, July 1999.

3. Author's interview with Dan Nix, July 1999.

4. *SF Chronicle*, July 22, 1999.

5. Smith and Rose comments appeared in *CEM*, August 17, 2001, No. 631 [13].

6. *San Diego Union-Tribune*, January 26, 2000.

Chapter Twelve: Preparation, Precautions, and Politics

1. *CEM*, March 17, 2000, No. 558 [15].

2. *CEM*, April 21, 2000, No. 563 [13-13.2], and April 28, 2000, No. 564 [18]

3. Energy NewsData, Western Price Survey, May 24, 2000.

4. For a more detailed description of California ISO's decision, see Chapter One.

5. California ISO Department of Market Analysis, *Report on California Energy Market Issues and Performance: May-June 2000*, August 10, 2000, p. 23.

6. *CEM*, June 11, 1999, No. 519 [16.2].

7. DMA report, *ibid.*, p. 26.

8. *Ibid.*, p. 1.

9. *CEM*, June 30, 2000, No. 573 [15.1].

10. DMA, *ibid.*, p. 22.

11. *CEM*, June 23, 2000, No. 572 [16].

12. *CEM*, June 30, 2000, No. 573 [15.1].

13. *CEM*, June 30, 2000, No. 573 [16].

14. Senate floor analysis, Senate Bill 96, August 30, 1999.

15. *CEM*, July 7, 2000, No. 574 [17].

16. California ISO board meeting minutes, July 6, 2000.

17. Governor Davis letter, June 15, 2000.

18. CPUC/EOB "Report to Governor," August 1, 2000.

19. *CEM*, July 28, 2000, No. 577 [14.1].

Chapter Thirteen: Thirty-Five Rabbits

1.   Davis news release, August 3, 2000.

2.   California ISO list of declared emergencies for 2000.

3.   CPUC direct-access reports for June 30, 2000.

4.   *Wall Street Journal*, November 27, 2000.

Chapter Fourteen: The Festival of Darkness

1.   In docket EL00-95-000, filed August 2, 2000.

2.   *CEM*, August 18, 2000, No. 580 [13].

3.   *CEM*, July 14, 2000, No. 575 [12].

4.   EL00-97-000.

5.   EL01-01-000.

6.   In EL00-95-000, November 1, 2000, 93 FERC ¶ 61,121.

7.   *CEM*, November 3, 2000, No. 591 [17] and [17.1].

8. *Ibid.*

9. *North County Times*, November 10, 2000.

10. Energy NewsData, Western Price Survey, December 8, 2000.

11. From testimony in FERC docket EL00-95; California ISO exhibits Nos. 38, 44 and 48.

12. *San Jose Mercury News*, December 6, 2000.

13. *CEM*, December 8, 2000, No. 596 [13].

Chapter Fifteen: Full Impacts

1. *Sacramento Bee*, January 18, 2001.

2. Assembly Bill 265, Davis/Alpert, September 7, 2000.

3. *San Francisco Chronicle*, January 18, 2001.

4. Energy NewsData, Western Price Survey, January 12, 2001.

5. SBx1-6, Burton/Bowen, May 16, 2001.

6. ABx1-5, Keeley, January 18, 2001.

7. *CEM*, January 26, 2001, No. 602 [17.2].

8. *CEM*, February 9, 2001, No. 604 [19].

9. *California ISO v. Reliant*, US District Court, Eastern District, S 01-238.

10. *CEM*, February 16, 2001, No. 605 [17].

11. California ISO market analysis report, January 16, 2001.

12. Monthly average-cost figures being generated by the Department of Market Analysis staff told a troubling tale:

November 2000	$171/MWh
December	$326/MWh
January 2001	$278/MWh
February	$363/MWh
March	$313/MWh
April	$370/MWh
May	$275/MWh

13. *CEM*, April 20, 2001, No. 614 [19.2].

14. Legislative analyst report, December 18, 2001.

15. FERC EL00-95-012. See *CEM*, February 2, 2001, No. 603 [15].

16. *CEM*, March 23, 2001, No. 610 [18].

17. *CEM*, July 13, 2001, No. 626 [12].

18. FERC IN01-3-000, AES Southland and Williams Energy Marketing and Trading, 95 FERC ¶ 61,167, April 30, 2001.

19. *CEM*, June 23, 2001, No. 623 [12].

20. Energy NewsData, Western Price Survey, March 23, 2001.

21. *Ibid.*

22. *CNN.com*, May 15, 2001.

23. *San Francisco Chronicle*, May 9, 2001.

24. EL00-95-012, April 26, 2001, in 95 FERC ¶ 61,115.

Chapter Sixteen: Recovery and Recriminations

1. CEC, "Summer 2001 Weather Comparison," September 21, 2001.

2. Lawrence Berkeley Laboratory report, "California Consumers Kept the Light On," *EEDT Newsletter*, summer 2002.

3. *Ibid.*

4. CEC, "Total Conservation in ISO Area," October 18, 2001.

5. *CEM*, November 9, 2001, No. 643 [11].

6. *Sacramento Business Journal*, May 2, 2001.

7. *CEM*, August 10, 2001, No. 630 [24.2].

8. *CEM*, January 18, 2002, No. 652 [23.1]

9. *SoCal Edison v. CPUC*, US District Court, Los Angeles, No. 00-12056-RSWL (Mcx), settled October 2, 2001.

10. *CEM*, June 22, 2001, No. 623 [16.1].

11. *CEM*, June 22, 2001, No. 623[13.2].

12. *CEM*, June 22, 2001, No. 623 [16].

13. Comments of ISO on FERC's order and additional analysis, November 22, 2000, and March 22, 2001.

14. DMA, *Impacts of Market Power in California's Wholesale Energy Market*, April 9, 2001. See Dow Jones NewsWire, June 20, 2001.

15. California ISO news release, July 9, 2001.

16. *San Jose Mercury News*, June 26, 2001, and Bloomberg, July 12, 2001.

17. In EL00-95-045, December 12, 2001.

18. *San Francisco Chronicle*, March 4, 2003.

19. California Parties' Supplemental Evidence filing in EL00-95-000, March 3, 2003.

20. FERC staff, *Final Report on Price Manipulation in Western Markets*, in PA02-02-000, March 26, 2003.

21. Ibid.

22. In EL00-95-000, CPUC analysis of FERC order and staff report of November 2000, Exhibit PUC-4.

23. CPUC, *Staff Investigative Report on Wholesale Electric Generation*, executive summary, September 15, 2001, p. 1.

24. California ISO comments on CPUC staff report, October 25, 2001.

25. FERC staff report, *ibid.*, p. 3.

26. Hildebrandt, *Did Any of Enron's Trading and Scheduling Practices Contribute to Outages in California?* November 15, 2001, pp. 1-2. Also, California ISO, *Revised Results for Analysis of Potential Circular Schedules*, January 17, 2003, and *Report on Analysis of Trading and Scheduling Strategies Described in Enron Memos*, October 4, 2002.

27. Transcripts, California Senate Energy, Utilities and Communications Committee; February 5, 2002.

28. *CEM*, November 9, 2001, No. 643 [16].

29. In Reliant Energy Power Generation, November 20, 2001, 97 FERC ¶ 61,215.

30. Transcript of hearing on update on various investigations, September 17, 2002, p. 2.

31. Morrow letter to CPUC, September 20, 2002.

32. Senate Bill 72, Dunn, introduced January 21, 2003.

33. FERC in EL01-35-000, et al., July 17, 2002, 100 FERC ¶ 61,059.

34. *FERC v. California ISO*, US District Court for DC Circuit, No. 1:02CV-1625; filed August 19, 2002.

35. Written statement of Feider to Subcommittee on Energy Policy, Natural Resources and Regulatory Affairs, February 22, 2002.

36. From NCPA regulatory affairs newsletter, August 2, 2002, p. 5

37. *San Francisco Chronicle*, December 25, 2002.

38. Jacobs, *supra*. See Chapter 11.

39. California ISO board agenda, January 17, 2003.

40. Reuters, January 23, 2003, and Dow Jones NewsWire, January 24, 2003.

41. The Inter-Agency Working Group consists of CPUC, CEC, EOB, CPA, and CERS/CDWR.

42. ISO Revised Proposal/IAWG comments.

43. ISO board agenda recommendation, *ibid.*

Chapter Seventeen: The Never-Finished Business

1. Vantage Consulting audit report, January 25, 2002. See *CEM*, February 1, 2002, No. 654 [17].

Appendix A: Jargon, Jokes, and Jingles

1. Deal and Kennedy, *Corporate Cultures*, p. 124.

2. Schein, *The Corporate Culture Survival Guide*, p. 42.

3. Stoft, *Analysis of the California WEPEX Applications to FERC*, October 1996, p. 1.

4. *Ibid.*, p. 63.

5. Original words and music by Richard M. Sherman and Robert B. Sherman.

6. Original words and music by John Phillips.

Bibliographic References

Breyer, Stephen. *Regulation and its Reform*. Cambridge, Massachusetts: Harvard University Press, 1982.

Chandler, Alfred. *Strategy and Structure: Chapters in the History of Industrial Enterprise*. Cambridge, Massachusetts: MIT Press, 1960.

Collins, James, and Jerry Porras. *Built to Last: Successful Habits of Visionary Companies*. New York: HarperCollins, 1994.

Deal, Terrence, and Allan Kennedy. *Corporate Cultures: The Rites and Rituals of Corporate Life*. Reading, Massachusetts: Addison-Wesley, 1982.

Drucker, Peter. *Concept of the Corporation*. New York: Mentor, 1983 (first published in 1946).

Fink, Steven. *Crisis Management: Planning for the Inevitable*. Lincoln, Nebraska: iUniverse.com, Inc., 2000.

Ford Foundation. *A Time to Choose: America's Energy Future*. New York: Ballinger, 1975.

Hirsh, Richard. *Power Loss: The Origins of Deregulation and Restructuring in the American Electric Utility System*. Cambridge, Massachusetts: MIT Press, 1999.

Hirsh, Richard. *Technology and Transformation in the American Electric Utility Industry*. Cambridge, England: Cambridge University Press, 1989.

Hughes, Thomas. *Networks of Power: Electrification in Western Society, 1880–1930*. Baltimore, Maryland: The Johns Hopkins University Press, 1983.

Jacobs, Jane. *Systems of Survival: A Dialogue on the Moral Foundations of Commerce and Business*. New York: Random House, 1992.

Kahn, Alfred. *The Economics of Regulation*. New York: John Wiley & Sons, 1970.

Kidder, Tracy. *The Soul of a New Machine*. Boston: Atlantic/Little Brown, 1981.

Micklethwait, John, and Adrian Wooldridge. *The Witch Doctors: Making Sense of the Management Gurus*. New York: Times Books/Random House, 1996.

Neuhauser, Peg, Ray Bender, and Kirk Stromberg. *Culture.com: Building Corporate Culture in the Connected Workplace*. Toronto, Ontario: John Wiley & Sons Canada, Ltd., 2000.

Packard, David. *The HP Way: How Bill Hewlett and I Built Our Company*. New York: HarperBusiness, 1995.

Peters, Tom. and Robert Waterman. *In Search of Excellence: Lessons from Amer-*

ica's Best-Run Companies. New York: Harper & Row, 1982.

Peters, Tom. *Thriving on Chaos: Handbook for a Management Revolution.* New York: HarperCollins, 1988.

Quirk, Paul. *Industry Influence in Federal Regulatory Agencies.* Princeton, New Jersey: Princeton University Press, 1981.

Schein, Edgar. *The Corporate Culture Survival Guide.* San Francisco: Jossey-Bass, 1999.

Schein, Edgar. *Organizational Culture and Leadership.* San Francisco: Jossey-Bass, 1992.

Smeloff, Edward, and Peter Asmus. *Reinventing Electric Utilities: Competition, Citizen Action, and Clean Power.* Washington, D.C.: Island Press, 1997.

Stragliano, Vito. *A Policy of Discontent: The Making of a National Energy Strategy.* Tulsa, Oklahoma: PennWell Corporation, 2000.

Williams, James. *Energy and the Making of Modern California.* Akron, Ohio: University of Akron Press, 1997.

Zemke, Ron, Claire Raines, and Bob Filipczak. *Generations at Work: Managing the Clash of Veterans, Boomers, Xers and Nexters in Your Workplace.* New York: American Management Association, AMACOM, 2000.

Regulatory References:

Energy Policy Act of 1992 (EPAct), Public Law 102-486, 106 Stat. 2776.

Public Utility Regulatory Policies Act of 1978 (PURPA).

Division of Strategic Planning. *California's Electric Services Industry: Perspectives on the Past, Strategies for the Future* ("The Yellow Book"). San Francisco: California Public Utilities Commission, 1993.

Order Instituting Rulemaking R.94-04-031 and Order Instituting Investigation I.94-04-032 ("The Blue Book"). San Francisco: California Public Utilities Commission, 1994.

Summary of Positions on Electric Industry, Prepared for the Independent Energy Producers. October 28, 1994.

Comments of Southern California Edison Company on Competitive Markets and Appropriate Market Institutions in a Restructured Electric Industry. July 26, 1994.

Status Report on Restructuring California's Electric Services Industry and Reforming Regulation. San Francisco: California Public Utilities Commission, January 24, 1995.

Audit Report Concerning Operations of the California Independent System Operator and Power Exchange. California Bureau of State Audits; March 22, 2001.

California Energy Markets: Pressures Have Eased, but Cost Risks Remain, Bureau of State Audits. December 2001.

California's Energy Crisis: A Time Line of the State in Crisis. Assembly Republican Caucus, July 12, 2002.

Initial Report in Fact-Finding Investigation of Potential Manipulation of Electric and Natural Gas Prices. Federal Energy Regulatory Commission, August 13, 2002.

Staff Investigative Report on Wholesale Electric Generation. California Public Utilities Commission, September 17, 2002.

Final Report in Fact-Finding Investigation of Potential Manipulation of Electric and Natural Gas Prices. Federal Energy Regulatory Commission, March 26, 2003.

FERC Staff Response to CPUC Report on Generation Withholding. March 26, 2003.

Restructuring Reports and Post Mortems:

Restructuring Backlash: How the Rate Reform Initiative Will Change Electric Restructuring in California and Across the US. San Francisco: Energy NewsData Corporation, 1998.

Restructuring in Perspective: Review of the Last Six Years. Jessie Knight, Jr., September 25, 1998.

Diagnosing Market Power in California's Deregulated Wholesale Electricity Market. Severin Borenstein, James Bushnell and Frank Wolak, University of California Energy Institute, February 1999.

Electricity Restructuring: Deregulation or Reregulation? Severin Borenstein and James Bushnell, University of California Energy Institute, February 2000.

How We Got into the California Energy Crisis. William Marcus and Jan Hamrin, Summer 2000.

California's Energy Market, Summer 2000: The Perfect Storm. Edward O'Neill, November 2000.

The Electric Summer, Symptoms-Options-Solutions. Edison Electric Institute, October 2000.

The California Story and Its Impacts on the Future of Electricity. Leonard Hyman, April 2001.

Impact of a Continuing Electricity Crisis on the California Economy. AUS Consultants, 2001.

Electricity Restructuring: The California Experience, What Went Wrong? Ann Cohn, Southern California Edison, October 2001.

Drift and Disarray: The California Energy Crisis Continues. William Ahern, Consumers Union, March 28, 2002.

Power to the People: An Economic Analysis of California's Electricity Crisis and Its Lessons for Legislators. Benjamin Zycher, Pacific Research Institute, May 2002.

Regulation's Rationale: Learning from the California Energy Crisis. Timothy Duane, in Yale Journal on Regulation, V.19 No. 2, 471, Summer 2002.

Manifesto on the California Electricity Crisis. Institute of Management, Innovation and Organization, University of California Berkeley, January 30, 2003.

The California Electricity Crisis: Causes and Policy Options. Christopher Weare, Public Policy Institute of California, January 2003.

About the Author

Arthur J. O'Donnell is an independent energy journalist and founding editor of the award-winning California Energy Markets newsletter. A nationally recognized expert on electric utilities, O'Donnell brings his unique understanding of these events and personalities to the telling of California ISO's history. O'Donnell resides in San Francisco.

0-595-29348-4

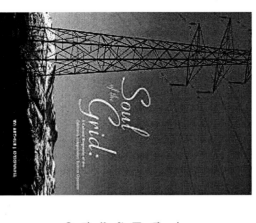

The Guilty Environmentalist